New York's Fighting Sixty-Ninth

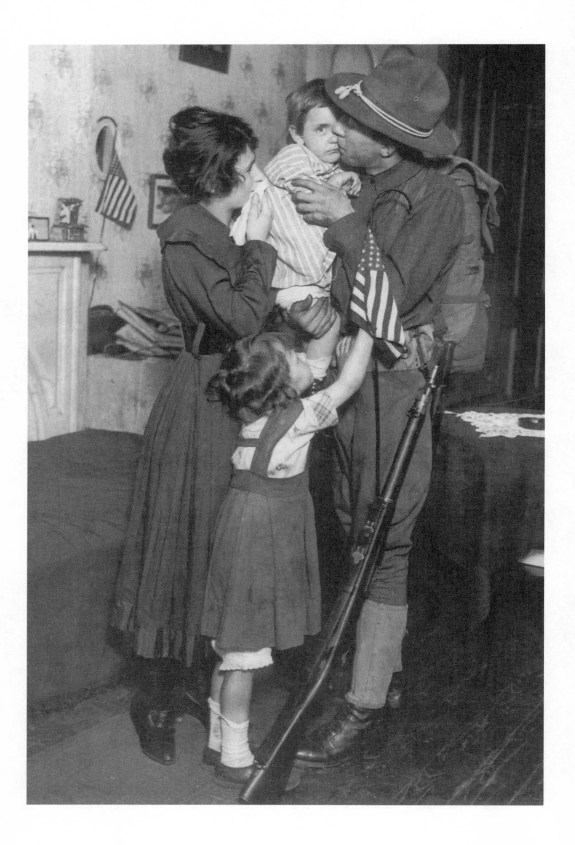

New York's Fighting Sixty-Ninth

A Regimental History of Service in the
Civil War's Irish Brigade and the
Great War's Rainbow Division

JOHN MAHON

McFarland & Company, Inc., Publishers
Jefferson, North Carolina, and London

Frontispiece: Private T.P. Loughlin of Manhattan says goodbye to his family following the summer 1917 activation of the 69th New York. Loughlin joined the regiment in October 1915, went overseas with Company B, First Battalion, 165th Infantry, and was wounded at St. Mihiel but returned safely with the rest of the regiment in May 1919 (New York State Archives, WWI Service card 89332, Thomas P. Loughlin).

LIBRARY OF CONGRESS CATALOGUING-IN-PUBLICATION DATA

Mahon, John, 1930–
New York's Fighting Sixty-ninth : a regimental history of service in the Civil War's Irish Brigade and the Great War's Rainbow Division / John Mahon.
p.   cm.
Includes bibliographical references and index.

ISBN 0-7864-1630-0 (illustrated case binding : 50# alkaline paper)∞

1. United States. Army. New York Infantry Regiment, 69th (1861–1865)
2. United States. Army. Infantry Division, 42nd.
3. United States—History—Civil War, 1861–1865—Regimental histories.
4. United States—History—Civil War, 1861–1865—Participation, Irish American.
5. United States—History—Civil War, 1861–1865—Campaigns.
6. World War, 1914–1918—Regimental histories—United States.
7. World War, 1914–1918—Campaigns.
I. Title.
E523.569th.M34   2004   356'.113'0899162073—dc22   2003025327

British Library cataloguing data are available

Cover painting by Don Troiani (www.historicalartprints.com)

Manufactured in the United States of America

McFarland & Company, Inc., Publishers
Box 611, Jefferson, North Carolina 28640
www.mcfarlandpub.com

To my wife, Mary, and children,
Jack, Maureen, Ann and Megan.
Special thanks to Mary,
who did all my typing,
and Megan, who was an
indispensable research assistant

Table of Contents

Preface

This is a history of the Fighting 69th, a regiment that served with distinction in the Civil War and World War I and World War II. It is the record of a militia unit, which was founded in 1851 by Irish immigrants and became one of the finest infantry regiments in the U.S. Army.

The staff of the 69th's regimental flag is topped by 23 streamers, one for each of the military campaigns in which the unit participated. The flagstaff is covered with 62 silver battle rings, one each for the bloody battles such as Fredericksburg in the Civil War, the Meuse River–Argonne Forest Campaign in the Great War and Saipan in World War II. Following the conclusion of the Second World War, the 69th had more battle rings than any other regiment in the American Army.

It is the story of the 69th New York State Militia (NYSM) at the Battle of Bull Run and the 69th New York Volunteers (NYV) in the Army of the Potomac during the remainder of the Civil War. This is also an account of the 165th Infantry, the federalized 69th, one of the best combat units to serve in the American Expeditionary Force (AEF) during the Great War.

The 69th NYV served in the Irish Brigade, Second Corps, Army of the Potomac, throughout the Civil War. The Brigade's combat record started with General McClellan's Peninsula Campaign, continued through epic battles at Antietam, Gettysburg, Spotsylvania, Cold Harbor, the Siege of Petersburg, and ended with the surrender of General Lee at Appomattox, Virginia.

The history includes the exploits of the 42nd Division, the famous Rainbow Division, in France during the First World War. The 165th Infantry, one of the Rainbow's best regiments, helped turn back the last German offensive of the war, participated in the Allies' counterattack with a heroic attack across the Ourcq River, spearheaded one of General Pershing's pincers during the American offensive at St. Mihiel, and then helped break the Hindenburg Line in the Argonne Forest.

Wartime experiences of the valiant guardsmen are emphasized. The book tells about Civil War combatants such as Brigadier Generals Corcoran, Meagher and Smyth; Colonels Nugent, Byrnes and Kelly; Chaplin Corby and enlisted men such as Color Sergeant Welsh, Corporal Clear and Private McCarter. The exploits of some Great War veterans, Colonels McCoy and Donovan; Majors Anderson,

1

McKenna and Kelly; Chaplin Duffy and enlisted men like Sergeant Kilmer, Corporal Hogan and Private Ettinger, are also related.

The triumphant returns of the regiment from Virginia and occupation duty in Germany following the conclusion of the Civil and Great Wars are described using excerpts from contemporary newspapers. Finally, the performance of the regiment in World War I is compared to that of other units in the Rainbow Division using an evaluation matrix devised by the author.

Calvary Cemetery is located in Long Island City, a working-class community separated from Manhattan Island and Brooklyn by the East River and Newton Creek. Veteran's Park sits in the middle of the old graveyard. The small square of land is dominated by an impressive obelisk, topped by the figure of a young woman holding a victory garland and cross. Full-size statues of Union soldiers are positioned at each corner of the pillar's base. The silent, steely-eyed guardians of the monument are an infantryman, an artilleryman, a cavalry officer and a pioneer. The last is a grizzled veteran hefting an axe. The obelisk's commemorative plaque bears the inscription: "To The Memory Of The Brave Men Who Gave Their Lives To Preserve The Union, 1861–65."

My fascination with military history, and the 69th in particular, stems from my early childhood. On Sundays, I used to take long walks with my father, a cemetery worker, in Calvary Cemetery. It was the final resting place of many brigade veterans who were mortally wounded in combat. We usually sat for a while and studied the monument, and I was impressed by the silent, imposing figures. I knew they represented those who fought in the Civil War, but I suspected they were modeled after men from the community's pride and joy, the Fighting Irish of New York State's militia.

Who were these men who deserved such a tribute? How did they help save the Union? Obtaining answers for those questions began my lifelong interest.

The militia made significant contributions to our nation's military successes from the Minutemen's role in the American Revolution to National Guard organizations participating in Desert Storm. The 69th Infantry was activated shortly after the terrorist attack on the Twin Towers on September 11, 2001. Mayor Rudolph Giuliani used its armory as a command center during the critical days immediately after the attack. Confrontation with President George Bush's "axis of evil" will require federalization of many guard units to augment the country's standing army and protect the nation's vital facilities. This history is a timely reminder of the importance of this country's National Guard.

Through the years, a number of books have been published relating the 69th's history in the Civil and Great wars. Recent works focusing on the former include Joseph Bilby's *Remember Fontenoy! The 69th New York and Irish Brigade in the Civil War* (1995) and Pia Seagrave's *The History of the Irish Brigade, A Collection of Historical Essays* (1999). The most recent work dealing with the regiment's history in the Great War is Albert and Churchill Ettinger's *A Doughboy with the Fighting Sixty Ninth, A Remembrance of World War I* (1992). My book details the regiment's story from its creation in 1851 through its sacrifice in the Civil War, service with General Pershing's Punitive Expedition on the Mexican Border, combat in the trenches of France and triumphant return from Germany in 1919.

Backdrops for the Civil and Great wars were condensed from a number of important works, including Craig Symond's *A Battlefield Atlas of the Civil War* (1983) and William Swinton's *Campaigns of the Army of the Republic* (1886). Corresponding works for World War I include Donald Smythe's *Pershing, General of the Armies* (1986) and S.L.A. Marshall's *World War I* (1964).

Unit histories were also derived from many old and recent volumes. Those for the Civil War include Francis Walker's *History of the Second Army Corps* (1886), William Fox's *Regimental Losses in the American Civil War, 1861–1865* (1889), Patrick O'Flaherty's *The History of the Sixty Ninth Regiment in the Irish Brigade, 1861–1865* (1986), and Seagrave's historical essays.

Corresponding information for the Great War was taken from a number of works, including Henry Reilly's *Americans All* (1936), Francis Duffy's *Father Duffy's Story* (1919), Martin Hogan's *The Shamrock Battalion of the Rainbow: A Story of the Fighting Sixty Ninth* (1919), James Cooke's *The Rainbow Division in the Great War, 1917–1919* (1994) and the Ettinger remembrances.

My research was also augmented by the following government works: *The War of the Rebellion, A Compilation of the Official Records of the Union and Confederate Armies* (1901), *42nd Division, Summary of Operations in the World War, American Battle Monuments Commission* (1944), *United States Army in the World War, 1917–1918* (1990) and *American Armies and Battlefields in Europe* (1938).

Personnel of the U.S. Army History Institute, Carlisle, PA, and Institute of Heraldry, Fort Belvoir, VA provided pertinent reference material and photographs from their historical holdings. The Centennial Park Library, Holiday, FL, responded to my requests for venerable as well as recent publications. Finally, a debt of gratitude is owed to Lt. Colonel Kenneth H. Powers, NYNG [Ret.], Regimental Historian, 69th New York, who reviewed my book and provided valuable assistance in its preparation.

Unit Insignia

Design of the distinctive unit insignia for the 165th Infantry (69th New York National Guard—the Fighting Sixty-Ninth) was originally approved on 26 April 1924. The design was modified a few months later by eliminating the regiment's motto. In March 1964, the emblem was redesignated for the 69th Infantry and in March 1993 for the 69th Air Defense Artillery. In December 1996, the insignia was once again designated for the 69th Infantry.[1]

Army heraldic crests are metallic, shield-shaped insignias identifying the wearer as a member of a specific military organization. Regimental insignia are worn by officers and enlisted men on the shoulder loops of dress shirts and by enlisted men on caps. Insignia design is based on a unit's lineage and battle honors. The symbolic presentation on a shield is usually configured in accordance with accepted rules of heraldry.[2]

The regiment's insignia highlights the long and honorable history of the Fighting Sixty Ninth. The field of the approximately one-inch-square shield is green, a color that calls to mind the New York City Regiment's Irish Catholic roots. Prior to the Civil War, the unit's dress uniform included a green jacket, a symbol of pride to the Fenian militiamen but an affront to many Nativists of the time.

A replica of the regiment's original coat of arms is located in the lower left corner of the crest. The insignia was used as a cap device prior to the Civil War and is displayed on regimental stationery. It consists of the numeral 69 superimposed on a gold oval shield supported by two Irish wolfhounds and a scroll.

A red trefoil or shamrock is located in the upper right hand corner of the shield. It was worn on the caps of soldiers in the First Division, Second Corps of the Army of the Potomac during the War Between the States. The Irish Brigade, in which the 69th Regiment served with distinction throughout the war, was the Second Brigade of the First Division.[3]

Between the two symbols is a section of rainbow, recalling the 165th Infantry's service with the famous 42nd (Rainbow) Division in World War I. In that conflict, the regiment was accorded battle honors for six campaigns, including the Aisne-Marne and Meuse-Argonne offensives. In the former action, on the Ourcq River, the 165th Infantry put up what has been called one of the great fights of the war.

Distinctive unit insignia of the 69th Infantry, New York Army National Guard (courtesy of Department of the Army, the Institute of Heraldry).

The regiment "forced a crossing without artillery support and then fighting alone on the enemy's side of the river, with its flanks unsupported, engaged a Prussian Guard Division and forced it to retire."[4]

The insignia was worn with pride by members of the 165th Regimental Combat Team during World War II. The unit, then part of the 27th Division, fought in the Pacific Theater, capturing Makin Atoll and participating in the seizure of Saipan and Okinawa. In that last battle of the war, one company of the regiment received a Distinguished Unit Citation and a private of another company was awarded the Congressional Medal of Honor.[5]

Introduction

Every year, New York City's annual St. Patrick's Day Parade is led up Fifth Avenue by elements of the Fighting Sixty-Ninth. At first glance, the national banner carried at the head of the marching guardsmen appears to be attached to a silver flagstaff. In reality, it is an elongated pole covered with 62 silver furls, one for each battle in which the regiment participated, and for many years more than any other regiment in the U.S. Army. The flagstaff's 23 streamers represent each campaign, including the Siege of Petersburg during the Civil War plus the Meuse-Argonne and Ryukus offensives in World Wars I and II.[1]

Early in the Civil War, the 69th New York Volunteers (NYV) was dubbed the Fighting Sixty-Ninth by General Robert E. Lee.[2] That sobriquet was a testament to the regiment's military prowess by the Confederacy's foremost soldier. The New York Irishmen considered themselves worthy of Lee's flattering appraisal and adopted it as their *nom de guerre*. It was an appellation that stuck to the unit through the years. The federalized regiment went to France as the 165th Infantry, but it was widely known as the Fighting Sixty-Ninth.

In the opening battle of the Civil War, the 69th New York State Militia (NYSM) was one of the few Federal units that acquitted itself well. It was in the thick of the action. Only one other outfit stopped more Rebel lead than the NY Irish.

William F. Fox was a nineteenth century authority on the fighting capability of Civil War units. In his *Regimental Losses in the American Civil War,* he stated, "The Irish Brigade was probably the best known of any brigade organization, it having made an unusual reputation for dash and gallantry."[3]

The Brigade served in the division that suffered more casualties than any other such unit in the Union forces. All five of the regiments in the Irish Brigade (63rd, 69th and 88th NYV, 28th Massachusetts and 116th Pennsylvania) are on Fox's list of the 300 Federal regiments that had the most battlefield casualties. The 69th NYV is sixth on that table. The regiment lost the most men in action, killed and wounded, of the 115 like outfits from New York State.[4]

In 1987, Colonel Paul F. Braim, a well known historian, compared the military prowess of 29 divisions in the American Expeditionary Force (AEF). His careful, well documented analysis indicates that the Rainbow Division was one of the four best combat divisions to serve in France.[5] Similar comparisons of the Rainbow's infantry units in this work support the claim that the Sixty-Ninth may have been the best of the division's four regiments.

The Irish were not expected to be enthusiastic supporters of President Abraham Lincoln's effort to suppress the rebellion in the Southern States. They distrusted the president's Republican Party, which had replaced the hated American Party.

Between 1846 and 1854, over a million Irish immigrated to the United States, primarily because of the potato famine in Ireland. Most had been tenant farmers on the estates of British aristocracy in Ireland. They were uneducated, had minimal technical skills and were desperately poor. The impoverished newcomers crowded into the worst of the North's urban areas, creating even shabbier neighborhoods and dangerous, disease ridden slums.

The Irish, like northern blacks, were willing to take the worst jobs for the lowest wages. By the mid–1850s, they had driven the blacks out of the more menial jobs available in the North. Prior to the start of the Civil War, Irishmen were the dominant source of labor for mining, canal building and railroad construction. The Irish were also finding employment as policemen and firemen.

Immigrant Irish detested blacks, the hatred resulting from intense economic competition in the unskilled labor market. They might be near the bottom of the social ladder, but in their opinion, blacks occupied the lowest rung. The Irish intended to keep them there.

In the 1850s, the United States was essentially a Protestant country. The nation's early colonists were frequently at war with their Catholic counterparts in French and Spanish controlled Canada and Florida. Resultant animosity and mistrust of Catholics continued well into the mid-nineteenth century. Many native Americans were suspicious of the newly arriving Irish Catholics. They were afraid the immigrants would undermine the government and turn it over to popish factions.

In the decade prior to the Civil War, the "American Party" rose to prominence in the United States. It was a Nativist movement dedicated to political warfare against recently arrived immigrants. Members were called "Know Nothings" because they refused to answer questions about their party's secret rituals. Nativists directed most of their political venom against Irish Catholics, railing against their religion and poverty. The newcomers were knocked for perceived tendencies toward drink and criminality, sins common to those near the bottom of the heap. Irish Catholics knew their enemies and sought political power in the Democratic Party, further widening the gulf between them and the Nativists. In addition, most of the recently arrived Irish wanted to free their homeland from English domination. They attempted to sow discord between the United States and Great Britain. This blatant animosity toward the British government troubled many Nativists interested in developing closer economic and political ties with the "mother country."

The slavery issue caused the American Party to be supplanted by the Republican Party. In 1860, the Irish had nearly as much reason to hate the Republicans as they had the Know Nothing Party. Most of the Nativists became ardent Republicans. More importantly, the Republican Party was dedicated to the liberation of black Americans from slavery. Emancipation would provide former slaves with an opportunity to rise above Irish Catholics on the economic ladder.

Surprisingly, when President Lincoln called for volunteers to suppress the rebellion, Irish immigrants flocked to the colors. Prominent leaders in New York City, such as Michael Corcoran and Thomas Meagher, had little difficulty in enlisting recruits for the expanded 69th NYSM and later the Irish Brigade.

Irish Americans had at least four reasons for their enthusiasm in joining Federal forces being organized to crush the rebellion.

1. The new immigrants were intensely nationalistic. They loved their adopted country's ideals. Most believed a debt was owed to the land that succored them in their hour of need. The oncoming war provided recent immigrants with an opportunity to demonstrate loyalty to the United States.

2. Great Britain was seen as a supporter of the Confederacy and the country which would most benefit by breakup of the Union. Irish Americans did not want the United States to lose power with respect to that hated nation.

3. Most Irishmen expected service in the Union Army to be a better occupation than their menial, low paying civilian jobs. Enlistment bonuses were huge inducements for poor immigrants to join the federal army. In addition, Irishmen had a natural affinity for military service.

4. Members of revolutionary groups, intending to forcibly liberate Ireland, hoped to gain requisite military experience for the task through service in the Union Army.[6]

As the Civil War dragged on and the number of casualties increased, support for the war diminished. This was especially true in Irish American communities, where the numbers of killed and wounded far exceeded corresponding percentages in the overall population. In addition, Lincoln's Emancipation Proclamation firmly established slavery's destruction as a primary goal of the Union war effort. Nevertheless, the 69th NYV and the Irish Brigade continued to serve with distinction and remained at the front with the Army of the Potomac throughout the war.

Immigrant Irish made a significant contribution to the success of federal armies in defeating the Confederacy and restoring the Union.[7] After the war, thanks in part to the exemplary performance of all Irish units such as the Fighting Sixty-Ninth, public opinion of Irish Catholics in the United States improved considerably.

The 69th NYSM was demobilized following the Battle of Bull Run and served in New York City for the remainder of the war. The unit was called out during the draft riots and helped restore order in the city during the turbulent summer of 1863.

The United States declared war on Spain in April 1898, the result of irreconcilable differences over the way Spain dealt with a popular uprising in Cuba. Sinking of the battleship *Maine* in Havana Harbor due to a mysterious explosion forced President McKinley to initiate hostilities against Spain. The 69th NYSM was federalized and in December 1898 was in Tampa, Florida, awaiting embarkation to Cuba when a peace treaty was signed in Paris.[8]

Mexico, at the turn of the century, was politically unstable. Insurrectionary factions fought each other for control of the country. In 1916, Pancho Villa, a Mexican revolutionary and bandit chieftain, raided Columbus, New Mexico. His men killed 16 people during the border town attack. President Woodrow Wilson ordered General John Joseph Pershing to conduct a "punitive campaign" into Mexico to destroy Villa's force. A number of militia units were federalized, including the 69th NYNG, for service with Pershing's expeditionary force.

The New York regiment was one of the best infantry units in Pershing's army. It set a marching record during the campaign, emulating that of the Irish Brigade prior to the Battle of Gettysburg, when its soldiers hiked 54 miles in about 21 hours' marching time. As in the Civil War, the physical endurance of the New York Irish in unhealthy environments was remarkable.[9] Pershing never collared Villa, and in early 1917, President Wilson recalled the expedition.

World War I erupted in August 1914. Russia went to war with Austria-Hungary when the latter declared war on Serbia. Germany backed Austria-Hungary and France supported Russia. When the Kaiser's army invaded neutral Belgium to get at France, England was forced to declare war on Germany and then her ally, Austria-Hungary. Colonies of the European belligerents were quickly drawn into the widening conflict. Eventually, other nations such as Bulgaria, Turkey, Italy, Romania and Japan became participants in what was then a world war. President Wilson attempted to keep the United States out of the struggle. Germany, however, began unrestricted submarine warfare in February 1917 and a number of unarmed American vessels were sunk on the high seas. Wilson's administration was forced to declare war on Germany and her allies in April of that year.

The 69th NY, which had returned to New York City from the Mexican border in March 1917, was recalled to federal service in August of that year. The U.S. Army increased the size of its infantry regiments from 2,000 to 3,600 men. The Sixty-Ninth had no problem recruiting healthy Irishmen to fill its expanded order of battle.

Irish Catholics rallied to the colors in spite of the fact they would be fighting alongside British troops, soldiers of the empire that crushed the Easter Rebellion in 1916 and summarily executed most of its leaders. Great Britain's heavy-handed response to the Dublin uprising launched guerilla warfare in Ireland against the British establishment. The old maxim "England's difficulty is Ireland's opportunity" was largely ignored in the United States. Patriotism and loyalty to one's adopted country overcame sentimental ties to the past and Fenian dreams for Ireland's separation from the British Empire. Undoubtedly, an opportunity to go to France with the Rainbow Division made enlistment in the Fighting Sixty-Ninth an attractive proposition.

This work relates the wartime experiences of heroic Irishmen and their non–Celtic comrades as they served their adopted country during two bloody conflicts.

Michael Corcoran (then a colonel) was being tried by court martial when Secessionists fired on Fort Sumter. He was defending himself against charges of insubordination—his refusal to parade the 69th NYSM during the city's celebration in honor of England's Prince of Wales. The desperate need for loyal troops in the nation's capital ended the trial. Colonel Corcoran led the regiment at the Battle of Bull Run and was one of the last Federal officers to leave the field when the Union forces collapsed. Corcoran was captured by Rebel cavalry and spent many months in a Confederate prison, most of the time under the threat of execution, before he was exchanged. His health ruined, Corcoran did not survive the war.

Brigadier General Thomas Meagher, an escapee from a British penal colony, organized the Irish Brigade. He led the unit during the Peninsular Campaign and battles at Antietam Creek, Fredericksburg and Chancellorsville, campaigns in which the Irish Brigade provided outstanding service to the Union. Meagher was loved and respected by his troops, but there were those in Lincoln's army who believed the general got his courage from the bottle. Meagher, unlike Corcoran, survived the war. He went on to become acting governor of the Montana Territory. In 1867, he disappeared from a river boat under mysterious circumstances. His body was never found.

Thomas A. Smyth, an Irish immigrant, commanded the Irish Brigade during bloody encounters at the Wilderness and Spotsylvania Court House. He led his command with bravery and determination. On 9 April 1865, he was mortally wounded by a sniper following the Battle of Farmville, Virginia. Smyth died two days later, while General Lee surrendered his army at Appomattox. He was the last Federal general killed in the war.

Colonels Richard Byrnes and Patrick Kelly were successive commanding officers of the Irish Brigade during General Ulysses Grant's bloody overland campaign in the spring of 1864. Both officers led their troops from the front. Byrnes was mortally wounded leading an assault at Cold Harbor. A few weeks later Kelly was shot through the head while storming a redoubt in the Petersburg defenses. The men were buried in the same Long Island City cemetery within a couple of weeks of each other's internment.

Fathers Ouellet and William Corby were chaplains of the 69th and 88th NYV, respectively. At times, they acted as padres for the entire brigade, often performing their religious duties while under enemy fire. Father Corby is best remembered standing on a boulder giving absolution to the brigade prior to its going into action at Gettysburg. The priests survived the war and Father Corby went on to become president of Notre Dame College at South Bend, Indiana.

Private William McCarter was one of General Meagher's orderlies. He participated in the brigade's disastrous assault on Marye's Heights during the Battle of Fredericksburg. McCarter was seriously wounded in that action. He was a skilled writer and his remembrances of the war provide valuable information about the Irish Brigade and General Meagher.

Peter Welsh, an immigrant from Ireland, served in the 28th Massachusetts of the Irish Brigade. He was a reliable soldier and at the start of General Grant's overland campaign was promoted to color sergeant. He was wounded in the arm during the Second Corps' famous attack on the "Salient" at Spotsylvania. A short time later, the wound festered and Welsh died. His widow preserved his wartime correspondence. Over a hundred years later, Kohl and Richard edited Welsh's correspondence and in 1986 published a collection of his letters. The work provides an insight into the mental attitude of a typical Irish Catholic soldier in the federal army. Welsh loved his adopted country. In a letter to a relative in Ireland, he wrote, "America is Irlands refuge, Irlands last hope...."[10]

Samuel Clear joined the 116th Pennsylvania in February 1864. He saw action with his regiment in the Wilderness, at Spotsylvania and Cold Harbor, plus major engagements during the siege of Petersburg. He kept a diary which provides eyewitness accounts of key battles fought by the Irish Brigade during 1864 and 65.[11]

Donovan, a Columbia Law School graduate, was called "Wild Bill" because of his prowess as a college football player. Active in the New York National Guard, he went to France as Major Donovan, First Battalion, 165th Infantry. He fought with conspicuous valor in all the Sixty-Ninth's battles and was awarded the Congressional Medal of Honor for heroism in the Argonne Forest. Donovan returned to New York City as the regiment's colonel. During World War II, he headed the Office of Strategic Services, progenitor of the Central Intelligence Agency.

Colonel Frank McCoy, a West Point graduate, went to France as a secretary on the staff of the AEF. General Pershing had a high regard for McCoy and when opportune, Pershing gave him command of the Sixty-Ninth. Obviously, Pershing believed the Colonel would be good for the regiment and that leadership of the combative New Yorkers would enhance his protégé's career. McCoy led the Sixty-Ninth during the intense fighting that blunted Germany's last offensive of the war. The performance of his unit was outstanding and McCoy was quickly promoted to the rank of brigadier general.[12]

Majors Anderson, McKenna and Kelly served as battalion commanders in France. The three proved to be outstanding officers. Anderson was awarded the Distinguished Service Medal and Legion of Honor. He survived the war and went on to command the Regiment in the interim between World Wars I and II. McKenna was killed in action during the Aisne-Marne Offensive. He was awarded the Distinguished Service Cross for heroism in that action. Kelly, who survived the war, won the Distinguished Service Cross and Legion of Honor.

Father Francis P. Duffy is probably the most famous chaplain in the history of the U.S. Army. He served with the Sixty-Ninth in all of its battles, often performing his religious duties in front line trenches. The Padre, an inspiration to the men of the regiment, was awarded the Distinguished Service Cross and Legion of Honor for heroism under battlefield conditions. In 1937, veterans of the regiment erected an impressive statue of the chaplain in NYC's Times Square. Father Duffy published a history of the 165th Infantry. The work emphasizes contributions of individual members of the regiment, enlisted men as well as officers, toward besting their opponents on the Western Front.[13]

Albert Ettinger went to France as a member of the Regiment's 3rd (Shamrock) Battalion. He served as a dispatch rider in France until seriously injured in a motorcycle accident. When recovered from his injuries, he was temporarily assigned to the regiment's intelligence section. Ettinger served with the infantry during the Argonne Offensive. He survived the war and recorded his experiences. In 1992, his son published a book based on those reminiscences, *A Doughboy with the Fighting Sixty Ninth*. The work recalls heroic, tragic and sometimes humorous incidents experienced by enlisted men in the Regiment.[14]

Martin Hogan was seventeen years old when he joined the 165th Infantry. Like Ettinger, he served in the Shamrock Battalion. Young Hogan was gassed in the Luneville Sector of the Western Front. He participated in the Champagne Defensive and the Aisne-Marne and St. Mihiel Offensives. Hogan was wounded during the regiment's attack on the Kremhilde Stellung during the Meuse River–Argonne Forest Campaign. He survived the war and later published his memoirs.[15]

Joyce Kilmer, an Episcopalian by birth, converted to Roman Catholicism while in his mid-twenties. When the U.S. went to war in 1917, he was a reporter for the *New York Times* and poetry editor for the *Literary Digest*. A poet of some note, he is best remembered for his sentimental verse "Trees." Kilmer claimed he was half Irish, although he was English by descent. His affinity for things Irish caused him to transfer from the Seventh to the 69th Regiment. Father Duffy, using connections in the former regiment, arranged his transfer into the Irish outfit.

Kilmer was 32 years old and married with a wife and three children when he joined the regiment. He was exempt from the draft but with his wife's blessing went overseas with the 69th, and had an unfortunate rendezvous with a sniper's bullet near the Ourcq River.

Father Duffy found nothing long haired about the poet, describing him as a sturdy fellow, manly, humorous and interesting. Sergeant Kilmer was recording the regiment's history in the Great War when killed. That task was completed by Father Duffy.

In summary, this work is the record of an outstanding infantry regiment and its gallant soldiers, from its creation in 1851 to its triumphant return from France in 1919.

CHAPTER 1

Beginning

The 69th Regiment was mustered into the New York State Militia (NYSM) on 12 October 1851, sixty-eight other regiments having already been accepted by the state. The unit, consisting of approximately 1,000 men organized into eight companies, was incorporated into the Fourth Brigade, First Division of the NYSM. More than 95 percent of the volunteers were born in Ireland or were first generation Irish-Americans.

Many of the citizen soldiers were Fenians, members of a revolutionary group committed to liberation of Ireland from English domination. The name Fenian was derived from the group's motto, "Sinn Fein," Gaelic for "ourselves alone," those who would free Erin.

The Fenian movement had at least two reasons for organizing militia regiments. First, to demonstrate loyalty to state and federal governments. Second, to establish a body of armed, trained military men who, should the opportunity present itself, would help overthrow the English establishment in Ireland. The goals were not kept secret. They were discussed openly at political meetings and published in many newspapers of the time.[1]

The St. Patrick's Day Parade of 1853 was the zenith of the Irish militia movement, with about 3,000 armed Hibernians parading on the holiday. Marching units received favorable reviews in the local press, including the *New York Herald*, *Daily Tribune* and *Irish American*. Later, on the Fourth of July, the men of the 69th Regiment appeared for the first time in their new dress uniforms: regulation hat with red plume, dark green coat with crimson facings and white pants. (The winter uniform of the 69th Regiment featured blue pants with a yellow stripe.) The prescribed blue coat was worn as a fatigue uniform.[2]

The American Party flourished from 1852 to 1860. This Nativist group included secret societies protesting against immigration and election or appointment of naturalized Americans, especially Irish Catholics, to official positions. Its members despised the Roman Catholic Church. Meetings of the American Party were usually held in secret and measures promoted never discussed openly. Whenever a party member was asked questions regarding his politics, the reply was usually, "I don't know." Constant repetition of the phrase gave the party its popular name, "Know Nothings." In state elections of 1854, the Know Nothings carried

Massachusetts. They also received a large number of votes in New York and Pennsylvania and gained considerable power in the South. In the election of 1856, however, the American Party split over the slavery issue and thereafter quickly disappeared.

In 1855, control of the Massachusetts and Pennsylvania state governments by the Know Nothing Party resulted in the disbanding of Irish militia units. There was no direct attack on New York regiments by local Nativists because of Irish Catholic political strength in New York City. Nevertheless, Nativist Americans continued outspoken criticism of the units. They focused on the green jackets of Irish formations, which they believed were blatant symbols of disloyalty to the U.S. "Wearing of the Green" was an anathema to many Nativists.

During the spring of 1855, racial and religious bigotry rose to a fever pitch in New York City. Leading city politicians feared the spectacle of thousands of armed Irishmen marching in green uniforms on St. Patrick's Day would inflame the passions of less moderate Nativists. They anticipated a pitched battle between paraders and radical elements of the Know Nothing Party. Accordingly, only civic groups received permission to march on the holiday. Irish militia groups were restricted to their parade grounds awaiting orders. Weather on 17 March was the worst on record and included violent hail storms. The number of paraders and onlookers was drastically reduced by the tempest and when the last of the marchers reached City Hall, there were more riot police than supporters and detractors combined.

The men of the 69th Regiment, as soon as they were released from the arsenal, marched with fixed bayonets down Broadway, through the Park and other major thoroughfares before they were dismissed at City Hall. The *New York Times* reported it as an empty gesture since there were few to cheer or jeer: "The storm had vanquished all save the gallant Sixty Ninth."[3]

The 69th Regiment saw its first active duty during the Quarantine War of 1858. The governor of New York believed Staten Island was in a state of insurrection, the result of violent civilian protests against the presence of an infectious disease hospital on the island. He called out the militia. The regiment was one of the units maintaining order in the troubled area. While on active duty, the 69th was inspected by a senior officer of the Adjutant General's Office and found to be "a serviceable and reliable organization."[4]

The parade on St. Patrick's Day in 1859 was held without incident. The 69th Regiment marched in full winter uniforms. The 450 man contingent looked sharp in gray overcoats over new blue uniforms. This was the first time the regiment marched without its distinctive green jackets. Presumably, the color guard wore the controversial Fenian coat, a tradition observed by the 69th Regiment to this day.

Michael Corcoran became the third commander of the 69th Regiment in July 1859. He was born in County Sligo, Ireland, on 21 September 1827. His father was a retired officer who served with the British Army in the West Indies. His

Opposite: **Colonel Michael Corcoran (courtesy of Massachusetts Commander Military Order of the Loyal Legion and the U.S. Army Military History Institute).**

mother was a descendant of Patrick Sarsfield, the Earl of Lucan, the most famous Irish soldier of his day.

As a young man, Corcoran ran into difficulty with the British establishment in Ireland and immigrated to New York City in October 1849. Due to his relatively good education and fine appearance (he was six feet, two inches and a sinewy 180 pounds), he became a prominent figure in Irish revolutionary circles and the organization of the 69th Regiment. In 1853, he was commissioned captain and given command of Company A. By August 1859, he was the 69th's colonel.[5]

The regiment flourished under Colonel Corcoran. The unit marched on Washington's Birthday and St. Patrick's Day in 1860 and was hailed by the *New York Herald* as "a splendid regiment of Irishmen."[6]

The 69th had achieved respectability in the eyes of the city's society. It was Americanized to the extent that the militiamen readily wore the blue coat of the Federal Army. In October 1860, however, an event occurred which threatened to mar its newly achieved good reputation.

President James Buchanan invited the Prince of Wales, who was touring Canada, to visit the United States. The heir to the English throne accepted the invitation and decided to travel incognito as Baron Renfrew. The upper class of New York was ecstatic and invited the prince to visit the city. Two events were scheduled to entertain His Highness, a giant ball and a military review.

The ball was a great success with Baron Renfrew dancing until five in the morning. Ladies who waltzed with him observed a European custom requiring those who danced with a prince not to traipse with lesser individuals for the rest of the evening. A female touched by royalty was apparently too enthralled to be embraced by ordinary mortals for at least 24 hours.[7] The upper class of New York City had forgotten their revolutionary past. Less than 85 years earlier, the military forces of the baron's monarchist's forbears were pursuing George Washington's colonial army as it retreated through Manhattan following defeat in the Battle of Long Island.

When the baron arrived in the city, he rode down Broadway from Bowling Green to his hotel on 23rd Street. He was cheered by thousands of New Yorkers lining both sides of the avenue. Renfrew was escorted by all of the First Division's regiments save one. The 69th Regiment refused to kowtow to his Royal Highness.

The reaction to the deliberate snub by Colonel Corcoran and the 69th Regiment to the Crown Prince was immediate and severe. Native American publications called for court martial of Corcoran and the regiment's disbandment. The unit was not broken up, but its colonel was ordered to submit himself for trial by court martial.

Corcoran was relieved of his duties as he awaited his trial. Meanwhile, the 69th, under the command of Lt. Colonel Robert Nugent, paraded on Evacuation Day, anniversary of the day the English flag was lowered forever in New York City. The 69th Regiment certainly supported that holiday and made a fine turnout. The *Military Gazette* said the regiment appeared to be in its best shape since acceptance into the New York State Militia.[8]

The court martial of Colonel Corcoran began on 20 December 1860. Corcoran was represented by Richard O'Gorman, a famous Irish lawyer. The trial continued through the spring of 1861. On 12 April 1861, the South Carolina militia under General P.G.T. Beauregard fired on Fort Sumter in Charleston Harbor. The Civil War had begun. Many officers and men of the 69th Regiment believed they shouldn't offer their services to the federal government until Colonel Corcoran was cleared of all charges and restored to his command. Corcoran sent a letter to his officers recommending they support the Union. He wrote, in part, "I stand ready to throw myself into the ranks for the maintenance, support and protection of the Stars and Stripes."[9]

The letter was read to an assemblage of officers, who subsequently voted unanimously to tender their services to the federal government. Shortly thereafter, all charges against Colonel Corcoran were dropped and he was restored to his command. The 69th set up recruiting offices and prepared for war in defense of the United States.

CHAPTER 2

Civil War, 1861

The Civil War started on 12 April 1861 and ended almost four years later on 9 April 1865, when General Robert E. Lee surrendered his ragged army at Appomattox Court House, Virginia. Shortly thereafter, the other Confederate armies capitulated.

The war was a turning point in the history of the United States. Slavery was ended. A way of life that depended on the labor of blacks was destroyed forever. The question as to a state's right to secede from the Union was firmly settled in the negative.

During the 1850s, quarreling between the South and other sections of the country was vitriolic and continuous. Senator William Seward of New York, later Lincoln's Secretary of State, called the controversy "an irrepressible conflict between opposing and enduring forces."[1] Most sectional disagreements had roots in the slavery issue. None of the compromises orchestrated by Congress defused the explosive situation.

In the presidential election of 1860, the Democratic Party split into Northern and Southern wings, nominating Stephen Douglas and John Breckenridge respectively as candidates for chief executive. Former Whigs, urging national unity, established the Constitutional Union Party. Their presidential candidate was John Bell. Republicans nominated Abraham Lincoln of Illinois.

The Republican platform went beyond mere opposition to slavery. Party leaders wanted to unite major economic groups in the North through a program favoring tariffs for manufacturers, free homesteads for farmers, central banking for merchants and financiers plus government subsidized railways for everyone.

The Republican platform was poison to the Southern states and many of them threatened to secede if Lincoln was elected. Honest Abe received only 40 percent of the popular vote but more than that tallied by any of his opponents. He then gained a majority of electoral votes and was elected president.

In December 1860, South Carolina adopted the Ordinance of Secession and became the first state to leave the Union. By the time Lincoln was inaugurated in March 1861, six other states had also seceded. They were, in order of withdrawal; Mississippi, Florida, Alabama, Georgia, Louisiana and Texas. Representatives from those states met in Montgomery, Alabama and established the

Confederate States of America. Jefferson Davis and Alexander Stephens were elected president and vice president of the new country.

The Civil War began in earnest with the attack on Fort Sumter. News of the subsequent surrender of the besieged federal bastion spread through the nation like wildfire. Government attempts at reconciliation with the rebellious states were over. President Lincoln issued a proclamation on 15 April 1861 calling for the loyal states to furnish 75,000 volunteers to put down the rebellion in the seven states. The fledgling Southern nation regarded his move as a declaration of war. Virginia, Arkansas, North Carolina and Tennessee promptly seceded from the Union and joined the Confederacy. Three other slave holding states, Maryland, Kentucky and Missouri, actively considered disunion. President Lincoln, with considerable political skill and government muscle, managed to keep the border states in the Union. Eventually, eleven states fought for the Confederacy and 23 others lined up for the Union. In May, the Confederacy's capital was established in Richmond, Virginia.

At the beginning of the war, neither government had formalized procedures for raising an army. Both sides relied on volunteer forces, a system that was initially successful. States, rather than the Union or Confederate governments, recruited most volunteers. Prominent citizens, desiring to organize a military unit, could do so. Thomas Meagher, for example, organized a company of zouaves prior to the Battle of Bull Run. As the war went on, however, volunteer enlistments decreased and both sides were forced to use conscription. The Northern program, begun in March 1863, made men between the ages of 20 and 45 subject to three years of military service. Both sides permitted draftees to avoid conscription by hiring substitutes. In the North, a draftee could also avoid service by paying a sum of $300 to the government.

The draft was extremely unpopular in many areas of the North. In July 1863, armed mobs in New York City set fire to buildings and took over parts of the city before police and militia units restored order. Most of the insurgents were Irish Catholics from poorer areas of the city. While they were rioting, their countrymen in the Irish Brigade were nursing wounds received in the Battle of Gettysburg. It should be noted that the 69th NYSM helped disperse the mobs.

Abraham Lincoln and Jefferson Davis chose their field commanders on the basis of what they or their advisors knew about the prospective officer's military skills. Many times, however, leaders were selected for political rather than military reasons.

Fortunately for Jeff Davis, he eventually chose Lee to take command of the eastern Confederate army, the Army of Northern Virginia. Lee's able lieutenants included Stonewall Jackson and James Longstreet. The Confederate commanders in the West—Albert Sidney Johnston, Beauregard, Braxton Bragg and Joseph E. Johnston—had less ability.

Lincoln tried several commanders for the Union's eastern army: Irwin McDowell, George B. McClellan, John Pope, Ambrose E. Burnside, Joseph Hooker and George Meade. All had serious weaknesses, Lincoln's western generals, Henry Halleck, Don Carlos Buell and William Rosecrans, also failed to measure up. None were effective commanders. But, as the war progressed, four great generals rose to prominence and eventually led the Union armies to victory. They were Ulysses S. Grant, William Sherman, Philip Sheridan and George Thomas.

With respect to human casualties, the Civil War was more costly than any other American struggle. About 1,000,000 men were killed or wounded. Deaths, including those from disease, totaled 622,511 men. The North lost 364,511 men and the South 258,000 men. Disease felled far more men than enemy action. Union and Confederate soldiers killed in combat totaled 110,000 and 94,000 men respectively.

Economic costs for the conflict were staggering. Estimated antes for the Union and Confederacy were more than $3 billion and $2 billion respectively. Total price tag for the reunited nation probably exceeded $15 billion.[2]

One of the more negative results of the Civil War was the hatred it generated. This was particularly true in the South. Southerners were the only Americans to experience military failure and subsequent occupation by enemy forces. Many grew bitter in defeat while some Northerners, especially the Radical Republicans, became vengeful in victory.

Early War

The Battle of Bull Run, fought on 21 July 1861, was the first major engagement of the Civil War. Thirty-five minor actions had already occurred between Confederate and Federal forces.[3] Following the battle, in which the Union forces were routed, there was only one other significant clash in the east during 1861. That engagement occurred in Port Royal, South Carolina on 7 November 1861. There, a combined force of Federal warships and troops captured Port Royal. Eventually, Union forces seized all of Port Royal Island and Beaufort, South Carolina. The Federal victory was significant, for in addition to providing an important base for blockading vessels, it demonstrated that steam-powered warships firing explosive shells could readily demolish Confederate coastal fortifications. Port Royal was the first in a string of Union victories along the South Atlantic and Gulf of Mexico coastlines.

The strategy of both sides in the west was affected by the ambivalence of Kentucky. After Fort Sumter, the state declared itself neutral. Nevertheless, both sides recruited troops in the region. For a number of months, neither side moved into the border state, but on 1 September 1861, Confederate troops seized Columbus, Kentucky on the Mississippi River. A short time later, Federal forces under Brigadier General Grant occupied Paducah, Kentucky.

Both sides continued to move troops into Kentucky. Confederate General Albert Sidney Johnston established a defensive barrier extending from Columbus through Forts Henry and Donelson (on the Tennessee and Cumberland rivers respectively), to Bowling Green, Kentucky and then east to the Cumberland Gap. At the close of the year, two major Federal armies menaced Johnston's defensive line. Brigadier General Grant's forces were moving on Forts Henry and Donelson while Brigadier Don Carlos Buell's troops were threatening Bowling Green.

On 10 August, at Wilson's Creek, Missouri, Confederate General Sterling Price, with an army of 12,000 men, defeated a much smaller Federal force under Brigadier General Nathaniel Lyons, placing southwestern Missouri under Rebel control.

Bull Run

Lincoln's volunteers were to serve for a period of three months. The 69th NYSM was federalized in late April 1861 and soon after ordered to Washington, D.C. During the first months of the war, it was one of six regiments defending the capital against a *coup de main* by Rebel forces gathering in nearby Richmond.

During the spring, the 69th NYSM built formidable earthworks on Arlington Heights and called it Fort Corcoran. The bastion was appreciated by other members of the capital's garrison, as evidenced by the following letter to the *Sunday Mercury.*

> To the Editors of the Sunday Mercury
> Seventy-Ninth Regiment
> Georgetown Heights, D.C., June 17, 1861
>
> ...Of all the regiments here, of whom New York ought to be proud, in my opinion, and I express it fearlessly, the Sixty-Ninth NYSM are entitled the first position to receive thanks of the citizens of New York and the United States.
> They have erected and completed as perfect a fortification as was ever finished by Todleben for the Russian Government during the Crimean War. Their strength in their present position is equal to ten regiments unprotected, and they are just the boys who will have a hand in where there is any fighting to be done.
> I must say that their officers are not excelled by any in the other regiments for perfection in drill and soldiery deportment....
>
> Yours sincerely,
> One of the Seventy Ninth NYSM[4]

In July 1861, Major General Irvwin McDowell, reluctantly responded to President Lincoln's prodding and led his amateur army against equally green Confederates under Brigadier General Pierre Beauregard at Manassas Junction, Virginia. Prior to the offensive, several militia regiments whose time was up left the area of contention and headed home. The 69th's term of service expired on 20 July 1861. To the Regiment's undying credit, its soldiers, after a stirring speech by Corcoran, elected to stay and took an active part in the forthcoming battle.[5]

The two armies came to grips on 21 July 1861 along Bull Run, a meandering creek in the vicinity of the junction. The Federal Army was initially successful, but as the day wore on, train loads of Confederate reinforcements under Brigadier General Joseph Johnston began to tip the scales. Late in the afternoon, a tactical error by McDowell coupled with the timely arrival of additional Rebel reinforcements on the right flank of McDowell's line caused his army to disintegrate.

Fort Corcoran—Colonel Corcoran and some of his officers are gathered around one of Fort Corcoran's heavy guns. Corcoran is on the extreme left and Major Meagher is standing behind the cannon. (Courtesy of U.S. Army Military History Institute.)

Aggressive Rebel cavalry and horse artillery turned the Federal retreat into a rout. McDowell's Army skedaddled all the way to Washington.

During the morning of 21 July, the 69th NYSM engaged the Fourth Alabama, Wheat's Louisiana Tigers and elements of the Virginia Black Horse Cavalry at Matthew's Hill. The New York Irishmen forced the Rebel units to withdraw. The regiment inflicted particularly heavy casualties on the Alabamians.[6]

In the late afternoon, the 69th NYSM assaulted strong Confederate positions on elevated ground called Henry House Hill. The attack was made at less than one-to-one odds against intense musketry and artillery fire. Colonel Sherman (later General Sherman of Georgia fame), the brigade commander, was unable to provide friendly artillery fire. Earlier, he imprudently left his guns on the Federal side of Bull Run. The regiment gained the crest of the hill and engaged the Rebel defenders, including remnants of the Fourth Alabama, in hand to hand fighting. Eventually, the Irishmen were driven off the hill. The failed attack was the last offensive action of the day by McDowell's army.[7]

Colonel Corcoran fought an unsuccessful rear guard action and was eventually captured with a number of his men by Rebel cavalry. The rest of the regiment made their way back to the fort on the outskirts of Washington, where they regrouped under Colonel Sherman and Major Meagher.

On 24 July 1861, President Lincoln released those militia units, including the 69th NYSM, that volunteered for three months of federal service at the start of

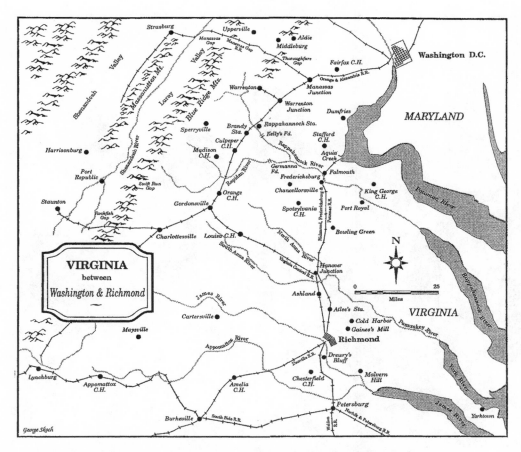

Virginia Battlefield (reprinted by permission of Perseus Books Publishers, a member of Perseus Books, L.I.C.).

the war. New Union armies would be comprised of regular army regiments and volunteer units enlisted for at least three years' service. The 69th NYSM returned to New York City and a tumultuous welcome.

Bull Run was the first and last battle fought by the 69th NYSM in the Civil War. The regiment, however, assisted in putting down the New York City draft riots in the summer of 1863.

The 69th proved its mettle at Matthew's and Henry House hills. Its solid behavior in the latter instance was verified by the after-action report of Colonel Andrew Porter, Commanding Office 16th US Infantry, First Brigade, Second Division: "The evanescent courage of the zouaves prompted them to fire perhaps a hundred shots, when they broke and fled leaving the batteries open to charge of the enemy's cavalry, which took place immediately. The marines also, in spite of the exertions of their gallant officers, gave way in disorder; The Fourteenth on the right and the column on the left hesitatingly retired, with the exception of the Sixty-ninth and the Thirty-eighth New York who nobly stood and returned the fire of the enemy for fifteen minutes..."[8]

The 69th New York State Militia at Bull Run, July, 1861.

A drawing of the 69th New York State Militia engaging in hand-to-hand fighting at Bull Run, July 1861.

Most of the regiment's men developed a fierce hatred of Colonel Sherman. They believed he mishandled his brigade during the battle. Many soldiers, including Corcoran, felt he lost his nerve near the end of the struggle and encouraged his troops to retreat while Corcoran was trying to rally his command. In addition, the Irishmen were of the opinion that Sherman shifted blame for the defeat from his shoulders to those of his troops. Meagher considered Sherman, "a rude and envenomed martinet."[9]

The regiment's performance at Bull Run was excellent but costly. The 69th

NYSM stopped more than its fair share of Rebel lead. It suffered the second highest number of casualties in killed and wounded, 97 men, of all Federal regiments
engaged.[10]

Organization of Irish Brigade

The 69th was mustered out of Federal service on 24 July 1861 and returned
to New York City from the capital on 27 July. The steamer carrying the veterans
arrived at the Battery around 0600 on a Saturday morning. Sometime later, they
marched past cheering crowds to the Essex Market Armory on Grand Street and
Fourth Avenue.

Members of the 69th were formally mustered out on 3 August and paid off
20 days later. Each man received $29.98, $2.68 having been deducted from their
pay for a pair of shoes and socks.[11]

Following deactivation of the 69th NYSM, Major Meagher and other prominent New York City Irish Americans organized the Irish Brigade. It consisted of
three infantry regiments; 63rd, 69th and 88th New York Volunteers (NYV) and
the Second New York Artillery Battalion. The 69th NYV, commanded by Colonel
Robert Nugent and comprised primarily of veterans from the old 69th, was the
first regiment to reach its quota of volunteers. The 745-man contingent left New
York City on 18 November after a rousing send off, and shortly thereafter joined
the Federal Army in Washington, D.C.

Prior to departure, city dignitaries, in an impressive ceremony, gave the regiment its colors. The battle standards consisted of a 6 × 6½", saffron fringed
national flag, an equally large saffron fringed deep green banner and two guidons.
"First Regiment (69th NYV) of the Irish Brigade" was embroidered on the national
flag's central stripe. A golden Irish harp was centered on the banner. A golden
sunburst was positioned above the harp and above that, a scroll identifying the
outfit, "First Regiment Irish Brigade." A wreath of shamrocks was located beneath
the harp, and below that, a second scroll bearing the regimental motto in Gaelic,
Riamh Nar Dhruid Spairn Lann ("Who Never Retreated Before the Clash of
Spears"). Each company of infantry was given a blue and white, swallow tailed
guidon, with "NY/69th" embroidered on it.[12]

The 69th carried the flags in all its battles through Antietam. In the fall of
1862, a group of 34 prominent New York merchants commissioned Tiffany and
Company to produce silk national and green regimental flags for the 69th as well
as the 63rd and 88th regiments. In late November, brigade officers returned the
original colors to the city and in a dignified ceremony received the new banners.
The Tiffany flags arrived at the front following the Battle of Fredericksburg.

Meagher returned the new flags to New York City before the start of the 1863
campaign. He claimed the brigade was too reduced in numbers to satisfactorily
protect the flags in combat: "These beautiful and sumptuous new colors remain
in New York, until the Irish Brigade, reinforced as it should be, shall have the
power to carry and defend them...."[13]

In December 1862, city officials presented stands of national and regimental

Brigadier General Thomas Meagher (courtesy of U.S. Army Military History Institute).

flags to its Irish regiments. Thereafter, the 69th, 63rd and 88th regiments carried the more modest civil banners into battle.[14] However, the Tiffany flags were borne by brigade veterans during the victory parade in the nation's capital following the war's end.[15]

Thomas Francis Meagher was born in Ireland in 1823. He was caught up in the revolutionary fiasco of 1848, arrested by the British authorities, convicted of treason and banished for life to Tasmania. He escaped to New York City in 1852. Meagher, a fiery orator, became active in Fenian circles and affairs of the 69th NYSM. Shortly after the start of the Civil War, he organized a contingent of Zouaves, which joined the regiment in Centreville prior to the Battle of Bull Run.

When the last elements of the brigade left New York City, Meagher was acting brigadier of the unit. On 3 February, he was promoted to the rank of brigadier general by President Lincoln and given formal command of the brigade.

Colonel Robert Nugent (Roger D. Hunt Collection at U.S. Army Military History Institute).

Robert Nugent, a Protestant, was born in County Down, Ireland. He was active in the regiment's organization and was its Lt. Colonel when the outfit went to Washington following the attack on Fort Sumter. Nugent, incapacitated by a riding accident, did not participate in the Battle of Bull Run. When the regiment paraded in New York City following its return from Federal service, he marched in the unit's rear by his own request since he had not actually fought at Bull Run.

Colonel Corcoran was held in captivity until 14 August 1862, when he was released in an exchange of prisoners. Most of his confinement was spent under threat of execution in retaliation for perceived political excesses by Lincoln's government. Corcoran refused offers of parole. Release required a sworn statement not to bear arms against the issuing government. Honor and patriotism required him to reject such offers of freedom.

Finally, on 14 August 1862, he and other prisoners were exchanged. Corcoran was badly weakened, having recently recovered from typhoid fever. His spirits soared, however, when he saw the American flag: "as my eyes fell upon its bright stars and stripes, my soul thrilled to its center and my Irish heart welled up with emotion such as it had never experienced before. And in the wild shout of delight that went up from the prisoners, I joined to the full extent of my voice."[16]

Shortly after his return to Washington, Lincoln promoted Corcoran to the rank of brigadier general. The Secretary of War offered him command of a newly formed brigade or the opportunity to raise his own unit. Command of the Irish Brigade was out of the question. Corcoran decided to organize another brigade of Irishmen for service in the Union Army. He then went on to raise the Corcoran Legion, which was eventually incorporated into the Second Corps. The unit fought with distinction at Spotsylvania, where it suffered heavy losses.

In the winter of 1863, Meagher, having resigned from command of the brigade, visited Corcoran at the Legion's camp in Fairfax, Virginia. On 22 December, while riding with Meagher, Corcoran suffered a stroke and died soon thereafter. He was 36 years old.[17]

Corcoran's embalmed body lay in state for two days in the Governor's Room at New York City Hall. He was buried in Calvary Cemetery, Long Island City, New York, following services at St. Patrick's Cathedral.

Journalist and author David P. Conyngham wrote, "Thus died in the prime of manhood, as brave a soldier and as sterling an Irishman as ever lived. He was a loss to America, for his name and reputation were talismanic to collect his countrymen to his standard. He was a loss to Ireland, for the dearest wish of his heart was to strike for her independence; and from his experience as a soldier, his wisdom as a general, and his prudence and foresight as a man, who knows what he might have accomplished had he lived?[18]

McClellan Replaces McDowell

On 27 July 1861, Major General George Brinton McClellan replaced McDowell as general of Federal forces defending the capital. General Scott remained overall commander of the Union Army. McClellan, a graduate of West Point and winner of minor victories in West Virginia, possessed excellent organizational skills. He used his talents in training and logistics to create the Army of the Potomac.

McClellan's vitality and enthusiasm had a positive effect on the army. It was no longer a motley, dispirited organization. When McClellan rode before his troops, they cheered him with fierce intensity and pride. "Little Mac's" men, including the 69th NYV, were ready to do whatever he asked of them. Unfortunately, McClellan, although a superb administrator, was not a fighter.

In March 1862, McClellan separated his army into four corps, each containing at least two divisions. The Irish Brigade became the Second Brigade, First Division, Second Corps. Organization of the Second Corps as it pertained to the brigade was as follows:

Second Corps:	Major General Edwin V. Sumner
First Division:	Major General Israel B. Richardson
Second Brigade:	Brigadier General Thomas F. Meagher
63rd NYV:	Colonel John Burke
69th NYV:	Colonel Robert Nugent
88th NYV:	Colonel Henry Baker
29th Massachusetts:	Colonel Pierce

The 29th Massachusetts, consisting primarily of native American Protestants, joined the brigade after the Battle of Fair Oaks.

CHAPTER 3

1862

The Battle of Bull Run was a bloody affair. The South lost almost 2,000 men: 387 killed, 1,582 wounded and 13 missing. The North lost over 2,800 men: 460 killed, 1,124 wounded and 1,312 missing.[1] Apparently, there was no turning back. It was to be all-out war between the United States and the Confederate States. President Lincoln issued a call for 400,000 volunteers to serve for a period of three years after the rout of his three-month summer soldiers. In the spring of 1862, the Confederate Congress passed a conscription act obligating all white males from the age of 18 to 45 years for military service.

During the first nine months of the year, the Confederacy was on the move, but by October, military momentum had shifted to the Federal armies. In the east, the Army of the Potomac renewed its efforts to capture Richmond. In the west, Union forces were threatening Chattanooga, Tennessee, and Vicksburg, Mississippi, on the Tennessee and Mississippi rivers. By late December, however, the Northern war machine was once again stuck on dead center. The eastern offensive received a bloody repulse at Fredericksburg. In the west, the advance on Chattanooga was halted by a sanguine draw at Stones River in Murfreesboro, Tennessee. On the Mississippi, Union attacks on Vicksburg were turned back decisively.

On the plus side of the Union's ledger in 1862 were seizures of Natchez, Mississippi, New Orleans, Memphis, and Baton Rouge. Another positive achievement was the narrow Federal victory in September at Antietam Creek, Maryland, allowing Lincoln to issue his "Emancipation Proclamation." The working class of Great Britain was solidly against slavery. Once the president liberated blacks in the rebellious states, there was little chance the British government would recognize the Confederacy.

Eastern Theater

General Joseph Johnston commanded the Confederate armies in the east, until he was wounded at the Battle of Fair Oaks (Seven Pines), Virginia, in late May. Jefferson Davis replaced the wounded general with Robert E. Lee. The latter was an excellent organizer and created the Army of Northern Virginia, which was more than a match for the Army of the Potomac. Lee was imaginative and daring and took chances other generals would not have considered. He believed in the fighting qualities of his men and in at least five campaigns, he out maneuvered the larger and better equipped armies that Lincoln's generals led against him. When numbers began to tell, and the "awful arithmetic" of Lincoln became a reality, Lee's army still held off defeat for nearly two years. McClellan's men respected him but Lee's troops practically deified their general.

While General Lee was audacious, McClellan was overly cautious. The latter always believed he was outnumbered by his Rebel opponents. He relied heavily on military intelligence gathered for him by the famous detective Allan Pinkerton. For some reason, the detective's estimates of enemy strength were always much higher than reality. He often exaggerated Confederate strength by over 100 percent.

McClellan began his advance against Richmond in March 1862. By mid–July, his so-called Peninsula Campaign had failed and his army was retreating toward Washington. As McClellan conducted the early stages of his campaign, a small Confederate force under General Stonewall Jackson raided the Shenandoah Valley. While there, he was a threat to Washington. Between March and June 1862, Jackson's army of approximately 16,000 men fought six battles and won five of them. He occupied nearly 60,000 Federal soldiers in a fruitless effort to bring his forces to bay. His threat to Washington kept McDowell's 40,000 troops from reinforcing McClellan on the peninsula at a key point in his advance on Richmond.

Jackson's forces rejoined Lee's army in late June. The latter launched a series of attacks on McClellan's army, the Seven Days Battles, which resulted in a Federal retreat to Washington, D.C. The brigade participated in nearly all of the struggles and received considerable praise from McClellan and his subordinates.

While McClellan was retreating before Lee's vicious attacks on the peninsula, Lincoln moved to consolidate his forces in the Shenandoah under a single commander. That man was Major General John Pope, who had won a minor victory on the Mississippi River, above Memphis, when he captured a Confederate strong point called Island No. 10. Pope designated his new command of 45,000 troops the Army of Virginia.

Lee decided to move against Pope while McClellan was slowly moving backward toward Washington. He sent Jackson with 20,000 men back to the Shenandoah Valley to check Pope's army, which had begun to threaten Richmond. On 9 August, Jackson's force crossed the Rapidan River and encountered Brigadier General Nathaniel Banks' Corps of about 8,000 men. In the resultant Battle of Cedar Mountain, Jackson mishandled his troops and was lucky to come away with a victory. Banks' beaten command escaped and joined Pope's main body. Jackson was reinforced by part of James Longstreet's Corps.

Jackson managed to elude Pope's larger army and destroyed the Federal supply base at Bristoe Station. Pope concentrated his forces and gave chase to Jackson's men. He believed he had the smaller Confederate force cornered. In reality, Lee had trapped Pope's army. On 29 and 30 August, he soundly whipped the Federal force during the Second Battle of Bull Run. Pope's shattered army retreated to Washington.

Following the defeat of Pope, General Lee invaded Maryland. He hoped to win a victory on Northern soil and thereby force Lincoln's administration to recognize the Confederacy's reality. Lee's advance into Maryland was checked by McClellan's army at the Battle of Antietam on 17 September. The brutal struggle was tactically a draw, but a strategic victory for the North. In the fighting, the Brigade suffered heavy losses, forcing the Rebels out of a strong position later called "Bloody Lane." General McClellan had driven the Confederate forces from Maryland and inflicted serious casualties on Lee's army in what would be the war's bloodiest day. Antietam was enough of a triumph to allow President Lincoln to issue the Emancipation Proclamation.

General McClellan did not pursue Lee's retreating forces after the Battle of Antietam. Instead, he was content to reorganize his 100,000 man army. Lincoln's repeated urgings and personal visits to McClellan's headquarters had no effect on his overly cautious general. Finally, in early November, an exasperated Lincoln relieved him of his command. He was replaced by Major General Ambrose E. Burnside.

Burnside, a graduate of West Point, saw active duty during the Mexican War. He led a brigade at First Bull Run. Later, he was given an independent command in North Carolina, where he achieved some minor success. His performance at Antietam, however, was lack luster. To his credit, Burnside did not consider himself capable of commanding the huge Army of the Potomac.

He attacked Lee's Army at Fredericksburg on 13 December. Although Burnside's forces enjoyed a two-to-one advantage in numbers, the resultant battle was an unmitigated disaster for the Army of the Potomac. The brigade was decimated in a heroic assault on a strongly defended hill. Assessing the results of the day's action, a Federal newspaper correspondent reported to his readers, "It can hardly be in human nature for men to show more valor or generals to manifest less judgment."[2]

The Battle of Fredericksburg was the last significant military action in the Eastern Theater during 1862.

Peninsular Campaign

General McClellan, after considerable prodding by President Lincoln, launched his Peninsular Campaign in the spring of 1862. He advanced on Richmond via the peninsula defined by the York and James Rivers, which flow into Chesapeake Bay. As McClellan's huge army inched toward Richmond, his flanks were protected by the U.S. Navy, which controlled both waterways.

The Federal Army reached the vicinity of Richmond in late spring. On 31 May 1862, General Joseph Johnston, commanding the opposing Rebel force, launched a surprise attack on a vulnerable wing of McClellan's army. The resultant Battle of Fair Oaks (Seven Pines) was a bungled affair. Nevertheless, the Rebels came close to destroying an isolated Federal corps.

Fair Oaks was indecisive but it had favorable results for the Confederates. The ferocity of the Rebel assaults convinced McClellan that he was seriously outnumbered and weakened his resolve to take Richmond. More importantly, General Johnston, who was wounded in the battle, was replaced by General Robert E. Lee.

Lee reorganized his forces and waited for an opportunity to strike McClellan's inert army. It came in late June, when Brigadier General Fitz John Porter's corps was separated from the bulk of the Federal Army by the Chickahominy River. General Lee began his assaults on 26 June. Over a period of seven days, he initiated a series of battles that ultimately forced McClellan from the peninsula. The Irish Brigade and the 69th New York Volunteers participated in the struggles at Gaines' Mill, Savage's Station, Peach Orchard (Allen's Farm), White Oak Swamp and Malverne Hill.[3]

At Gaines' Mill, the timely arrival of reinforcements from the Second Corps (Meagher's and French's brigades) saved the hard pressed Fifth Corps from being overrun. General McClellan wrote,

> These brigades advance boldly to the front, and by their example, as well as the steadiness of their bearing reanimated our own troops and warned the enemy that reinforcements had arrived. It was now dusk. The enemy had been repulsed several times with terrible slaughter and hearing the shouts of the fresh troops, failed to follow up their advantage; and this gave an opportunity to rally our men behind the brigades of Generals French and Meagher, and they again advanced up the hill ready to repulse another attack. During the night our thin and exhausted regiments were all withdrawn in safety, and by morning all had reached the other side of the stream.[4]

Francis Walker, in *History of the Second Army Corps*, described the arrival of Meagher and French as follows:

> And now an unaccustomed cheer rises along the slender Union line. It is the cheer of men overweighted and worn, when they learn help is at hand. Mingled with it is the easily distinguishable cheer of brave men who know that they are sorely wanted, and see that they have come in time. It is reinforcement from the Second Corps; two brigades of those which a month ago, crossed the river to the relief of Keyes [Fair Oaks] and now as gladly and as hotly crowd the bridge for Porter's rescue. Good brigades, good men! There wave the green flags of the Irish regiments of the rollicking, irrepressible, irresponsible Meagher. Here comes the brigade of French, the grim old artillerist at the head."[5]

In the last of the Seven Days battles, which occurred on 1 July 1862, the 69th New York Volunteers played a prominent part in defending Union positions on Malverne Hill. The high ground dominated Harrison's Landing, McClellan's base on the James River. At the close of the day, the regiment and the 88th New York Volunteers turned back a violent, all-out attack spearheaded by elements of the Louisiana Tigers. The fighting was hand-to-hand, in many cases Tigers wielding knives against Irishmen using muskets as clubs.[6]

The Battle of Malverne Hill cost the Louisiana Tigers more than 400 men. The bloody scrap added to their reputation as fierce fighters. The 69th and 88th New York Volunteers Regiments clashed with the First or 10th Louisiana, although they mistakenly thought it was Wheat's desperadoes. (Major Roberdeau Wheat's

Special Battalion, Louisiana Volunteers, clashed with the 69th New York State Militia during the Battle of Bull Run.)

After the battle, the regiment licked its wounds and requested new muskets to replace those destroyed on Malverne Hill. General Sumner at first refused to issue new weapons, thinking the men had discarded them during the long retreat. He changed his mind, however, when he was shown a pile of muskets with cracked and splintered stocks, bent barrels and twisted bayonets—evidence of the vicious hand-to-hand scrap with the Tigers. A sergeant brought the general up to speed: "The boys got into a scrimmage with the tigers, and when the bloody villains took their knives, the boys mostly forgot their bayonets, but went to work in the style they were used to, and licked them well sirs."[7]

Lieutenant John H. Donovan, Company D, 69th New York Volunteers was initially counted among the dead left on the battlefield. He had been shot through the right eye by a ball that exited through his ear. When the young man recovered his senses, he found himself a prisoner of the Rebel Army.

The next morning, Generals Hill and Magruder questioned captured Federal officers. When they came to Donovan, Hill requested his sidearms. According to Conyngham, Donovan replied that he sent them to his regiment by his orderly after falling: "I think," said the General, "from the apparent nature of your wound you won't have much need of them in the future."

> "I think differently, General," replied the other indignantly. "I have one good eye left yet, and will risk that one in the cause of the Union. Should I ever lose that, I'll go blind."
> "What command do you belong to?"
> "Meagher's Irish Brigade."
> "Oh indeed!" said the other passing on.[8]

Donovan recovered from his wound and was later exchanged. Although blind in his right eye, he fought at Fredericksburg. He was seriously wounded and later transferred to the Veteran's Reserve Corps.

The Seven Days were costly for the Irish Brigade. It suffered 493 casualties in killed, wounded and missing. The 69th New York Volunteers sustained the brigade's highest regimental losses, 208 men.

Antietam

The initiative in the east passed to the Confederacy with McClellan's withdrawal from the peninsula and Pope's defeat at Second Bull Run. General Lee decided to carry the war into Northern territory. A victory in Maryland or Pennsylvania might be enough to force Lincoln's government to accept the Confederacy's reality.

The Rebels crossed the Potomac and invaded Maryland on 7 September 1862. McClellan learned of Lee's plans and intercepted his much smaller army at Sharpsburg, Maryland, a small hamlet on the Potomac River, about 50 miles northwest of Washington.

Regimental Losses in the Civil War
69th NYV

Battles	Killed	Wounded*	Missing†	Totals‡
Fair Oaks, Va.	1	12	1	14
Gaines' Mill, Va.	0	1	1	2
Peach Orchard, Va.	1	1	4	6
White Oak Swamp, Va.	2	15	28	45
Malvern Hill, Va.	17	110	28	155
Antietam, MD	44	152	0	196
Fredericksburg, Va.	10	95	23	128
Chancellorsville, Va.	3	7	0	10
Gettysburg, PA	5	14	6	25
Bristoe Station, Va.	0	0	2	2
Wilderness, Va.	7	37	8	52
Spotsylvania, Va.	17	82	23	122
Totopotomy, Va.	1	2	3	6
Cold Harbor, Va.	5	31	5	41
Petersburg, Va.	3	22	18	43
(Assault 16–18 June 1864)				
Siege of Petersburg, Va.	11	26	8	45
Deep Bottom, Va.	1	5	0	6
(Assault 14–18 August 1864)				
Ream's Station	0	6	46	52
Hatcher's Run, Va., 25 March 1865	9	85	0	94
White Oak Road, Va., 31 March 1865	0	0	0	0
Sutherland Station, Va., 2 April 1865	1	6	0	7
Amelia Court House, Va., 6 April 1865	2	7	0	9
Farmville, Va., 7 April 1865	0	4	0	4
TOTALS	140	720	204	1064

Includes mortally wounded
†*Includes captured*
‡*Regiment also present at Yorktown, Savage Station, Mine Run, Po River, North Anna, Strawberry Plains, Fall of Petersburg and Appomattox*
   Casualty figures for battles at Hatcher's Run, White Oak Road, Sutherland Station, Amelia Court House and Farmville based on Lt. Colonel Smith's after-action reports, 34 and 35, in OR, Series I, Volume XLVI, Part I, Reports. All other data from Fox's Regimental Losses in the Civil War, *p 204.*

Lee concentrated his army in a good defensive position, at a bend in the Potomac River, near Sharpsburg. Most of his army was positioned along a rapidly moving stream called Antietam Creek. McClellan had a two-to-one superiority in numbers, 80,000 vs. 40,000 men, and should have ordered a coordinated assault which might have overwhelmed Lee's army. On 17 September, he committed his troops piecemeal. Lee shifted his units adroitly from crisis point to crisis point. His lines bent but never broke and in the end, McClellan failed to destroy his enemy. He lost his nerve and never committed his reserve.

The Irish Brigade had a stand-up fight with regiments from Major General Daniel Hill's Division in the center of the Rebel line. The Irishmen traded fire with the 6th Alabama, 2nd, 14th, 4th and 30th North Carolina, and Posey's Mississippians at a distance of 50 yards. Most of the brigade were equipped with U.S. Model 1842 .69-caliber smooth bore muskets. Its standard load of ball and buckshot was fearsome at close range. Meagher's men fought upright as if on parade. Their fire took a heavy toll on the Rebels. The Rebels, however, got in their licks.[9]

Richardson's Division continued its attack and eventually the Rebels, blasted from front and flank, broke to the rear. The Federals had pierced the center of Lee's line. Richardson was mortally wounded as his triumphant troops moved to within musket range of Sharpsburg. General Lee managed to scrape together enough men and guns to halt the fought-out Union division. At that point in the battle, McClellan should have committed his reserves. He didn't, and lost a golden opportunity to smash through the center of the Rebel Army. Later in the day, General Burnside crossed a hotly contested bridge over the Antietam and threatened to roll up Lee's right flank. The timely arrival of A.P. Hill's Corps from Harper's Ferry halted the Federals' final thrust on 7 September.

The bloodiest day of the war ended with both sides still facing each other. It is believed that Confederate killed, wounded and missing exceeded 14,000 men and that Federal casualties were about 12,400. The day after the battle, Lee's forces remained in position, arrogantly awaiting a renewed assault by the Army of the Potomac. McClellan chose not to attack. On the night of 18 September, Lee, having demonstrated his army's toughness, retreated across the Potomac.

McClellan won a strategic victory—he checked Lee's invasion of Maryland and inflicted heavy losses on the Rebel army. President Lincoln used the questionable achievement to justify his announcement of the Emancipation Proclamation. Lee won a tactical victory. His outnumbered army had fought the mighty Army of the Potomac to a standstill and left the field of battle only after the Unionists showed no inclination to renew the conflict.

The Irish Brigade fought with distinction. Its gallant attack on the Rebels in the sunken road was colorfully described by Johnson and McLaughlin:

> Longstreet at this point took R.H. Anderson's division and Rode's fresh division sized brigade and counterattacked. The 4,000 fresh troops broke through French's thinning ranks, planting their battle flags at the Roulette Farm, 500 yards deep in what had been French's rear. There, flush with victory, they ran into the Irish Brigade. With their bands drumming, their washerwomen cheering them from behind, and their green flag bearing the golden harp fluttering in the wind, the men of the "Fighting 69th," the pride of the New York regiments, hurled themselves at Longstreet's Virginia and Alabama infantry. Soon their commander, Colonel Thomas Francis Meagher, fed in the rest of his brigade, mostly Irish immigrants raised in New York City. The 88th and 63rd New York and the 29th Massachusetts closed up the gap. The other brigades of Major General Israel B. Richardson, commanding the last of Sumner's three divisions, passed behind the Irish and also swept toward the Sunken Road.[10]

General McClellan praised the unit for its bravery under fire. In his opinion, "It [the Irish Brigade] sustained its well deserved reputation."[11]

The Irish Brigade lost heavily in the action with 540 total casualties: killed—133, wounded—422, and missing—5. Four captains and ten lieutenants were either killed on the battlefield or mortally wounded. Among the wounded were Lieutenant Colonel James Kelly and Major Bentley, Commanding Offices 69th and 63rd New York Volunteerss respectively. (Colonel Nugent was recovering from wounds suffered during the Peninsular Campaign.)

The 69th New York Volunteers sustained 196 total casualties: killed—44, wounded—152, and none taken prisoner. Those losses were a staggering 61.8 percent of the men engaged in the battle. The New York Irish suffered the third highest percentage casualties of all Union regiments participating in the action. By comparison, the British Light Brigade, in its heroic charge at Balaklava during the Crimean War, sustained 247 total losses out of a command of 673 officers and men, a percentage loss of 36.7 percent.[12] Total losses sustained by the 69th New York Volunteers as a result of the Peninsular Campaign and Antietam were 418 men killed, wounded and missing.

Following the battle, Major General Darius Couch replaced Sumner as commanding officer of the Second Corps. Major General Winfield S. Hancock took command of the First Division, General Richardson having been killed at Antietam.

The 28th Massachusetts, a predominately Irish unit, replaced the 29th Massachusetts in the brigade. Its commander, Colonel Richard Byrnes, was born in County Cavan, Ireland. His family immigrated to the United States when he was a youngster. Byrnes served 15 years in the Regular Army as a cavalryman on the western frontier. Byrnes received numerous promotions for gallant and meritorious service. Commissioned in July 1861, he ranked directly below George Armstrong Custer. Byrnes distinguished himself as a cavalry officer during the Peninsular Campaign. Noted as a tough disciplinarian, he was given command of the 28th in September 1862 and quickly turned the hitherto lackluster regiment into tough, reliable outfit.[13]

The 116th Pennsylvania, raised in Philadelphia and primarily comprised of Irish immigrants and German-Americans, was assigned to the Brigade in the fall. Its commanding officer, Colonel Dennis Heenan, was severely wounded at Fredericksburg and replaced by Lt. Colonel St. Clair Mulholland.

Fredericksburg

Burnside attacked Lee's Army at Fredericksburg on 13 December. Although his forces enjoyed a two-to-one advantage in numbers, the resultant battle was a debacle for the Army of the Potomac.

General Lee located his army along high ground on the western side of the Rappahannock River. He had a very strong position in the center of his lines at Marye's Heights, which dominated the town of Fredericksburg. There, a shoulder high retaining wall fronted a sunken road which ran along the crest of the hill. Confederate troops piled earth up against the outside of the wall, creating a formidable infantry parapet.

On 13 December, Burnside ordered attacks all along his line. He launched six separate assaults on Marye's Heights, all were unsuccessful. Union forces sustained over 10,000 casualties and none of the charging bluecoats reached the crest of the hill. The Irish Brigade, although drastically thinned by the Rebel fire, was one of the few Federal formations to get close to the Confederate works.

The portion of Rebel line assaulted by the Irish Brigade was held from left

Cobb and Kershaw's troops engage the Irish Brigade from behind the stone wall.

to right by Phillip's Legion plus the 24th and 18th of Cobb's Georgia Legion. The 46th and 27th North Carolina of Cooke's Brigade plus the 3rd, 7th and 2nd South Carolina of Kershaw's Brigade were behind the Georgians.[14]

The 1,200 man Irish Brigade lost 545 men, a casualty rate of 46 percent. Colonel Nugent led the charge and was seriously wounded in the groin. (General Meagher was temporarily incapacitated because of an ulcerated shrapnel wound in one of his knees.) Major James Cavanaugh, Commanding Office 69th New York Volunteers, took command of the brigade after Colonel Nugent was struck down. He rallied the troops before the heights, yelling, "Blaze away and stand to it boys, remember what they will say about us in Ireland."[15] A short time later, Cavanaugh was seriously wounded.

Following the repulse, remnants of the Brigade hung on to positions behind boulders and in hillside depressions. In many instances, the bodies of fallen comrades were used as shields against sharpshooters' minnie balls. After almost 45 minutes, orders were given to fall back. Elements of the 69th New York Volunteers, pinned down by Rebel fire, were unable to retire until darkness.

General Kershaw reported, "An embroidered guide flag [guidon] of the 69th New York Regiment is among the trophies taken by my command."[16] During the truce, the regimental color bearer's body was recovered by his comrades. He and his flagstaff lay near the stone wall. The 69th's colors were safely hidden inside his blouse.[17]

The 69th New York Volunteers lost 128 out of the 238 men attacking Marye's Heights, a casualty rate of 54 percent. Sixteen out of 18 officers were seriously wounded.[18]

Assault on Marye's Heights, painting by Don Troiani (www.historicalartprints.com).

Private William McCarter, Meagher's secretary, was shot in the shoulder during the assault. He was carried off the battlefield by his comrades during the night of 13–14 December. His wound didn't heal properly and he was discharged from the Army in May 1863. McCarter was permanently disabled and received a lifetime federal pension.

McCarter, a Protestant, was born in Derry, Ireland. Soon after the 116th Pennsylvania joined the brigade, his expertise with pen and ink came to the attention of General Meagher, who needed a soldier with good penmanship. McCarter filled the bill. He could have avoided the attack on Marye's Heights since Meagher ordered him to a place of safety with the wagon trains. McCarter disobeyed the general and surreptitiously joined his buddies.[19]

Some sections of the Confederate line cheered the oncoming Yankees. General George S. Pickett, who months later would lead the most famous attack of the war at Gettysburg, described the spontaneous Rebel applause to his fiancee, "Your soldier's heart almost stood still as he watched those sons of Erin fearlessly rush to their death. The brilliant assault on Mayre's Heights of their Irish Brigade was beyond description. Why, my darling we forgot they were fighting us, and cheer after cheer at their fearlessness went up all along the lines."[20]

A correspondent for the *London Times* who had viewed the attack from behind the Southern lines, and who had no particular reason to praise the Irish (many of whom refused to parade for Baron Renfrew), wrote later, "Never at Fontenoy, Albuera or a Waterloo, was more undaunted courage displayed by the sons of Erin than the six frantic dashes which they directed against the almost impregnable position of their foe ... the bodies which lie in dense masses within 40 yards of Colonel Walton's guns are the best evidence of what manner of men they were who presses on to death with the dauntlessness of a race who gained glory on a thousand battlefields and never more richly deserved it at the foot of Mayre's Heights on the 13th day of December 1862."[21]

Total battlefield casualties for the 69th New York Volunteers then reached over 546 men; Peninsular Campaign—222, Antietam—196, and Fredericksburg—128 men.

General Lee's comment on Meagher's brigade's assault on Marye's Heights was precise and to the point: "The gallant stand which his bold brigade made on the heights of Fredericksburg is well known. Never were men so brave...."[22]

CHAPTER 4

1863

By mid–1863, the Confederate States scored a series of impressive military victories causing optimism in the South and pessimism in the North. General Lee won a stunning victory at Chancellorsville and invaded Pennsylvania, threatening Philadelphia, Baltimore and Washington. The South's sense of invincibility was ended in early July, however, when Lee's army was turned back at Gettysburg and General Grant captured Vicksburg, the Rebel bastion on the Mississippi River.

A score sheet for the war tallied at the beginning of 1863 would have indicated a fairly even contest. The Confederacy controlled most of its territory, except for small Federal enclaves in western Tennessee, northern Arkansas, the Carolina coast and New Orleans. Such a comparison, however, would be misleading. The Confederacy was not capable of fighting a lengthy war on widespread fronts. Even in its greatest triumphs, the South was being bled white. At Fredericksburg and Chancellorsville, Federal and Confederate armies sustained 29,000 and 18,000 casualties respectively. At a quick glance, comparative losses indicate victory points for the Rebels. When the figures are expressed as percentages of those engaged, however, Confederate losses were proportionally greater, 32 percent versus 26 percent. In addition, the Confederacy had a finite source of manpower from which to make good its losses. The North, on the other hand, had a relative abundance of manpower based on its much larger population, continuous immigration from Europe and a willingness to use Negro troops.

The Confederacy also began to realize a serious degradation in the quality of its officer corps. Unlike many of their Federal counterparts, Rebel brigade and division officers led their respective units from the front and were easy targets for Yankee lead. For example, General Jackson was killed while reconnoitering along the battle line at Chancellorsville and every brigade commander in Pickett's charge at Gettysburg was either killed or wounded. Lee was unable to find suitable replacements for Stonewall Jackson and other key officers struck down in combat.

President Lincoln realized the Union's advantage in numbers. He confided to Secretary Stoddard that "at Fredericksburg, the Potomac army lost 50 percent more than the enemy army, yet if the two should re- fight the battle with the same result every day through a week of days, the enemy would be wiped out and the Potomac army would still be a mighty host."

As Stoddard recorded it, the President said, "No general yet found can face the awful arithmetic, but the end of the war will be at hand when he shall be discovered."[1]

There was a further question, however. Would the men in the ranks of the Army of the Potomac be willing to face a war of attrition?

Apparently, some of the people on the Northern home front were beginning to face the "awful arithmetic" and they were not happy about it. In many urban areas, the struggle was called "a rich man's war but a poor man's fight." The national draft, introduced in early 1863, was not popular among lower classes in Northern society. Sporadic protests against conscription occurred in most of the North's larger cities. The worst were the New York City draft riots of July 1863. The insurrection of the city's mostly Irish population must have provided encouragement to the struggling Confederacy.

There was little chance that Britain would recognize the Confederacy because of the Emancipation Proclamation. The British working class would never support a war to preserve slavery. Napolean III of France was impotent without the acquiescence of Britain. The only real chance for the Confederacy was that the North would simply become war-weary and let the South go its separate way.

In the east, General Burnside failed at Fredericksburg and later nearly drowned the Army of the Potomac in a sea of mud. His successor, General Hooker, lost his nerve during the Battle of Chancellorsville and permitted his army to be mauled by the numerically smaller Army of Northern Virginia. Late in June, as Lee's army invaded the North for a second time, President Lincoln replaced Hooker with General Meade, who held on to defensive positions at Gettysburg and defeated General Lee's aggressive army. Through the rest of the year, the cautious Meade tried to get Lee to attack him again in Gettysburg-like fashion. Lee, on his part, attempted to pull a Chancellorsville-like coup on Meade's army at Mine Run, Virginia, in late November, to no avail. Meanwhile, as Lincoln experimented with new commanders for the Army of the Potomac, the long-suffering men in the ranks stoically did their duty. By the end of 1863, it was they and not their lackluster commanders who were beginning to wear down the Confederacy.

In the west, General Grant captured Vicksburg on 3 July. Port Hudson, Louisiana, surrendered a few days later and an exuberant President Lincoln later stated, "...The Father of Waters [the Mississippi] again goes unvexed to the sea."[2]

By the end of the year, Chattanooga and most of Tennessee were firmly under Union control. In spite of the great Confederate victory at Chickamauga Creek in western Georgia, a Federal army under General Sherman was poised to move against Atlanta, Georgia, in early 1864.

The western forces of the Confederacy appeared to be inferior to their Federal antagonists, but in the eastern theater, the Army of Northern Virginia remained a force to be reckoned with.

Eastern Theater

General Burnside was not deterred by his disastrous defeat at Fredericksburg. He informed President Lincoln that he still intended to cross the Rappahannock

River. Accordingly, on 19 January, his army began fording some miles upstream from Fredericksburg. The movement started off in fine fashion but then the rains intensified and the Federal army became mired in a sea of mud. By 23 January the troops were returning to their original camps. The infamous "Mud March" was another abysmal Federal failure. The morale of the Army of the Potomac was at an all time low.

On 25 January, President Lincoln relieved General Burnside (by his own request) of his command and replaced him with Major General Joseph Hooker. Generals Sumner (by his own request) and Franklin were also relieved of their commands.

Hooker concentrated on restoring the fighting spirit of his demoralized army. During the late winter and early spring, he established a more efficient intelligence system and reorganized the Federal cavalry. He also introduced the use of corps badges, an idea enthusiastically received by the troops. Besides being a source of pride to the various corps, the devices were useful to the army's officers. Combat units on the march or on the battle line could be quickly identified. Members of the Irish Brigade wore a red trefoil (shamrock) on their kepis.

General Hooker did not begin to move against Lee's army until late April. He used the early months of 1863 to refit and train his army. When his campaign started on 26 April, the Federal army was in good fighting shape.

Hooker surprised Lee by successfully carrying out a flanking maneuver, placing a large Federal army on the same side of the Rappahannock as the Rebel army defending Fredericksburg. Surprisingly, Hooker lost his nerve and went on the defensive in a heavily wooded area called the Wilderness. His lines were located near Chancellorsville, a small crossroads hamlet. General Lee seized the initiative and attacked Hooker's stalled force. During the period 1 to 4 May, his army soundly defeated the much larger Federal force. The Irish Brigade was Hooker's rear guard as his battered legions retreated across the Rappahannock River.

In June, the strength of Lee's army increased to about 70,000 men when General Longstreet's Corps rejoined the Army of Northern Virginia. Longstreet's men had been campaigning in the Carolinas. Lee reorganized his command. He formed three corps: First Corps—Major General Longstreet; Second Corps—Major General Richard S. Ewell; and Third Corps—Major General Ambrose P. Hill.

General Lee decided to carry the war into northern territory for the second time. In early June, his army began to move. General Hooker recommended a rapid descent on Richmond but President Lincoln rejected his plan. He reminded Hooker that General Lee's army, and not Richmond, was his true objective. Aggravated, Hooker moved his army northward. He attempted to intercept Lee while keeping the Federal force between the Army of Northern Virginia and Washington, D.C.

General Hooker got into a squabble with his superiors—Edwin M. Stanton, the Secretary of Defense, and General Halleck—over the garrison at Harper's Ferry. Hooker wanted the arsenal evacuated as soon as possible. Lincoln's high command demurred and General Hooker threatened to resign if his military recommendations were not immediately followed. President Lincoln, dissatisfied with Hooker's performance, called his bluff and accepted the resignation. On 27 June, Major General George Gordon Meade became the Army of the Potomac's new commander.

Meade, born in 1815, was a West Point graduate. He was promoted to major general from the rank of brigadier general of volunteers after his success at Fredericksburg. There, his Pennsylvania reservists had broken through General Jackson's line. The unexploited success was the only bright spot during the Fredericksburg fiasco. Meade was considered a capable fighter and administrator. A professional soldier, he was businesslike and strong on discipline. Meade was a perfectionist and cautious by nature. He was not the general most likely to win a rapidly changing offensive, but could be relied upon to keep his head and make the correct moves in a defensive struggle.

The Confederate and Federal armies continued to move northward on roads that were essentially parallel, roads that converged at Gettysburg, a small college town in southern Pennsylvania.

The Battle of Gettysburg was fought over a three day period, 1, 2 and 3 July. On the first day of the struggle, the Rebels battered their Federal opponents. Through the efforts of General Hancock, the Union Army managed to establish strong defensive positions on high ground called Cemetery Ridge. On the second day, General Lee attacked the left flank of the Federal line. The Second Corps was heavily engaged in this action and the Irish Brigade fought heroically in a part of the battlefield later called the "wheat field." The second of July was a bloody day with each side losing about 10,000 men. General Lee, on at least three occasions, came very close to breaking Meade's lines. Having attacked both flanks of the Union line, the Rebel leader decided to assault the Federal center. The fighting on 3 July culminated with "Pickett's Charge." With the failure of that assault, the battle's ferocity subsided. Federal and Confederate casualties for the three-day struggle were estimated to be 23,000 and 28,000 men respectively.

On the night of 4 July, General Lee's army retreated toward Virginia. Meade made no serious effort to harry the defeated Rebel columns.

Congress passed the Federal Conscription Act in March 1863. The so called 'draft act' was very unpopular with the masses. What began on the morning of 13 July in New York City as a demonstration against the draft erupted into a full scale riot. For five days, the city was under siege. Angry rioters burned draft offices, closed factories, destroyed railroad tracks and hunted policeman and soldiers. Before long, the insurgents turned their wrath against the black community. Most of the rioters were from poor Irish Catholic wards in the city. The uprising was eventually put down by the city police with the help of local militia units, including the 69th New York State Militia and five regiments of Federal troops from the Army of the Potomac at Gettysburg. At least 105 people were killed, making the draft riots the most violent insurrection in American history.

General Meade cautiously followed General Lee's army as it retreated across the Rapidan River and by 4 August, both armies were back at their approximate starting points of the Gettysburg campaign. In the west, Major General Rosecrans had captured Chattanooga and was threatening to invade Georgia. His Confederate adversary, Major General Bragg, needed help. Since Meade showed no signs of moving against his army, Lee transferred two divisions from Longstreet's Corps to the western theater. The troops were on the move by 8 September and arrived on the Georgia-Tennessee border in time to participate in the Battle of Chickamauga. It was a slick use of the South's feeble railroad system.

After the Confederate victory at Chickamauga, General Halleck ordered Howard's and Slocum's corps to Chattanooga to support the partially besieged Rosecrans. The reinforcements were commanded by General Hooker. General Grant took command in the west and during the period 23 to 25 November, routed Bragg's army. The siege of Chattanooga was lifted and the Rebels driven from Tennessee.

The belligerents' innovative use of railroads during the Chattanooga Campaign was studied by the Prussian Army. Lessons learned helped Germany develop the military rail system it used so effectively during World War I.

Transfer of the two corps to Rosecrans reduced Meade's numerical superiority over Lee's army from 2 to 1 to about 8 to 5. Lee decided to take advantage of the reduced odds and give the Federal army a hard knock. In general, he hoped to use tactics successfully employed against Hooker. Lee started to move on Meade's flank. The latter decided to get his army out of the constricting V of the Rapidan and Rappahannock rivers. He retreated along the Orange & Alexandria Railroad toward Manassas. Lee's advance assaulted Meade's rear guard, elements of the Second Corps, at Bristoe Station on 14 October. The result of the short but bloody encounter was a Union victory. The Confederates lost 1,850 men versus 300 men for the Federal force.[3]

In late November, bolstered by his success at Bristoe Station and his numerical superiority, Meade decided to come to grips with Lee's army. He hoped to smash the Confederate right flank at Mine Run, Virginia. Since Lee's line was about 30 miles long, the Union general believed he could overwhelm the Rebel left before Lee could concentrate his forces. The Federals didn't move fast enough, causing another failed campaign. On 1 December, General Meade ordered his troops back to positions at the start of the campaign. Total Federal and Confederate losses for the Mine Run campaign were 1,653 and 629 men respectively.[4] Lee was disappointed with the results of the Mine Run operation, believing he missed an opportunity to inflict a second Chancellorsville on the Army of the Potomac.

Following the Mine Run fiasco, both armies went into winter quarters. The Army of the Potomac had fought well in 1863 but their inept commanding officers had failed to capture Robert E. Lee.

Chancellorsville

General Hooker did not intend to attack the Rebel defenses at Fredericksburg. His plan was to hold Lee's corps in position while part of his army performed a grand flanking movement. With a sizeable Federal force across the Rappahannock and Rapidan rivers, Lee would be forced to abandon his lines at Fredericksburg and accept battle with Hooker's much larger army in the open country south and west of the city.

In late April, he sent three full corps, almost half his army, on a long march up river. Hooker was confident his remaining forces were strong enough to beat back any Rebel thrusts across the Rappahannock River in the vicinity of Fredericksburg. Hooker's flanking force uncovered previously guarded fords close to Fredericksburg and two more Federal corps crossed the Rappahannock. By 30 April, five of Hooker's seven corps were across the river and concentrated at Chancellorsville.

General Lee realized his army was in a precarious situation. There were a number of options open to the Confederate general, but being audacious, he chose a plan which, although dangerous, offered the best chance to defeat Hooker. He decided to outflank the flanker. He left a small force to cover Fredericksburg and moved the bulk of his army into the dense forest to meet Hooker. The Federal general lost his nerve and his advance slowed in the Wilderness. On 2 May, Lee sent General Jackson, with more than half his force, on a long march around Hooker's army. In the late afternoon, Jackson's troops hit the Federals' vulnerable right flank. The surprise attack from a supposedly impenetrable forest stampeded a Federal corps and other elements of Hooker's army.

General Hooker lost the initiative and never regained it. General Lee adroitly moved his forces from front to front and hammered away at the disorganized Federal army. Hooker's army retreated across the Rappahannock River on the night of 3–4 May.

General Meagher commanded the rear guard of the Federal Army during its retreat across the river at U.S. Ford. As his men moved toward the embattled bridgehead covering the ford, one of them was heard to say,

"What are we goin here for?"

"We're making history, Barney," answered his friend.

"Faith I'm glad to hear it, there won't be many of us to read it.[5]

During the fighting withdrawal, the Fifth Massachusetts Battery was moved to a forward position covering the ford. Subsequently, in a furious artillery duel, almost all of the Federal artillerymen were either killed or wounded. Shortly thereafter, the troops in the perimeter were ordered back to fortified positions closer to the river. Before the Federals could retire, however, the Fifth Maine's artillery pieces had to be saved from capture by the on coming Confederates. A detail of men from the 116th Pennsylvania, using heavy ropes, pulled the guns out of the mud. The Rebels continued to fire on the artillery pieces, killing or wounding a number of men laboring to remove the field guns. Eventually, all of the weapons were hauled from the field.[6]

The Federals and Confederates suffered 16,000 and 13,000 casualties respectively. Lee, outnumbered by two to one, had once again humiliated his Union opponent. The Confederate victory, however, was marred by the death of Lee's brilliant lieutenant, Stonewall Jackson.

The Irish Brigade was not heavily engaged until 3 May, when it covered the retreat. Nevertheless, it lost a total of 102 men: killed—8; wounded—63; and missing—31. Since the brigade entered the battle with a total of 520 men, its loss was about 20 percent of those engaged. The 69th New York Volunteers, led by Captain James McGee, lost a total of 10 men; three killed and seven wounded.

Meagher Resigns His Command

Meagher lost a fifth of his command at Chancellorsville. Once again, he requested his regiments be sent home to recruit volunteers for their decimated ranks. The request was denied; General Hooker could not spare the reliable brigade. In disgust, Meagher resigned his commission. Surprisingly, it was quickly accepted by Lincoln and his immediate subordinates. It must be noted that some high ranking officers in the Federal Army considered Meagher to be a military upstart and occasional drunkard. Unfortunately, it was an appraisal that could be applied to many officers in Lincoln's army.

Walker doesn't mention Meagher's resignation in his History of the Second Army Corps. It appears to be a deliberate omission. Following each account of an important battle, Walker in addition to providing a list of officers killed or wounded in the action, identifies senior officers who were promoted, resigned or were dismissed from the service. One is forced to conclude that Walker's oversight was a deliberate snub of Meagher. At the very least, he probably believed the general's resignation was ill timed since it was submitted when Lee was showing signs of once again invading the North.

Meagher, like McClellan, was highly regarded by the brigade. In combat, he always demonstrated exceptional bravery. Conspicuous astride his white horse (killed at Antietam), he was reckless with his life. He believed his obvious courage under fire would inspire the brigade and compensate for his lack of military expertise.[7]

Private McCarter had the following to say about the general:

> He was a gentleman of no ordinary ability in thorough military skill and courage and bravery on the battlefield, he was second to none in the Army of the Potomac.
> In polished, gentlemanly manners and bearing [when himself], he was head and shoulders above any other man occupying a similar position in the army that I ever knew or heard of....
> He was one of the very few military leaders who never required or would ask of his command to go where he would not go himself. Meagher was the first to lead the way. He was a soldier who not only prided in doing his duty but encouraged and helped all under him to do theirs. Glory, honor and praise to his memory as a soldier, firm and true to his government and country."[8]

At the conclusion of the war, President Andrew Johnson rewarded Meagher for his wartime service. He was appointed Secretary of the Montana Territory in September 1865. A year later, the governor of the territory resigned. Meagher became *de facto* governor. He acted in that capacity for almost a year. During that time, he became embroiled in political issues and made powerful enemies. On the night of 1-2 July 1867, Meagher disappeared from a Missouri River steamboat docked at Fort Benton, Montana. His body was never found. Whether he met with foul play, committed suicide or accidentally fell overboard was never determined.[9]

Colonel Patrick Kelly, 88th New York Volunteers, took command of the brigade after Meagher's resignation. Kelly was born in County Galway, Ireland. He served with distinction as a company commander in the 69th New York State

Militia at First Bull Run. He later fought at the Battle of Shiloh and was breveted to major for bravery in that action. When the Irish Brigade was formed, Kelly obtained a promotion to the rank of Lt. Colonel and an appointment to the 88th New York Volunteers as its second in command. He led the regiment during the battles of Fair Oaks and Antietam. Kelly was promoted to colonel and directed the 88th's assault at Fredericksburg, where his uniform was riddled with bullets. Later, he commanded the regiment during the rear guard action at Chancellorsville.

General Couch, dissatisfied with Hooker's performance at Chancellorsville, asked to be relieved of his command. His resignation was accepted and command of the Second Corps was given to Major General Winfield S. Hancock. Command of the First Division was given to Brigadier General John Caldwell.

Gettysburg

The Battle of Gettysburg began around 0800 on 1 July, when lead elements of Lee's Third Corps engaged Federal cavalry. The intensity of the fighting escalated as additional troops arrived on the battlefield. By day's end, Lee's forces had routed the two Federal corps opposing them. The retreating Yankees, however, managed to establish a good defensive position on Cemetery Ridge, high ground a few miles southeast of Gettysburg. Union reinforcements, including Hancock's Second Corps, arrived on the scene during the night and helped solidify the Federal line.

The remainder of Lee's army, minus Pickett's Division and Stuart's cavalry, were on the field by 2 July. The Confederate general realized he was outnumbered, 50,000 Rebels vs. 60,000 Yankees, but decided to continue the battle, a decision heavily influenced by his force's overwhelming success the previous day. Lee ordered vigorous assaults on the left flank of the Union line and at the close of the day an all-out attack on the extreme right of Meade's positions. The Federal lines were battered but never broke. It turned out to be a bloody day with each side suffering about 10,000 casualties.

General Meade considered retreating on the night of 2-3 July, but his corps commanders convinced him to fight it out in his current positions. At the conclusion of the meeting, Meade expressed the opinion that Lee would strike the Federal center the next day.

During the night, Pickett's Division and Stuart's cavalry joined Lee's army at Gettysburg. The Confederate general, as Meade predicted, decided to assault the center of the Federal line on Cemetery Ridge. The attack would be spearheaded by Pickett's fresh division supported by eight other brigades, a total of 12,500 men.

At 1300, the Confederates started to shell the Federal lines. Federal artillery answered the enemy fire. Around 1400 Meade's gunners slacked their fire and at 1500 ceased firing altogether. The Rebel officer responsible for the bombardment recommended that the attack begin. General Longstreet, per Lee's orders, sent Pickett forward.

The advancing Rebels were blasted with artillery fire from the center of the Union lines plus enfilading fire from Cemetery Ridge and the Round Tops. Huge gaps were created in the ranks of the assaulting columns. Nevertheless, a small remnant of the attacking force managed to charge in among a Federal battery. Timely Union reinforcements shattered the last of the Rebel units that had reached the traditional "high water mark" of the Confederacy.

At 1630 on 2 July, the Irish Brigade was ordered to fall in and prepare to advance. As the Brigade moved out, it paused for a general absolution by the unit's chaplain. Father Corby stood on a large boulder so that he would be visible to the entire brigade. The stirring moment has been the subject of many inspirational paintings and sculptures.

Father Corby became chaplain of the 88th New York Volunteers near the end of 1861. He was with the brigade through all of its major operations from the Peninsular Campaign to the Siege of Petersburg. He missed a few engagements due to illness but was at Antietam, Fredericksburg, Chancellorsville and later the Wildernesss and Cold Harbor. For long periods of time, Father Corby was the only priest in the Army of the Potomac.[10]

The Irish Brigade moved into a wheat field and passed through retiring Federal troops of the Third Corps. The soldiers moved rapidly through the waist high wheat in two ranks, with their regimental flags flying and their weapons at right shoulder shift. Lt. Colonel Elbert Bland, Seventh South Carolina, as he watched the advance of Kelly's Brigade, remarked to his commanding officer, "Is that not a magnificent sight?"[11]

Brigadier General Kershaw, of course, had seen the banners before at Marye's Heights, where his Carolinians helped mow down Meagher's men.

The exultant advance of Kershaw's South Carolinians was checked by Irish buck and ball. The brigade, under the command of Colonel Kelly, fought hand-to-hand with their Rebel adversaries. The Confederates were pushed back, but the arrival of 1,400 Georgians on the scene forced the Federals to retreat. Getting out of the wheat field was harder than getting into it and the brigade suffered heavily while retiring. Nevertheless, the Irish Brigade and the rest of the First Division had taken the fight out of the Rebels in their section of the battlefield. General Hancock posted the remnants of the First Division on Cemetery Ridge close to their original jump off sites. During the night, the troops dug in and awaited the dawn of 3 July.

The brigade completed their breastworks early in the morning of 3 July. Colonel Kelly characterized the Rebel bombardment preceding Pickett's attack as "probably the heaviest artillery fire ever heard."[12]

The men of the brigade could see the entire spectacle that was Pickett's charge, as the bulk of the Rebel attack struck the Federal line to their left. The Confederate brigades of Wilcox and Perry were directly in front of Hancock's men. The Rebels disappeared for a moment due to a sharp decline of ground. The men waited to see the Confederate flags come over the hill, but instead of the red flag of the Rebellion, a man crawled over the crest waving a white handkerchief and ten minutes afterwards the larger part of Wilcox's brigade walked quietly into the Union line as prisoners.

Father Corby's Absolution (courtesy of Massachusetts Commander Military Order of the Loyal Legion and the U.S. Army Military History Institute).

General Hancock was shot in the thigh during the final repulse of Pickett's charge. The wound was serious, but the general remained in the saddle until the last of the Rebels, who had reached the Federal lines, were either killed or captured. Casualties on 3 July were light except in the brigade's battery, which was almost annihilated. Losses in killed, wounded and missing for the three day battle were 202 men out of 530 men engaged, a 38 percent casualty rate.[13]

After the war, Confederate General Kershaw commented on the fight in the wheat field, "I have never been in a hotter place."[14]

The 69th New York Volunteers Regiment lost 25 men: killed—5; wounded—14; and missing—6; a casualty rate of 33 percent. Captain Richard Moroney, who led the 69th into the wheat field, was shot in the leg, sustaining a fractured thigh bone. Command of the regiment then passed to First Lieutenant James J. Smith.

The Irish Brigade and its 69th New York Volunteers had suffered more than 30 percent casualties for the fourth time in the war. Some military experts believe units which twice suffer losses greater than 30 percent are destroyed mentally.[15] It didn't matter though, there were only 328 men left in the Brigade and 50 men in the 69th New York Volunteers.

There is little doubt that the action in the wheat field had taken its toll on the Irish Brigade. Peter Welsh, 28th Massachusetts, wrote in a letter to his wife, "We lost heavily. The killed and wounded of our little regiment is over a hundred.

Out of the five regiments that form this brigade there is but enough to make three full companies...."[16]

New York City Draft Riots

The New York City draft riots occurred during the period 13 to 17 July 1863. The insurrection started on Monday morning, when a mob of draft protesters assaulted government officials who were conducting a draft lottery. The unruly crowd sacked and burned the Ninth District Provost Marshal's Office at Third Avenue and 47th Street. The insurrection spread throughout Manhattan and by noon the rioters had essentially brought business activities to a standstill. The mob's wrath was directed at police officers, war industries, prominent Republican leaders and, toward the end of the day, negroes. Police Superintendent Kennedy was almost beaten to death.[17]

On Tuesday, the insurrection took on a different characteristic. Many industrial workers who actively protested the draft on Monday did not join the mob on Tuesday. Local fire fighting organizations returned to their duty stations. Most German American groups stayed in their wards. The rioters were then primarily comprised of Irish Catholic laborers and their families.[18]

Metropolitan police and local militia units, such as elements of the Seventh and 69th (redesignated NY National Guard in 1862), not trained in urban warfare, were unsuccessful in putting down the growing insurrection. Around noon on Tuesday, Mayor Opdyke asked Secretary of War Stanton for Federal troops. General Halleck was advised by prominent New Yorkers that among the state militia only the native born and largely Protestant Seventh Regiment could be trusted with riot duty. Apparently, many of the city's upper crust still mistrusted the 69th New York State Militia in spite of its exceptional performance at Bull Run.[19]

Stanton sent ten thousand infantry and three batteries of artillery from Meade's army in Virginia to the city. Very few of the units were from New York. The troops arrived Wednesday evening and got to work immediately.[20] "We saw the grim batteries and weather stained and dusty soldiers tramping into our streets as if into a town just taken by siege," a witness recorded in his diary. According to him, the action was brief and bloody: "There was some terrific fighting between the regulars and insurgents, streets were swept again and again by grape, houses were stormed at the point of the bayonet, rioters were picked off by sharpshooters as they fired on the troops from the housetops, men were hurled dying or dead into the streets by the thoroughly enraged soldiery, until at last, sullen and cowed and thoroughly whipped and beaten, the miserable wretches gave way at every point and confessed the power of the law."[21]

During the riots, a mob wrecked Colonel Nugent's apartment on the upper floors of a building at 156 East 86th Street. His ceremonial sword was stolen.[22] Nugent, recovering from his Fredericksburg wound, was then New York's Acting Assistant Provost Marshal. In that temporary duty, he was directing the initial stages of the draft lottery when the insurrection erupted. Apparently, in the mob's opinion, Nugent's status as a brigade hero didn't trump his participation in the hated draft. The colonel's sword was later found in possession of a little boy on the East Side. The blade was broken and jewels pried off its hilt.[23]

Casualty estimates ranged from less than 300 to more than 1,000 persons. Some Democrats later claimed the figure had been enlarged by Republican propagandists. Democrats stated that the maximum number of victims was 75.

Careful research by Adrian Cook established that 105 people were definitely killed, and another dozen or so deaths may have been linked to the rioting. Eleven of those killed were black victims of the mob, eight were soldiers and three were policemen; the rest were rioters.[24]

Nativist's Opinion of Rioters

Most of the draft rioters came from lower class Irish Catholic communities. That sad fact rekindled Nativist hatred of immigrant Irish Catholics. George Templeton Strong was one of the harshest critics of the immigrant Irish. Strong was a respected lawyer and a leading member of the Union League Club. The club, founded in early 1863, was made up of men of "ancient" New York heritage—leading scientists, literati and respected professionals. These men were representative of the so-called "Black Republicans," a group targeted by the rioters.[25]

Strong kept a diary and his writings illustrate the contempt that many of his class had for Irish Catholics. (Excerpts from his diary were quoted in Ken Burns' highly acclaimed TV series, *The Civil War*.) On the first night of the rioting, Strong urged Mayor Opdyke to declare martial law and request the use of Federal troops to put down the insurrection.[26] In his epitaph to the draft riots, Strong wrote, "For myself, personally, I would like to see war made on the Irish scum as in 1688."[27] (The time of the Wilhemite Wars in Ireland, which included the Battle of the Boyne in 1690 and ended with the Treaty of Limerick in 1691.) Apparently, Strong and his colleagues viewed their differences with the Irish American community as the most dangerous fault line in the Christian republic.

It is interesting to note that in 1864, Strong hired a substitute to take his place as a draftee in the Union army. An entry from his diary on August 29, 1864, in New York City states:

> To office of Provost Marshal of my district this morning [Captain Manione], where, after waiting an hour, I purveyed myself, a big "Dutch" boy of twenty or thereabouts, for the moderate consideration of $1,100. Thus do we approach the alms-house at an accelerating rate of speed. My alter ego could make a good soldier if he tried. Gave him my address, and told him to write to me if he found himself in the hospital, or in trouble, and that I would try to do what I properly could to help him. I got myself exempted at this high price because I felt all day as if some attack of illness were at hand.[28]

In 1863, substitution was outlawed in the Confederacy. It continued to flourish in the North and was widely criticized. A rich conscript could hire a soldier to fight in his place. In the opinion of some, Templeton had no plausible excuse for exemption, except for being near-sighted and wealthy.[29]

Soldier's Opinion of Riots

It is difficult to determine what brigade soldiers thought about the rioters. It is suspected that most of them held the insurrectionists in contempt. There is no doubt that Sergeant Peter Welsh, 28th Massachusetts, loved his adopted country and had a poor opinion of the rioters. He said as much in letters to his wife, Margaret Pendergast Welsh, and to her father in Ireland.

In a letter to his father-in-law, dated 1 June 1863, Welsh explained his reasons for fighting against the Confederacy: "America is Irlands refuge Irlands last hope—destroy this republic and her hopes are blasted. If Irland is ever free the means to accomplish it must come from the shores of America. To the people of different nations who have immigrated here and become part of its native population Irland owes nothing in fact they are rather her debtors. But to this country Irland owes a great deal. How many thousands have been rescued from the jaws of the poor house and from distress and privation by the savings of the industrious sons and more particularly by the daughters of Irland who have emigrated here...."[30]

Welsh's opinion of the New York City rioters are expressed in the following letters to his wife.

> Pleasant Vally Maryland, July the 17th/63
>
> "...I am sorry to hear that there is such disgraceful riots in New York I hope it will not get near to you nor anoy you i read a full account of it in yesterdays paper the report was up to twelve oclock wensday night i see they tried the virtue of grape and canister on them and it had a very good efect the originators of those riots should be hung like dogs those they are agents of jef davis and had their plans laid to start riots simultanesly with Lees raid into Pensilvenia i hope the authorutys will use canister freely it will bring the bloody cuthroats to their censes...."[31]
>
> In camp near Kelly's ford August 2nd/63
>
> "I hope that disturbance is all put down in New York i hope it did not come near enough to you to anoy you i am very sorry that the Irish men of New York took so large a part in them disgraceful riots. God help the Irish. They are to easily led into such snares which gives their enemys an oppertunity to malighn and abuse them...."[32]

CHAPTER 5

1864

The American Civil War was the last old style war and the first modern war. It was essentially a romantic conflict in 1861 and '62, but in 1863, the grim realities of the struggle forced Union and Confederate leaders to prepare their nations for total war—a conflict in which every facet of society was marshalled and directed at the enemy.

The change worked to the advantage of the Federals, who possessed significantly greater economic, industrial and manpower resources. By 1864, the Lincoln administration was finally able to take advantage of its vastly larger population. Union armies were starting to wear down their Confederate opponents. The Federal draft was not efficient and it wasn't fair. It certainly wasn't popular, but the draft riots of the previous year were not repeated in 1864.

President Lincoln found a general who understood the "awful arithmetic" when, on 1 March 1864, he made Ulysses S. Grant commander of all Union forces. Grant and his principal lieutenants, Generals Sherman and Sheridan, waged unrelenting warfare on the Confederate States. Heavy Federal losses sustained by Union armies during the spring campaigns of 1864 were made good by the Lincoln administration. On 1 February 1864, the President issued a draft call for 500,000 more troops, twice as many men as were then in the Rebel armies. It seemed as though new immigrants were marched from landing piers straight to Union Army encampments.

More and more Negro regiments were being incorporated into Federal armies. Most of these units were used in non-combat assignments, but they permitted the transfer of white outfits to front line armies. Some black regiments, however, such as the 54th Massachusetts, provided heroic service in numerous hotly contested battles. The Confederacy did not use black troops, thereby exacerbating their deficiency in numbers.

All-out warfare tested the resiliency of each side's economic fabric; transportation system and industrial base. Sources of a nation's power became legitimate military targets. Cotton could be sold overseas to provide cash for badly needed war supplies. The commodity became a target for Federal raiders, who routinely burned bales of cotton wherever they were found. Both sides used railroads to move troops and supplies to various theaters of action. Therefore, rolling stock, railroad track and trestles were constantly under attack.

By 1864, an effective method of railroad destruction was developed by Yankee raiders. Troops pried up sections of rail and underlying ties. The ties were burned and central areas of the rails heated in the resultant blaze. When the iron glowed red hot, the rails were bent around nearby tree trunks or telegraph poles. Twisted sections of track were called "Sherman's hair pins." Federal railroaders replaced damaged sections of track much faster than their Confederate counterparts. Factories and forges, whether or not they produced war materials, were also targets for advancing Federal forces and Confederate raiders.

Napolean is supposed to have said, "An army travels on its stomach." In the Civil War, sources of food became a military target. As the war dragged on, soldiers in opposing armies became callous and not averse to making war on the civilian population. Farms, plantations and crops became fair game for marauding troopers.

General William Tecumseh Sherman, a man disliked by the 69th New York State Militia, was the Union officer most closely associated with the horrors of total war. He realized it was necessary to break the South's spirit to obtain victory. Sherman's "March to the Sea" in November and December of 1864 created a 20 mile swath of destruction in Georgia. As promised, he made the state "howl." To this day, his name evokes a negative response from most Southerners.

The Shenandoah Valley was the breadbasket for Lee's Army of Northern Virginia. In 1864, General Sheridan's forces devastated the area. Sheridan claimed a crow flying over the area would have to bring his own supplies. Both Sherman and Sheridan argued that any action, no matter how reprehensible, that served to shorten the war was in reality humane and therefore justified.

In the early part of the struggle, fighting behind breastworks was considered unmanly. General Lee, in early 1862, was derisively called the "King of Spades" when he ordered defensive entrenchments constructed during the early stages of McClellan's Peninsular Campaign. By 1864, however, both sides dug in whenever they could. Units that stopped for a night dug rifle pits. If time permitted, gun parapets were constructed. In a 48 hour period, both armies could produce formidable fortifications featuring slashes and lunettes providing interlocking fields of fire. In a week, the soldiers of 1864 could construct defensive positions presaging the sophisticated trenches of World War I.

During this last phase of the struggle, there were only two parade ground style assaults on fortified positions similar to those conducted at Fredericksburg and Gettysburg. One was ordered by Grant at Cold Harbor, Virginia, and the other by Confederate General Hood at Franklin, Tennessee. Both were bloody failures.

Grant was promoted to the rank of lieutenant general and given command of all Union forces, a rank last held by George Washington. He met with Lincoln and his military advisors in Washington during early March. The result of the conferences was a straightforward plan of operations. The Army of the Potomac would go after Lee. General Sherman's army in northwest Georgia would move against General Johnston's army at Dalton, Georgia. Sherman was to destroy the Confederate force, move far into Georgia and inflict all the damage he could on the South's resources. Generals Banks and Frederick Steele, commanders of the

Department of the Gulf and Arkansas respectively, were to move up the Red River and seize Shreveport, Texas. Following capture of East Texas, Banks was to return to New Orleans, leaving Steele to control the captured territory. From New Orleans, Banks was to move against Mobile, Alabama. He was to coordinate his operation against the port with Rear Admiral David G. Farragut's gulf squadron.

Grant's tenacity and ability to correctly assess the strategic situation in early 1864 infused a new sense of purpose into the hitherto lethargic Federal command in the East. Shortly after receiving his commission, Grant ordered the Army of the Potomac across the Rapidan. He began a campaign that ended with Lee's army pinned in front of Petersburg, Virginia. Once Grant came to grips with the Army of Northern Virginia he never released it, no matter how severely his forces were battered Grant's army suffered enormous casualties and he was called a "butcher" by friend and foe alike. Nevertheless, he understood the awful arithmetic, never lost the initiative and bought the vaunted Army of Northern Virginia to bay by June of 1864.

Eastern Theater

General Meade remained in nominal command of the Army of the Potomac. General Grant didn't stay in Washington, deciding to travel with the Eastern Army. Meade was in nominal control of the force but in reality, General Grant called the shots. Grant enjoyed two advantages over Lee that his predecessors did not have.

The first was a distinct superiority in numerical and industrial strength. Grant assumed operational control over Burnside's hitherto independent command of 20,000 men. In addition, he reduced the size and number of garrisons around the capital and incorporated the newly available troops into the Army of the Potomac. In early spring, Grant fielded a reorganized army of about 120,000 combat troops to Lee's 62,000 men of all arms.

Grant's second advantage over his predecessors was his position as commander in chief. He coordinated the efforts of all Federal armies in the field. Previously, General Halleck had the responsibility but he was not forceful. The former insisted his lieutenants keep pressuring their Confederate opponents.

When Grant left Washington for Meade's army, he intended to relieve Meade as commander of the Army of the Potomac. He believed the eastern general had been too cautious during the Mine Run campaign. Grant changed his mind after meeting with Meade and decided not to can him. Meade, however, would be subject to Grant's orders at all times and was told, "Wherever Lee goes, there you will go also."[1]

While Meade's army was engaging Lee's forces, General Grant ordered Major Generals Franz Sigel in the Shenandoah Valley and Benjamin Butler on the Yorktown Peninsula to launch simultaneous offensives of their own. Both men were political generals and Grant did not have much confidence in either of them. Sigel was a well known German national in an army that relied heavily on German and German American recruits. Butler, a prominent Democrat from Connecticut, had

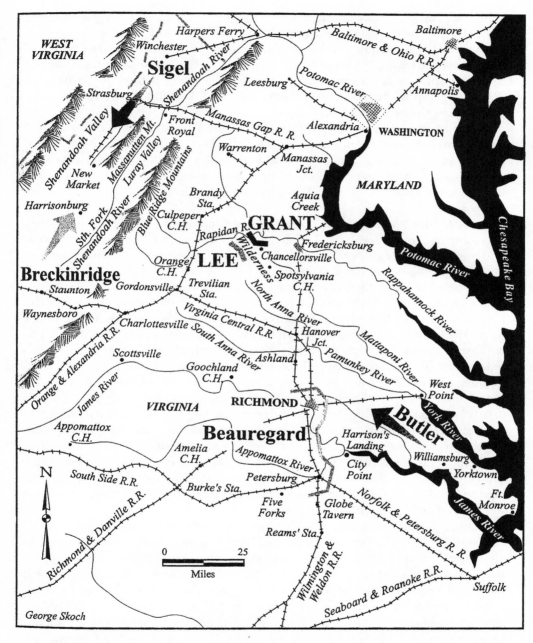

Grant's strategic plan—The map shows the relative situation in the east on 1 May 1864 (reprinted by permission of Louisiana State University Press from *To the North Ana River: Grant and Lee, May 13–25, 1864,* by Gordon Rhea; copyright 2000 by Louisiana State University Press).

considerable political power in New England. Both men were facing inferior forces, and if Grant kept the pressure on Lee, Sigel might pacify the Shenandoah

Valley and Butler could possibly move up the peninsula and into Richmond. The key to Grant's strategy was simultaneous operations on all fronts.

On 4 May, the Army of the Potomac crossed the Rapidan and moved into a thick forest called the Wilderness. Over a period of 40 days Grant and Lee fought a series of bloody battles that forced the Rebel army into trenches in front of Petersburg and Richmond. These battles included the Wilderness, Spotsylvania, North Anna Crossing and Cold Harbor.

Grant had a number of opportunities to seize Petersburg, but Lee managed to outmaneuver his generals on each occasion. The Dimmock Line, a defensive position in front of Petersburg, was assaulted on 17 and 18 June. The attacks were uncoordinated and only partially successful. Similar thrusts on the 19th also failed when reinforcements from A.P. Hill's Corps arrived in time to bolster the city's defenses.

On 22 June, Grant sent two corps against Confederate positions on the Weldon Railroad, to the south of Petersburg. Hill's troops attacked each of the Federal units separately and drove both back in turn. Thereafter, operations around Petersburg settled into trench warfare.

General Butler began his offensive on 5 May, the day Lee's army attacked Grant's troops in the Wilderness. His force of about 30,000 men debarked at the plantation landing of Bermuda Hundred where the Appomattox joins the James River. His force of five divisions began to move westward toward Petersburg. Butler's army sortied three times, in ever increasing strength, against thinly held Confederate lines across the peninsula. Each assault was repulsed. Butler then tried to move against Richmond. His forces again proceeded tentatively and by 16 May were stalled in front of the city. Beauregard, defending the Rebel capital, launched a surprise attack on Butler's army. In the resultant battle, each side lost about 4,000 men. Butler's troops retreated back to their original jump off positions. Beauregard's forces followed and entrenched about a mile west of the Federal lines. The net result of Butler's offensive was that he was bottled up in the Bermuda Hundred cul de sac by a force one quarter the size of his army. General Grant's assessment of Butler's situation was concise and to the point. He was as useful as if he were "in a bottle strongly corked."[2]

On 29 April, General Sigel, with a force of nearly 8,000 men, began to move cautiously southward from Martinsburg, West Virginia. Sigel's army proceeded along the Virginia Central Railroad toward Staunton. A small force of about 1,500 Rebel cavalrymen slowed Sigel's advance. Confederate General Breckinridge, with two small brigades totaling 2,500 men, occupied Staunton on 8 May. Breckinridge's army was reinforced by 250 cadets, aged 14 to 18 years, from the Virginia Military Institute. The Rebel force moved northward and met Sigel's advancing blue coats at New Market, Virginia. There, on 15 May, the smaller Confederate force soundly whipped Sigel's army. The thoroughly demoralized Federals retreated back up the Shenandoah Valley toward Winchester. Sigel's threat to the valley was over. Breckinridge was able to send some 2,500 men to Lee, who was preparing to meet Grant at Cold Harbor.

After the Battle of Cold Harbor, General Lee realized that Grant was forcing his army into a defensive mode and that he was losing his ability to take the initiative. On 13 June, Jubal Early, with a force of about 9,000 men, left Cold Harbor and headed for the Shenandoah Valley. Early's mission was to threaten Washington and hopefully cause General Grant to loosen his death grip on Lee's army.

At Lynchburg, General Breckinridge's small force was incorporated into Early's army. Early then proceeded to move against the Federal forces of Generals Sigel and Hunter. Both Union armies retreated in front of the Confederate raiders. Early forces plundered Harper's Ferry and then crossed the Potomac River near Sharpsburg. His raiders demanded and received $20,000 and $200,000 respectively from the citizens of Hagerstown and Frederick, Maryland, payment for not torching their cities.

A small Federal force of about 7,000 men blocked Early's approach to Washington on the Monocacy River, just east of Frederick. The Federals, under Major General Lew Wallace (he later wrote *Ben Hur*), were easily defeated by Early's men on 9 July. The Battle of Monocacy, however, cost Early a full day in his march toward the Federal capital. When the Confederate raiders reached the outer fortifications of Washington on 11 July, it was too late, reinforcements from Meade's army were already manning the city's defenses. That night the Rebel army retreated toward Leesburg in friendly Virginia.

General Early's raid was successful, he had regained control of the Shenandoah Valley, won a victory at Monocacy and threatened the Union's capital. The thrust caused Grant to reinforce the nation's capital, but did lessen his attacks on Lee's army.

In April 1864, General Grant gave command of Meade's cavalry to Major General Phillip H. Sheridan. On 6 August, Sheridan was ordered by Grant to pacify the Shenandoah Valley. Sheridan's forces then proceeded to carry out Grant's instructions to turn "the Shenandoah Valley [into] a barren waste ... So that crows flying over it for the balance of the season will have to carry their provender with them."[3]

Sheridan's and Early's armies fought it out in the valley. On 19 October, after series of bloody battles, Sheridan routed Early's army at Cedar Creek, Virginia. The Shenandoah Valley was open to Sheridan's wrecking crew for the remainder of the war.

Reorganization

General Grant reorganized the Army of the Potomac in March 1864. The First Corps was incorporated into the Fifth Corps, commanded by Major General G. K. Warren. The Third Division of the Third Corps was transferred to the Sixth Corps, commanded by Major General John Sedgwick. The First and Second Divisions of the Third Corps were transferred to the Second Corps, commanded by Major General Hancock.

The First, Second and Third Divisions of the Second Corps were commanded by Brigadier General Francis C. Barlow, Brigadier General John Gibbons and Major General David Birney respectively. Barlow, while in the Eleventh Corps, commanded a brigade at Chancellorsville and a division at Gettysburg. One of the youngest generals in the Federal Army, he was brash and courageous. Correspondence with his mother indicates contempt for immigrant soldiers, especially the Germans under his command. According to Conyngham, he was exceedingly unpopular not only with the brigade but with the First Division.

The Irish Brigade remained the Second Brigade of the First Division, and consisted of the five regiments that fought at Gettysburg; 63rd, 69th and 88th New York Volunteers, 28th Massachusetts and 116th Pennsylvania. Command of the Irish Brigade was given to Colonel Thomas A. Smyth. Smyth, born in County Cork, Ireland, in 1832, immigrated to Philadelphia in 1854. The following year, he joined William Walker's expedition to Nicaragua. Walker, a soldier of fortune, led a successful revolution in the Central American country. He ruled as president for almost a year before he was forced out. Smyth returned to the United States after Walker's downfall. He settled in Wilmington, Delaware, gaining employment as a carriage maker.

At the outbreak of the Civil War, Smyth organized a company of infantry which became part of the all-Irish 24th Pennsylvania. The regiment was mustered out of the Federal Army after 90 days' service. Soon thereafter, Smyth obtained a majority in the First Delaware Infantry. He subsequently fought with distinction at the Battles of Antietam, Fredericksburg and Chancellorsville. At Gettysburg, Smyth commanded the Second Brigade, Third Division, Second Corps.[4]

In early 1864, surviving veterans of the Irish Brigade were given a thirty day reenlistment furlough. The regiments recruited heavily and by April 1864, brigade strength had risen to over 2,000 men. Major Richard Moroney, recovered from his Gettysburg wound, commanded the rejuvenated 69th.

The Wilderness

The Army of the Potomac crossed the Rapidan River on 4 May and advanced into a dense forest of cedar and pine known locally as The Wilderness. General Lee, aware that Grant was on the march, determined to hit the Federal army while it was in the impenetrable woods. There, Grant's superiority in numbers and artillery would be neutralized.

Two Confederate corps struck lead elements of Grant's army on 5 May. The Rebels were initially successful but by day's end Federal numbers began to tell and Lee's men were forced to dig in. The next day, the Second Corps, under General Hancock, was on the verge of breaking Lee's lines when a surprise flank attack on the Federal left by Lee's remaining corps temporarily routed Hancock's men. The Confederates achieved local successes elsewhere in the Wilderness and at a critical point in the fighting almost rolled up the Federal right flank.

General Hancock (not yet fully recovered from Gettysburg wound) commented in his official report on the brigade's solid performance on 5 May, "During this contest, the Irish Brigade, commanded by Colonel Smyth of the Second Delaware Volunteers and Colonel Brooke's Fourth Brigade, both of Barlow's division, attacked the enemy vigorously on his right and drove his line some distance.

The Irish Brigade was heavily engaged, and although four fifths of its members were recruits, it behaved with great steadiness and gallantry, losing largely in killed and wounded."[5]

Colonel St. Clair Mulholland, 116th Pennsylvania, reported that a sergeant in the Irish Brigade who was blasted through the lungs with a minnie ball complained loudly when no one offered to help him to the rear. "Why Cassidy," called out a nearby soldier, "there's a man with all of his head blown off and he's not making half as much fuss as you are."[6]

Late in the day on 6 May, the Confederates launched an all-out attack on Hancock's positions on the left flank of the Federal line. The Rebels came on with unprecedented ferocity. A reporter on the scene described the attack as the "most wicked assault thus far encountered—brief in duration, but terrific in power and superhuman momentum."[7]

The assault appeared doomed to failure when a large fire broke out in the breastworks before Mott's Brigade, to the right of Smyth's Irishmen. The Federal defenders fell back and a South Carolina brigade seized the opportunity and breached the Union lines. Hancock's defensive line on Brock Road was severed, but Federal artillery and reinforcements from other Second Corps' units sealed the breach. The Irish Brigade played an important part in restoration of the Federal line.

Corporal Sam Clear, 116th Pennsylvania, described the fight as short and sharp. In his diary, he wrote, "On they came with a woman-like scream, then we let them have the buck and ball from behind the old logs and brush. The burning paper fell into our old logs and they took fire...."[8] The Irish Brigade stood their ground, firing blind volley after volley through the blazing barrier until the Confederates withdrew. At 1730, General Hancock reported to Meade that the enemy had been "finally and completely repulsed."[9]

Hancock visited Grant's headquarters around 2000. Grant was in a cheery mood but very fatigued. He reached into his pocket, intending to offer Hancock a cigar. He only had one left. Grant had smoked 20 cigars, "all very strong and formidable in size." It had been a long and hard day for Grant. He never again equaled that record in use of tobacco.[10] Grant died of throat cancer in 1885. One wonders how much the trials of 5 and 6 May contributed to his subsequent health problems.

At day's end, Federal and Confederate losses were 17,600 and 8,000 men respectively. The Rebels had turned both Federal flanks. Lee had achieved one of his greatest victories. Grant, however, was not deterred by the rough handling of his army and during the night of 7-8 May began moving his forces southward. The brigade was not involved in the initial move toward Spotsylvania and Corporal Clear had an opportunity to survey the battlefield. The opening line in his diary is poignant: "This is a fine morning, I went over to our front they had piled the Rebs in holes during the night, but the old hats of every kind, shape, color and make laid around by the hundreds."[11]

The Irish Brigade sustained heavy casualties. Five officers were killed or seriously wounded. To that point in the war, thirty-six officers of the brigade had been slain. The 69th lost 52 men; seven killed, 37 wounded, and eight missing.

Spottsylvania

Grant's next target was Spotsylvania Court House, a small crossroads hamlet about 15 miles southeast of his headquarters in the Wilderness. The fighting at Spotsylvania Court House, which started on 8 May, reached a crescendo four days later, when General Grant sent nearly 60,000 men against a vulnerable protrusion in the Confederate line that both sides called the "Mule Shoe." Hancock's corps burst through the enemy lines and charged into the salient. The rapid advance disorganized the Federals and a reserve enemy division was able to counterattack and regain possession of the Mule Shoe. The Federals pushed out of the salient and clung to the outside wall of the Rebel works. Both sides fought muzzle-to-muzzle throughout the day and into the night. The Mule Shoe earned a new nickname that day—Bloody Angle. The Irish Brigade participated in the assault of 12 May and sustained a high number of casualties.

Heavy rains during the period 13 to 16 May prevented Grant from continuing his battering of the Confederate positions. On 18 May, however, he renewed his assault on Lee's army. Hancock's troops were again featured in the operation with support from two other corps. Again, the Irish Brigade was deeply involved in the advance. The attack ended in a bloody repulse of the Union forces.

Twelve May. Smyth's Irish Brigade marched on 12 May in inky darkness, through dense woods, with rain falling in torrents, to jump-off spots for the attack on the salient. The troops reached their positions without incident and at 0435 stepped off toward the Confederate lines, shrouded in fog. The Rebels were caught off guard and the advancing Federals moved through the abatis and into the Confederate works. Corporal Sam Clear, 116th Pennsylvania, described the action, "Then such a yell as only the old Irish Brigade can give, and in we went, like as if the devel had broke loose, over the works in among the Johnnies, and many of them lost their lives by the bayonet. We captured and sent to the rear hundreds of prisoners."[12]

Color Sergeant Peter Welsh, 28th Massachusetts, was wounded in his left arm during the attack on the Mule Shoe. Welsh was carried to the rear and eventually ended up in Carver Hospital, Washington, D.C. In a letter to his wife from a field hospital, dated 15 May 1864, he described his wound: "It is a flesh wound in my left arm just a nice one to keep from any more fighting." He went on, "we had been 8 days constantly fighting before I got hit that was the greatest battle of the war we licked the saucepans out of them...."[13]

When Welsh was admitted to the hospital, it was determined that he had a fractured bone in his forearm. Bone fragments and the spent bullet were removed from his arm in a short operation. Initially, he did well, but then the wound became infected. Welsh, veteran of Gettysburg and the Wilderness, died of septic poisoning. He was buried in Calvary Cemetery, joining many other recently deceased members of the brigade. Welsh's wife ultimately received a widow's pension of $8 a month plus $342.86 covering back pay and a reenlistment bonus. She never remarried.[14]

The men of Smyth's Brigade, scattered along a captured section of log revetment, fought furious Confederate attacks throughout the daylight hours of 12

A contemporary drawing illustrating the Federal penetration of the salient shows hand-to-hand fighting at Bloody Angle (courtesy of Massachusetts Commander, Military Order of the Loyal Legion, and the U.S. Army Military History Institute).

May. A drenching, chilling rain began but had no effect on the incessant fire. Soldiers shot at the enemy through crevices in log fortifications. They stabbed at their adversaries from the top of parapets. Crazed combatants would leap up on works and fire down on the enemy. Freshly loaded muskets were handed up to them and they continued blasting away until they too, were felled. The dead and dying were heaped up on opposite sides of shell blasted barriers. Periodically, the dead were tossed out of the trenches to make room for those still able to fight.[15]

Corporal Clear believed that the artillery fire was the worst of the horrors facing the adversaries in the Mule Shoe: "...from dawn until after dark, the roar of guns was ceaseless. A tempest of shells shrieked through the forests and ploughed through the fields; I went over the works and seen the Johnnies laying in piles, the dead laying on the wounded holding them tight, and hundreds torn in pieces by shells after they were dead. It was an awful sight, and our boys, they laid dead and wounded by the hundreds...."[16]

Around midnight, the exchange of gunfire began to slacken. The combatants were physically and mentally exhausted. Somewhat later, the Rebels on the firing line began retiring to General Early's hastily constructed earthworks about a half mile distant from the Mule Shoe.[17]

Historian Gordon Rhea provides eyewitness accounts of the struggle in the salient: "'Nothing can describe the confusion, the savage blood-curdling yells, the murderous faces, the awful curses, and the grisly horror of the melee,' a veteran remarked. Another referred to the fight as 'a seething, bubbling, roaring hell of hate and murder.' An officer termed the salient a 'hissing cauldron of death.'"[18]

Colonel Byrnes, commander of the 28th Massachusetts, returned from recruiting duty in Boston on 17 May and, being senior to Smyth, took his place as commander of the Irish Brigade. The following day, Smyth was reassigned as commander of the Third Brigade, Second Division, Second Corps.

Eighteen May. The Federal attack on 18 May began at 0400. This time the Confederates were ready; their defenses were formidable and supported by artillery. The Irish Brigade was once again in the forefront of the attacking columns.

The lead brigades advanced to the edge of the abatis on their front. Brigadier General Barlow informed Hancock that the barrier was the thickest he had ever seen and that he did not believe his men could penetrate the obstacle. Nevertheless, the attack went ahead. Many soldiers in the Irish Brigade tried to cross the abatis and were cut down while entangled in tree limbs. The attacking Federals received heavy canister fire from the front and enfilading fire from the left. Barlow ordered his men to lie down while he awaited further orders from Hancock.[19]

At 0830, Hancock informed headquarters that Barlow, after personally studying his front, considered it impossible to carry out his orders. The abatis was dominated by seven artillery pieces whose fire was chewing up Barlow's men. Hancock added, that if nothing further was going to be done in the immediate future, he wanted to withdraw Barlow's troops from their exposed position. General Meade called off the operation when he received Hancock's message.[20]

Cannon fire took a heavy toll on the Irish Brigade. At one point in the stalemate, Captain Blake, 69th New York Volunteers, grabbed the regimental flag and advanced into the abatis. He waved the banner, encouraging his men to move forward, "Come on boys, and I will show you how to fight!" A short time later, he fell mortally wounded.[21] Corporal Clear was struck by a bullet and knocked to the ground senseless. When he came to, he realized a minnie ball had hit his belt buckle, knocking him flat on his back.[22]

The Union attack of 18 May was a complete failure. The assault was broken up by artillery fire alone. Wounds of Federals able to reach dressing stations were severe. Most of the stricken had been hit by shell fragments and canister. Many of the wounded and dead in the abatis were blown apart. Meade later admitted, "We found the enemy so strongly entrenched that even Grant thought it useless to knock our heads against a brick wall."[23]

Aftermath. The Irish Brigade suffered heavy casualties as a result of the Federal attacks of 12 and 18 May. The brigade, like the whole of the Second Corps, was being rapidly used up by Grant's unrelenting attacks on Lee's army.

On the evening of 19 May, the Second Corps was directed to make yet another attack on the Confederate Army. General Morgan, Hancock's Chief of Staff, was incensed by the order, as recorded by Walker: "There is an old adage that it is the willing horse that is worked to death." Morgan then broke out into an indignant recital of the marches and battles of the Second Corps from 3 to 18 May, closing with, "and now on the third consecutive night, it was proposed to send it on a flank march over twenty miles, to attack vigorously in the morning...."[24]

The regiment sustained 122 casualties at Spotsylvania; killed—17, wounded—82, and missing—23. To date, the regiment had lost a total of 757 soldiers.

Cold Harbor

On 21 May, Grant abandoned his lines in front of Spotsylvania and again attempted to get between Lee's forces and Richmond. Over the next several days, elements of both armies were in continuous combat. Significant engagements were fought while Grant's army crossed the North Anna and Totopotomy rivers. On 2 June, the Federal army arrived at Cold Harbor, a small crossroads village less than 10 miles northeast of Richmond. At the same time, Lee's army began digging in front of the hamlet, expecting Grant to attack the next day.

General Lee aligned his forces as necessary to strengthen defenses in the vicinity of the crossroads. That night, Lee's troops confidently awaited dawn and the expected Federal attack. Both flanks of their defensive position were securely anchored on rising streams, the Chickahominy River and Totopotomy Creek. Earthworks were formidable and afforded overlapping fields of fire along seven miles of front. Confederate artillery was plentiful with guns registered on fields over which the Yankees were expected to advance. Richmond was only ten miles away but the hunkered down Confederates asked for nothing better than a Federal attack in the morning.

The assault was made at dawn, with Grant's sledgehammer striking three points along the center and right center of the Confederate lines. The advance and predictable results foreshadowed the disastrous British offensive on the Somme in 1916. Never before had so large a body of troops been subjected to such concentrated firepower. As the advancing Federals neared the concave Rebel line, crossfire intensified. Advancing soldiers were sometimes hit two or three times. Colonel Oates, 15th Alabama, recorded, "I could see the dust fog out of a man's clothing in two or three places where as many balls would strike him at the same moment. In two minutes not a man of them was standing. All who were not shot down had lain down for protection."[25]

The assault was over in about eight minutes. Grant lost in excess of 7,000 men on June 3, Lee less than 1,500. Most of the Federal casualties occurred in the first minutes of action.[26]

Hancock's corps attacked the right flank of Lee's line. The Irish Brigade was in the second wave. The Third Brigade was in support. The first wave of troops overwhelmed the Rebels to their front. They advanced into the Confederate works, seizing 300 soldiers, 3 cannon and regimental colors. The Rebels brought up reinforcements to halt the successful Federal thrust. The first wave's initial success was cut short as Confederate artillery blasted Second Corps men in the captured trenches. Despite devastating enfilading fire, the first wave held on. Byrnes brought up his brigade through the malestorm.[27] The 69th New York Volunteers was led by Major John Garrett.

Garrett who was born in Ireland, fought in the Mexican War and at the start of the Civil War served with the 15th New York Volunteers. He commanded the regiment during the fighting around Spotsylvania and at the North Anna and Totopotomy rivers.[28]

Many of the Irish Brigade succeeded in gaining the main works. There, they joined the rest of the division defending the newly won section of trenches. Enfilading fire intensified and Byrnes ordered men who had not reached the captured trenches to fall back. Those soldiers retreated a short distance and then dug in. Shelters were temporary and generally inadequate against the increasing ferocity of Confederate fire.

Samuel Clear, then a sergeant, was one of the soldiers forced back from the Rebel works: "[We] charged them, captured 3 cannons and several hundred prisoners. Our second line failed to come up soon enough and the Rebels rallied and forced us back, but not to our old lines, only a few yards and they could not get us any further. We lay about 40 yards apart. If they showed themselves we let them have it and they returned the compliment when they had the chance.... So we had to lay, the fighting going on continuously. They were using solid shot, shell, grape and canister and small arms.... We dug holes with our bayonets to protect ourselves and more than one poor fellow was shot before his little dugout would protect him. We lay there expecting every minute to be gobbled up and sent south."[29]

It is believed that Colonel Byrnes was wounded while extracting his troops from the captured Rebel earthworks. A minnie ball hit him in the middle of the back, lodging near his spine. He was carried to a field hospital, where his wound was judged mortal. Major Garrett was also seriously wounded in the ill-fated assault.

The Third Brigade's tardy advance nullfied Barlow's fleeting opportunity to capture Watt's Hill, a critical position in Lee's line. Seizure of the prominence might have unhinged the Rebel defenses.[30]

The brigade, commanded by Colonel Kelly, Byrnes' replacement, was once again a shadow of its old self. It had lost 974 men since the beginning of Grant's overland campaign. Total losses by regiment in killed, wounded and captured were: 28th Massachusetts—286 men; 63rd New York Volunteers—167 men; 69th New York Volunteers—221 men; 88th New York Volunteers—98 men; and 116th Pennsylvania—201 men. At Cold Harbor, the regiment lost a total of 41 men; killed—5, wounded—31 and missing—5.

General Morgan, Second Corps Chief of Staff, summed up the effect of Cold Harbor on Hancock's men: "The Second Corps here received a mortal blow, and never again was the same body of men." General Morgan went on to say that between the Rapidan and the Chickahominy rivers, in a period of about 30 days, the corps' losses averaged over 400 men daily. "It was not in numbers only that the loss was grievously felt. Between those rivers the corps lost terribly in its leaders: the men whose presence and example were worth many thousand men. Hays, Merriam, Carrol, Webb, Brown, Coons, Tyler, Byrnes, Brooke, Haskell, McKeen, McMahon, Porter and the Morrises, and many other gallant men were dead or lost to the corps; and though there were many brave and efficient officers left, the place of those who had been taken could not be filled."[31]

Barlow's breakthrough at Cold Harbor (reproduced from the collection of the Library of Congress).

By 6 June, Colonel Byrnes had been moved to Armory Square Hospital in Washington, D.C. There it was determined, as suspected, that his wound was fatal. Byrnes died on 12 June. According to Father Corby, "He lived, I was told, to be transported to Washington, where his loving, faithful and weeping wife and children met him and embraced him before he departed for the unknown future."[32]

His funeral was held in Jersey City on 19 June. Among those in attendance were Colonel Robert Nugent, 69th New York Volunteers, and Lt. Colonel George Cartwright, 28th Massachusetts, both recovering from wounds. The 69th New York State Militia, under the command of Colonel James Bagley, escorted the casket through the streets of Long Island City as the cortege made its way toward Calvary Cemetery, Byrnes' final resting place.

Byrnes had a strong premonition of his death. A few days before the attack on Cold Harbor, he gave Father Corby the following letter for his wife should he be killed in the action:

May 17, 1864

My Dear Ellen: I am well. No fighting yesterday; but we expect some to-day. Put your trust and confidence in God. Ask his blessing. Kiss my poor little children for me. You must not give in to despair—all will yet be well. My regiment has suffered much in officers and men. I am in good health and spirits. I am content. I fear nothing, thank heaven but my sins. Do not let your spirits sink;

we will meet again. I will write you soon again; but we are going to move just now. Good bye, Good bye; and that a kind and just God may look to you and your children is my fervent prayer.

Richard[33]

Siege of Petersburg

Spotsylvania and Cold Harbor demonstrated to Grant the near impossibility of smashing through or moving around Lee's army. Nevertheless, he was determined to get between the Confederate forces and Richmond. He decided to cross the James River and move against Petersburg from the east and south.

Petersburg is located on the south bank of the Appomattox River. Linked to the James River by rail and water, it has access to the Atlantic Ocean via the Chesapeake Bay. In 1864, five railheads, two planked roads and numerous smaller thoroughfares met at the city of approximately 18,000 people. When Grant targeted Petersburg, it was an essential supply center for the Army of Northern Virginia.[34]

On the evening of 12 June, the Union army began a march of 50 miles, during which a half-mile-wide river, over 90 feet deep, was rapidly crossed. It was a surprisingly rapid advance with lead elements of the Federal army reached Petersburg within 72 hours. The movement caught General Lee by surprise. Grant had disengaged his huge army and deployed it in the Confederate rear. Lee missed an opportunity to attack the Federal columns while on the move. The result of such an attack could have been another disaster for the Union cause. Grant had orchestrated a brilliant military maneuver—an operation equaling his envelopment of Vicksburg in early 1863.[35]

When lead elements of Grant's army reached the outskirts of Petersburg, they were confronted with the Dimmock Line. The line was laid out by Confederate Captain Charles Dimmock in 1862, in response to General McClellan's Peninsular Campaign. It was about 10 miles long and approximately 20 feet wide. Although studded with redoubts and lunettes, many parts of the line were not formidable. Critical areas, however, featured impressive earthworks fronted with dry moats, abatis of entangled tree limbs and *chevaux-de-frise*. In some places the Dimmock Line was more of a fort than a line of field works.

Around 1900, on 15 June, the Eighteenth Corps assaulted a section of the Dimmock Line. The sector was sparsely defended and the Federals easily seized over a mile of the Rebel earthworks. The gate to Petersburg and probably Richmond was wide open. As it was getting dark, the Federal commander on the scene hesitated and then decided to attack Petersburg the next day. By then, 75,000 troops, including the Second Corps, would be at the Dimmock Line. Unfortunately, General Beauregard beefed up the city's defenses during the night.

On June 16, Hancock's three divisions launched a series of assaults on the jury-rigged Confederate line. The attacks were bloodily repulsed. The First Division, including men of the Irish Brigade, managed to capture three redoubts and connecting lines of earthworks.

The attacking Irishmen were led by Colonel Kelly. They and the rest of the

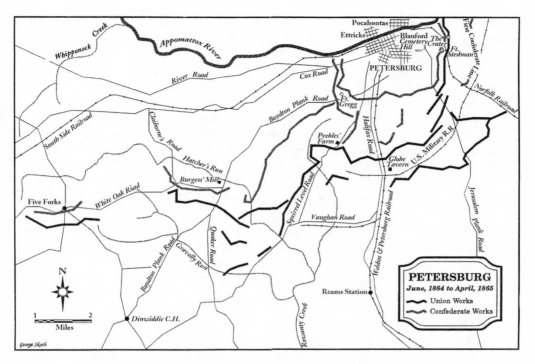

Petersburg, June 1864 to April 1865 (James Studios).

First Division went through the abatis and overran the works. For a few moments, there was hand-to-hand fighting. The melee was quickly over and the brigade took possession of a section of the Dimmock Line. The Rebels, however, took a heavy toll on the attackers. Kelly was among the casualties, shot through the head and killed instantly. Lieutenant Colonel James McGee, then commanding the 69th New York Volunteers, was wounded during the assault.

On June 17 and 18, the Federal army continued its attacks on Beauregard's line. Poor staff work resulted in uncoordinated and costly thrusts that bent the Rebel line back but never severed the patchwork defense. All the Federals achieved was the capture of a few more miles of Rebel trench. The Irish Brigade participated in the attacks. At that point in the campaign, the brigade was led by Major Richard Moroney, 69th New York Volunteers.

Moroney, born in Lockport, New York, served in the First New York Volunteers during Mexican War. Later, he worked as a machinist in New York City. Moroney was active in the 69th New York State Militia and fought as a lieutenant at Bull Run. He received a captaincy in the 69th New York Volunteers and led a company with distinction at Antietam. Captain Moroney commanded the regiment at Gettysburg and was shot in the thigh during the struggle in the wheat field. He returned to duty in August 1863.[36]

Thus ended the last of the massed assaults upon the Petersburg entrenchments. General Meade finally became satisfied that it was foolhardy to storm the enemy lines. On the night of 18 June, Beauregard's troops evacuated the Dimmock Line and manned prepared interior defenses. Lee was then certain that Petersburg was Grant's target. He sent the remainder of his army rushing toward the beleaguered city.

Colonel Kelly was buried in Calvary Cemetery on 22 June, just three days after Colonel Byrnes' interment. The "large and imposing" funeral procession was escorted by the 69th New York State Militia, Colonel Bagley commanding. Colonel Nugent was among the pall bearers. Kelly had a premonition of his death. The day before he was killed at Petersburg, he grieved over the recent loss of his horse, "I've lost my black horse, and my black dog, and now they'll have 'the little black man' [Kelly himself]."[37]

Williams's Farm

On 22 June, Grant ordered the Sixth and Second Corps to extend the Federal lines around Petersburg to the left, with the objective of cutting the Weldon Railroad. The Sixth Corps was on the left of the Second Corps. The success of the operation depended upon the two corps maintaining a solid, unbroken front. During the flanking movement, the Sixth Corps fell behind schedule and made the left flank of the Second Corps vulnerable to attack.

General Lee, aware of the flanking movement, ordered General Mahone with three brigades of infantry to drive back the Federal advance. Late in the afternoon, Mahone saw his opportunity and struck the vulnerable flank of the Second Corps. Caught by surprise, two divisions of Hancock's corps were routed.

The Irish Brigade on the extreme left of the line was hit first. All of its regiments were able to make an orderly retirement but could not form a firm line. Eventually, the brigade joined the rest of the Second Corps and fell back in some disorder. As the New York regiments retired, they delivered scattered but effective fire which "did fearful work."[38]

Mahone then attacked the unsupported Sixth Corps and drove it back as well.

Grant's attempt to seize the Weldon Railroad had failed. Total losses for the Second and Sixth Corps were 2,392 and 150 men respectively. Second Corps losses included 1,742 prisoners. Total Confederate losses were 572 men.[39]

Grant's relentless style of warfare was destroying the proud Second Corps as well as the Army of the Potomac.

Reorganization

In the seven weeks from 5 May to 22 June, the Army of the Potomac experienced casualties equal to 60 percent of its original strength. "Never has the Army of the Potomac been so demoralized as at this time," wrote an artillery officer while a sergeant penned, "Our immense army has been wasted in battles and marches until now it is too weak to work with."[40]

The sadly depleted Second Corps was also at its breaking point and in need of reorganization. Accordingly, the unit was reorganized in late June. One significant change was the breakup of the Irish Brigade.

In late June, the 28th Massachusetts and 116th Pennsylvania were transferred to other brigades in the Second Corps. The 63rd, 69th and 88th New York Volunteerss were combined with seven other depleted New York regiments to form a "Consolidated Brigade." The survivors of the Irish Brigade were depressed. They were now part of a hodgepodge unit with no fighting reputation and a bleak future. Major Moroney, who commanded the remnants of the three Irish regiments, was relieved by Major Byron prior to events at Ream's Station.[41]

Sergeant Clear's diary had the following entry for 24 June: "They have broken up the 'old Irish Brigade,' and distributed us into the other Brigades, our Regt the 116th Penna goes into the Fourth Brigade. It was awful to hear the men swear when they found the Regiments forming the Irish Brigade had to separate, some of the men swore they would never charge again."[42]

Deep Bottom

After the terrible experiences of May and June, generated by disastrous frontal assaults on entrenched positions, the months of July and August were dedicated to flanking operations. These thrusts were largely rapid movements first to the right, then to the left, sometimes thirty to forty miles in length, in the hope of somewhere, at some time, getting on the flank of an unprepared enemy.

On 27 June, Grant ordered Hancock to proceed to Deep Bottom and to attack the supposedly weak Confederate defenses in that area. (Deep Bottom was the site of a Federal bridgehead on the James River, about five miles southeast of Richmond.) When the Rebel lines were severed, Sheridan's cavalry was to make a dash on Richmond. Even if the plan failed, it would draw Confederate forces away from another section of the Petersburg defenses, which General Burnside planned to attack following the detonation of a large mine.

Confederate defenses at Deep Bottom were formidable and the attack was called off. More than half of Lee's army confronted Hancock's and Sheridan's men. Rebel strength facing Burnside, however, had been significantly reduced. Burnside exploded his huge mine on 30 June but his subsequent attack (later called the Battle of the Crater) was a botched affair. Grant, in a message to General Halleck, aptly described the failed attack: "It was the saddest affair I have witnessed in the war. Such an opportunity for carrying fortifications I have never seen and do not expect to have again."[43] The fiasco had one positive feature, however, General Burnside was politely put out to pasture.

The Second Corps suffered 135 casualties, killed, wounded and missing in the Deep Bottom operation. The Consolidated Brigade had minimal casualties. No officers were killed or wounded.

Second Deep Bottom

Between 31 July and 12 August, the Second Corps remained in camp near its section of the Petersburg line. During that period of time, General Grant decided to make a second assault on Lee's left flank in the vicinity of Deep Bottom.

On 13 August, the Second Corps faked movement to Washington via the

James River and City Point and then returned at night to make a primitive amphibious landing at Deep Bottom. The enlisted men were bitterly disappointed. They had been completely faked out, believing the Second Corps was about to get a well earned rest in the capital.

Elements of the Second Corps began debarking around 0230 on 14 August. The surprise attack was supposed to start before dawn. It was almost noon, however, before all of Hancock's attack force was ashore. Finally, around 1600, Hancock ordered Barlow to begin the assault.

Barlow's strike force consisted of about 10,000 dispirited men. The young brigadier was ill and his attacks were poorly coordinated. Nevertheless, the Irish regiments of the Consolidated Brigade managed to seize a line of works.[44] In spite of that and other initial successes, the Federal attack was easily repulsed by the Rebels. Barlow complained of his troops' performance. General Morgan supported his low opinion of the Second Corps. "It is evident," concluded Morgan, "that assaults all along the line had left very little of the old material there."[45]

During the next few days, Hancock tried to penetrate Lee's defenses. By 18 August, it was obvious that Lee had turned back the Federal thrust. Casualties for the Second Corps were 915 men. The Irish regiments lost 40 men, six of which were from the 69th New York Volunteers.

On 18 August, General Barlow, not fully recovered from wounds received at Antietam and Gettysburg, and suffering from other maladies, gave up command of the First Division. He was replaced by Brigadier General Nelson Miles. Miles had previously commanded the division's First Brigade.

Ream's Station

On 24 August, the First and Second Divisions of the Second Corps were engaged in destroying sections of the Weldon Railroad in the vicinity of Ream's Station. The railroad depot was about eight miles south of Petersburg. Hancock's troops were separated from the main body of Grant's army and in a precarious situation. Lee decided to strike the overextended Federal wrecking force. Accordingly, on the afternoon of 25 August, eight brigades of infantry plus cavalry attacked the isolated Federal divisions. Just when it appeared that a last all-out Rebel assault would be beaten back, a part of the Federal line held by the Seventh, 52nd and 39th New York Volunteers, gave way in confusion. The Yankees were soon routed. A makeshift battle line was established by sundown but the Federals were unable to retake any of their lost positions. Later that night, the battered Second Corps retreated to its encampment near Petersburg. As Hancock gave the order to withdraw from Ream's Station, the thoroughly discouraged general exclaimed, "Colonel I do not care to die, but I pray to God I may never leave this field."[46]

Ream's Station was a stunning Confederate victory. Union and Rebel casualties were 2,602 and 814 men respectively Federal losses included 2,046 prisoners. The Confederates also captured nine artillery pieces and 12 stands of colors.[47] Those of the 69th were not taken.[48]

The battle was a complete disaster for Hancock, the Second Corps and remnants of the Irish Brigade. The Brigade lost 94 men, most of whom were captured. The 69th New York Volunteers suffered 52 casualties, 6 wounded and 46 captured. Major Byron was among the Rebel prisoners.

When the Consolidated Brigade took its position in the earthworks at Ream's Station, Byron deployed a sufficient number of skirmishers to cover his defensive positions. The trenches were manned by a thin screen of soldiers about a pace apart. Ideally, the line should have been manned by two ranks of soldiers standing shoulder to shoulder.

The New York regiments took a heavy toll on the advancing Confederates. Many Rebels were pinned down by the deadly Federal fusillades and raised their hands to surrender. When the Rebels broke through at a railroad cut, the Irish regiments, holding their ground and blasting the enemy on their front, were in immediate danger of being surrounded.

It was a matter of falling back quickly or being taken. Those who continued to fight were either struck down or captured. The 69th New York Volunteers, then commanded by Major John Gleason, had 46 men captured. It appears that the men of the regiment were among the last to abandon the Union defenses when the Rebels broke through.

Ream's Station provided conclusive proof that Grant's overland campaign, 100 days of almost continuous fighting and marching, had used up the Second Corps. Its proud regiments, including the three New York units, were victims of the 'awful arithmetic.' Hancock's veteran outfits could not be spared for rest and rehabilitation at their cities of origin. They were penalized by a policy favoring creation of new, often useless regiments with politically connected colonels. Morale in the Irish regiments was further degraded by replacement of their beloved brigade with the hodgepodge Consolidated Brigade.

Defeat at Ream's Station all but ended Hancock's military career. The despondent general, still suffering from his Gettysburg wound, was sent home, supposedly to organize a corps of veterans. The war was over for General Hancock but his erstwhile command still had to soldier on.

Boydton Plank Road

On 26 October, the Second and Third Divisions of Hancock's Corps moved out of the Petersburg line as part of an advance against the South Side Railroad. The First Division and the New York Regiments, then commanded by Colonel Denis Burke, remained in the lines. The plan to sever the railroad failed completely. The First Division, however, launched a series of successful trench raids which brought Grant's siege line somewhat closer to Petersburg. The Consolidated Brigade sustained 14 casualties; three killed, and 11 wounded, all from the 88th New York Volunteers.[49]

Reorganization

General Hancock was relieved by Major General Andrew A. Humphrey on 26 November. Humphrey had been Chief of Staff, Army of the Potomac.

Earlier Colonel Nugent and Lieutenant Colonel James McGee, both recovering from wounds in New York City, were successful in recruiting men for the decimated Irish Brigade. By October, the three regiments, especially the 69th New York Volunteers, were nearly at full strength. Early in November, Colonel Nugent returned to the Second Corps and assisted in the reorganization of the Irish Brigade.

The 28th Massachusetts, which had also been considerably reinforced, was once again reunited with the New York regiments. The Seventh New York Heavy Artillery (NYHA) was assigned to the reborn Second Brigade in lieu of the 116th Pennsylvania. Colonel Nugent was given command of the brigade and Major Moroney that of the 69th New York Volunteers, Lt. Colonel McGee being permanently disabled. The 116th Pennsylvania could not be effectively reunited with the brigade because its commander, Colonel Mulholland, outranked Nugent.

Hatcher's Run

The Irish Brigade was involved in Grant's last raid on the Weldon Railroad in 1864. On 8 December, the First Division marched on Vaughan Road out to Hatcher's Run. The brigade was then under the command of Colonel Duryea, Seventh NYHA, Colonel Nugent being temporarily reassigned. The division encountered enemy pickets, drove them across the stream and then continued on to a place called Armstrong's Mill. The reconnaissance in force, having found the railroad stoutly defended, returned to its camps. The First Division and the Irish Brigade sustained minimal casualties in this last operation of 1864.

Terrain in the area of Hatcher's Run was rugged with dense underbrush and stands of trees. Enemy patrols routinely surprised each other as they reconnoitered. In some instances, the startled combatants exchanged gunfire and in others a short truce permitted the exchange of tobacco for coffee. If members of the Irish Brigade were involved, swigs from whiskey-laced canteens might be available. Sometimes sudden encounters with the enemy provided unusual results. According to one account:

> An officer of the 88th New York Volunteers walked into the middle of a band of Rebels and thinking they were prisoners asked, "Where is the Provost Guard?"
> "We uns aint got none," came the reply in an unmistakable southern drawl.
> "What troops?" asked the officer.
> "Fourth Alabama," came the reply.
> "Good men, push on," replied the Irishman who fortunately did not have a northern accent. Off went the Fourth Alabama in one direction and the 88th man in the other.[50]

Perhaps some of their progeny would enjoy fisticuffs in Mineola taverns and comradeship in the Argonne Forest.

CHAPTER 6

1865

The war in the east ended on 9 April, when General Lee surrendered remnants of his once formidable army to General Grant at Appomattox Court House. President Lincoln didn't have much time to enjoy his victory. He died on 15 April, after being mortally wounded the previous evening by John Wilkes Booth in Washington's Ford Theater.

General Joseph Johnston surrendered the Confederacy's major western army to General Sherman in the vicinity of Hillsborough, North Carolina, on 26 April. Sometime later, Confederate Generals Richard Taylor, Bedford Forrest and Kirby Smith capitulated. Confederate Generals Jo Shelby, Sterling Price and John Magruder chose not to yield. They and a small group of Rebel diehards escaped to Mexico, where they offered their services to Emperor Maximilian. The French puppet ruler was actively fighting democratic insurgents led by supporters of Benito Juarez. The ex–Rebels had once again embraced a losing cause.

President Davis and his fleeing entourage were brought to bay at Abbeville, Georgia, on 10 May. He was taken to Fort Monroe, Virginia, where he was held prisoner under indictment for treason. Two years later, he was released without trial.

Eastern Theater

During the winter of 1864–1865, a relative quiet settled over no-man's land between the Confederate and Federal lines at Petersburg. Both sides waited the coming of spring, Grant with optimism and Lee with apprehension. Both realized the final decision was near.

Lee's army in Petersburg depended upon the fragile South Side Railroad, which carried an inadequate amount of supplies into the city from a rapidly diminishing logistics base. Lee had one desperate chance left. He intended to break Grant's grip on Petersburg and march his command south. He hoped to join General Johnston's army in North Carolina, and with their combined strength, crush Sherman's army. The joint forces would then turn and confront Grant's massive Army of the Potomac. In reality, it was a harebrained scheme, but it was the only option left to Lee other than surrender.

Before General Lee could withdraw, however, he had to loosen Grant's stranglehold on the city. To achieve that goal, he ordered Major General John B. Gordon to attack an important fort in Grant's siege line. That strong point was Fort Stedman. General Lee hoped that Gordon would capture the fort and then drive into the rear of the Federal line. Grant would be forced to seal the breach and hopefully draw troops away from roads leading out of Petersburg.

The initiative was carefully planned and on 25 March, Gordon's surprise attack captured the fort. Federal counterattacks, however, checked the Confederate advance and Gordon's raiders were compelled to retreat. The attack cost Lee some 3,500 men, at that time about ten percent of his army.

General Grant realized Lee's intentions and, surmising that Lee had "robbed Peter to pay Paul," decided to once again try to turn the Confederate right. He sent Warren's Fifth Corps and Sheridan's Cavalry on a wide sweep toward the South Side Railroad. The Federal flankers were halted at Dinwiddie Court House but on 1 April, at Five Forks, the Rebel right wing under General Pickett was shattered. Suddenly, General Lee's position in Petersburg was untenable.

Flushed with success, General Grant ordered attacks all along the line. The next day, General Wright's corps broke through the Rebel positions at Popular Springs. General A. P. Hill was killed in the battle.

On the night of 2 April, General Lee began evacuating Petersburg and Richmond. His immediate goal was the railway junction at Lynchburg, Virginia. From there, he could start transferring his troops south. Again, General Grant guessed his intentions. Five miles southwest of Amelia Courthouse, lead elements of Lee's army were intercepted by General Sheridan's cavalry. On 5 April, finding his retreat blocked, Lee moved his army to the west.

Grant pursued relentlessly. The next day, Lee's army of about 20,000 effectives turned to fight off Sheridan's cavalry. During the resultant Battle of Sayler's Creek, the Confederate line was rolled up. Nearly, 8,000 dispirited Confederate veterans were captured. Lee, his army reduced to less than 13,000 men, pushed on toward Lynchburg. The vaunted Army of Northern Virginia was finally trapped at Appomattox Court House. Sheridan's cavalry and two Federal corps were across Lee's line of march, the remainder of Grant's army was closing on his rear guard. The jig was up. Some of Lee's lieutenants suggested that his army disperse and carry on the struggle via guerrilla warfare. General Lee would have none of it. He shook his head and said, "There is nothing left for me to do but to go and see General Grant, and I would rather die a thousand deaths."[1]

On 9 April, 1865, General Lee met with Grant at the home of Wilmer McLean in the small village of Appomattox Court House to surrender his army. General Lee, in his best uniform, arrived first at 1300. Grant, with several Federal officers, including Generals Sheridan and Ord, arrived at 1330. Grant was dressed in his campaign uniform. Grant attempted some small talk but Lee got right to the purpose of the gathering: "I suppose, General Grant, that the object of our present meeting is fully understood. I asked to see you to ascertain upon what terms you would receive the surrender of my army."[2]

Grant's terms were lenient. The Rebels would lay down their arms and pledge not to fight again. Lee agreed and asked Grant to put it in writing. Grant then wrote out the terms, exempting the officer's side arms, horses and personal baggage from the surrender.

Lee read the document carefully and then asked a favor of Grant. Would the Federal commander allow enlisted cavalrymen and artillerists who used their own animals to retain them after the surrender? Grant considered Lee's request and agreed to incorporate it in the surrender document.

A clean copy of the revised surrender terms was prepared and shortly after 1500 both parties signed the document. Lee and Grant shook hands one more time and parted, Grant to the congratulations of a grateful nation. Lee, then a paroled prisoner of war, rejoined the ragged and hungry remnants of the Army of Northern Virginia.

Winter Siege of Petersburg

Nothing of importance occurred during the month of January of 1865. On 5 February, however, General Grant ordered a thrust against the roads in the vicinity of Dinwiddie Court House, with the intent of interrupting Lee's supply routes in that area. The assault was led by Gregg's cavalry and supported by General Warren's Fifth Corps. General Humphrey, with the Second and Third Divisions, was to maintain communications with the flanking force and the extreme left of the Federal entrenchments. Those trenches were held by General Miles' First Division, including the rejuvenated Irish Brigade.

Lee countered Grant's thrust and heavy fighting occurred on 5 and 6 February. The result of the above operations was the extension of Federal lines around Petersburg to a point where the Vaughan Road crossed Hatcher's Run. The Second Corps held the left of Grant's lines.

The greater part of March passed without noteworthy incident, the days and weeks being devoted to inspection, drill and discipline, military routines to minimize the negative effects of soldiering in harsh weather and the preceding campaign's heavy losses.

St. Patrick's Day, 1865

The St. Patrick's Day celebration began, as usual, with a solemn High Mass celebrated by Father Ouellett. Father Corby had resigned and returned to a monastery in Indiana. After mass, brigade members and guests assembled on a field serving as a race track. A large roofed stand, recently erected, sheltered a spacious refreshment area, in which brigade officers passed out sandwiches and spiked punch to hungry and parched guests.

Among officers present were Generals Humphrey, Warren, Crawford, Miles and Meagher. Colonel Nugent acted as race course clerk. Festivities included several flat and steeplechase races. Apparently, Colonel Nugent's horse "Harry" performed well, winning at least one event. As usual, horse races were fiercely contested and several riders were seriously injured. Second Lieutenant

McConville, 69th New York Volunteers, suffered a fractured skull and subsequently died.

Enlisted men competed in sack and foot races. A soldier of the 88th New York Volunteers won both races, pocketing about forty dollars per event. For some reason, there was no mule race that year. Army regulations did not allow enlisted men to drink alcoholic beverages at the shindig. The honored guests had to make do with sandwiches and punch liberally laced with "commissary whiskey."

Sergeant Clear attended the festivities. Some of Clear's observations follow:

> We found a nice track like a Fair Ground, but they had four hurdles built three feet high across the track and between these hurdles a ditch three feet deep, four feet wide and forty feet long....
> And then the word was given and away they go. Some went over the hurdles and ditches, some flew the track and ran through the crowd of soldiers. A sergeant of the 69th New York was trampled to death and half a dozen others badly wounded. The ambulance was hauling dead and wounded away all day. The second round the Black Stallion of the Dutch Col. fell over a hurdle and broke his neck and both arms of the Colonel. They sent the Colonel to the hospital, rolled the dead horse out of the way and went ahead as if nothing had happened....
> Never did I see such a crazy time. I will have to alter my mind if I ever go to see another Irish Fair.[3]

The festivities were relatively subdued compared to previous events. Four years of hard campaigning had mellowed all but a few of the surviving brigade members. On a positive note, national acceptance of the 69th New York Volunteers had improved dramatically since the dark days of the 1850s.

Fort Stedman

At 0330 on 25 March, General Gordon launched his surprise attack on Fort Stedman. Lee hoped to sever Grant's communications with his vital base at City Point. Initially successful, the surging Rebels were eventually forced back with severe losses.

When General Humphreys learned of the Rebel attack, he immediately ordered each of his division commanders to launch a series of reconnaissances in force along their lines. The resultant attacks were made with such vigor that the entire entrenched Rebel picket line facing his divisions were captured. The Confederate main line was then tested at several points but found to be strongly defended. Second Corps troops were content to hold the captured picket line. Subsequent Rebel attacks to regain the captured trenches were beaten back.[4]

At that point in the campaign, corps, division, brigade and regimental commanders were Humphreys, Brigadier General Nelson Miles, Nugent and Lt. Colonel James Smith. The Seventh NYHA had been replaced by the Fourth NYHA.

Smith, while a lieutenant, took command of the brigade after Moroney was shot at Gettysburg. Smith was wounded in August 1864 during a bayonet charge at Deep Bottom and again at Ream's Station. He worked his way up through the ranks and by the start of Grant's '65 campaign was a lieutenant colonel.

Skinner's Farm–Hatcher's Run

As soon as General Humphreys learned of the attack on Fort Stedman, he proceeded to probe the enemy's front for weaknesses. Reconnaissances in force were ordered along the Second Corps front. One such probe was launched by the brigade on a section of line fronting Skinner's Farm. The site was located near Hatcher's Run. According to Conyngham, "The contest was conspicuous to the rest of the corps, who appeared to be, as it were, spectators at an exciting melodrama in a huge theatre, and on every side the most flattering admiration was expressed for such a spectacle of unflinching bravery."[5]

Captain Mulhall of the 69th New York Volunteers commanded the Federal skirmishers. He was badly wounded, a ball shattering the bone in his lower leg, as he led his men in the advance. He fell between the contending lines of troops. Finally, after a period of about two hours the Confederates gave way and Mulhall was rescued.

The brigade was relieved in the early evening. Humphrey having determined that the Rebel positions to his front were still formidable, ordered his command back to its jump off positions.

The brigade lost heavily in this action. Losses were: 69th New York Volunteers—nine killed and 85 wounded; 28th Massachusetts—seven killed and 35 wounded; 63rd New York Volunteers—one wounded; and 88th New York Volunteers—four wounded.[6]

White Oak Road

On 31 March, Confederate General Pickett, with six brigades of cavalry and five brigades of infantry, attacked Sheridan's cavalry in the vicinity of Dinwiddie Court House. The Confederates eventually drove the Federal cavalry back to the Court House.

Meanwhile, the Fifth Corps was moving toward Five Forks with the intent of severing Pickett's communications with the rest of the Rebel army. General Lee, realizing the situation's seriousness, personally directed a counterattack by four brigades of infantry, which caught Warren's lead units by surprise. The Fifth Corps was forced back in some disorder, forcing Warren to ask General Humphreys for support. The latter sent Miles to his aid with the brigades of Madill and Ramsey supported by Colonel Nugent's Irish Brigade.

Miles' impetuousness caused Lee's troops to fall back. The First Division captured in excess of 300 prisoners and a Rebel flag before the Confederates returned to their trenches.[7] Sometime later, General Warren re-formed his troops and gained the advanced trenches of the enemy. During this action, the First Division lost 331 men, including 45 killed, 245 wounded and 41 missing.

As a result of the action on 31 March, General Warren was subsequently relieved of his command by Sheridan. Conyngham described the attitude of the brigade toward Warren's relief: "The course taken by General Sheridan in relieving Warren was very much regretted by the army generally, and by none more than the brigade, by whom Warren was held in high estimation."[8]

Five Forks

On 1 April, Sheridan's cavalry and the Fifth Corps routed Pickett's force at Five Forks. Over 4,000 Confederate soldiers were taken prisoner. Total Rebel losses were much greater than Lee could accommodate, considering he was attempting to hold 40 miles of entrenchments from Petersburg to Richmond.

The remnants of Pickett's forces fell back on the South Side Railroad. During the night, he was reinforced by four brigades from Lee's right. The Confederate General, however, realized he had to evacuate the Petersburg defenses.

While the Battle of Five Forks was in progress, the First Division under General Miles severed White Oak Road to prevent Lee from reinforcing Pickett from the Petersburg defenses. Miles was subsequently ordered forward to reinforce Sheridan at Five Forks.

Sutherland Station

On 2 April, the Sixth and Ninth Corps broke through the Confederate lines at Petersburg. General Humphreys was instructed not to assault the lines in front of his corps until the First Division was returned to him. Nevertheless, Humphreys ordered a series of probing attacks that were generally successful. During the night, General Miles' First Division rejoined the Second Corps.

General Meade ordered Humphreys to send the Second and Third Divisions toward Petersburg to support the Sixth Corps in exploiting its earlier breakthrough. These divisions were to move by the Boydton Road. Miles' division was to advance toward Petersburg via the Claiborne Road after crossing Hatcher's Run.

Miles, moving quickly, encountered a Confederate force of four brigades under General Cooke, whose men were behind hastily erected entrenchments. Notwithstanding the numbers opposing him and strength of the enemy's position, Miles attacked with the Irish and Madill's Brigades. The vigorously delivered attack was repulsed. Undeterred, Miles re-formed his lines and attacked again. The Federals were repulsed with heavy losses. Miles repositioned his artillery and attacked a third time. This time his men carried the Rebel works, capturing two artillery pieces and over 600 prisoners.[9]

Colonel Nugent reported his men charged the works with the Third Brigade and, owing to terrific enfilading fire of artillery and musketry, were repulsed. The men of the brigade immediately re-formed and charged again, this time capturing a section of the Confederate defensive works with about 150 prisoners, two cannon and one battle flag.

In its last major battle of the war, which was fought near Sutherland Station on the South Side Railroad, the brigade lost 91 men, killed, wounded or missing. The 69th had one killed and six wounded.[10]

Appomattox

General Lee's army evacuated Petersburg and Richmond during the night of 2 April. The Second Corps joined Sheridan's cavalry and the Fifth Corps in pursuit of Lee's retreating army. Lee's immediate objective was Burksville Junction on the Richmond and Danville Railroad.

On the afternoon of 4 April, General Sheridan encountered the Irish Brigade. Irishman Sheridan rode up to Colonel Nugent and asked him what troops he was leading. Nugent responded, "The Irish Brigade, First Division, Second Corps." Sheridan replied, "Ah indeed!" with a smile. A spontaneous cheer rose up from the throats of over 1,000 men in the brigade. General Sheridan rode away, acknowledging the compliment.[11]

The Confederate last stand was made at Sayler's Creek on 6 April. General Sheridan struck the enemy's rear guard and detained it until the Sixth Corps arrived on the scene and joined the attack. When the combined arms of cavalry and infantry struck the Rebels, they were quickly routed. Between 6,000 and 7,000 prisoners were taken. During the fighting at Sayler's Creek, the Second Corps captured a large train of Confederate baggage at Amelia Station. According to Conyngham, "The trophies of the Second Corps included, in addition, several pieces of artillery and thirteen flags. Of these the brigade captured the largest number and some of the officers were subsequently dispatched with the trophies to Washington, where they received a decoration from the War Department."[12]

The Second Corps, resuming pursuit of the Rebel forces, encountered a portion of Lee's army strongly entrenched near Farmville, Virginia. General Smyth was killed while reconnoitering the Confederate positions. It was quickly determined that Lee's troops, approximately 18,000 men, were dug in covering the stage and plank roads to Lynchburg.

General Meade ordered the Sixth and Twenty Fourth Corps to proceed to Farmville to assist Humphreys in attacking Lee's army. Before either of the corps arrived on the scene, Humphreys began his advance. General Miles directed his First Brigade to assault a perceived weakness in Lee's line. The resultant attack was repulsed with loss. After that, there was a sporadic firing until dark. Later that night, Lee's army continued its retreat.

Total Second Corps casualties at Farmville were 571 men killed, wounded and missing. Thirty-four of those losses were sustained by the Irish Brigade. Four men of the 69th were wounded.

The death of General Smyth was a severe loss to the brigade. He was loved and admired by his former command. Conyngham had the following to say about the fallen leader,

> In appearance General Smyth had few superiors; tall of muscular frame with a native dignity and commanding grace about him, you could scarcely see a finer or truer specimen....
>
> [He] always tried to correct evils in camp more by contrast and moral effect than by punishment. On this account, his camps were always remarkable for their cleanliness, his men for their order, sobriety and efficiency. While commanding the Irish Brigade he had so ingratiated himself with the troops that they actually wept when he left, and the officers presented him with an address....
>
> The greatest hope of his life was to strike a blow for his freedom, for like most Irishmen, he felt the degradation of being a race without a country, and winning renown on foreign battlefields, while his countrymen, at home were a

starved and despised race. In him and General Corcoran, Ireland lost two of her noblest and purest patriots—England two of her bitterest foes....[13]

Following Farmville, Lee's army continued its retreat toward Lynchburg via Appomattox Court House. The Second Corps was in hot pursuit of the Rebel force, closely followed by the Sixth and Fifth Corps. On the afternoon of 8 April, elements of Sheridan's cavalry seized Appomattox Court House. Lee's retreat to Lynchburg was blocked by a large force of Federal horsemen.

During the previous two days, Grant sent messages to General Lee via General Humphreys suggesting that the Confederate General surrender his beleaguered forces. On 9 April, Humphreys sent a third such message through the lines to Lee. The latter was forced to accept Grant's offer and at 1600, it was announced to the Army of the Potomac that the Army of Northern Virginia had surrendered. The war in the east was over.

Second Corps' casualties for the period 29 March to 9 April were 8,268 men killed and wounded plus another 1,676 men missing, for a total of 9,944 Federals. It is assumed that Humphreys' Corps exacted an equivalent number of casualties on the Rebel ranks. General Lee's failure to admit defeat had caused unnecessary blood to be shed and lives, including General Smyth's, to be needlessly lost.

Final Movements

After the surrender of Lee's army at Appomattox, most of Grant's army rested at Burkesville for a few days. While there, the army was stunned and saddened by the assassination of President Lincoln.

The Army of the Potomac marched through Richmond on the way to Alexandria, Virginia. The brigade received mixed reviews in the Confederate capital. The Federal army and the brigade rested for several weeks at Alexandria. While there, Nugent was promoted to the rank of brevet brigadier general.

A review was held in Washington on 23 and 24 May. The Army of the Potomac marched on the first day and Sherman's western army paraded the following day. The reviews were held in the presence of President Andrew Johnson and his cabinet. Also in attendance were representatives of foreign powers and a large crowd of local gentry. The soldiers of the brigade marched with sprigs of evergreen in their caps, reminders of their sacrifice at Fredericksburg. The unit was led by Colonel Nugent, who was astride a lively black horse. The animal had been presented to him by admirers in New York City.

Homecoming

The Irish Brigade, about 800 men strong, arrived in New York City early in the morning of 3 July 1865. The three New York regiments were temporarily quartered in the Battery Barracks. The 28th Massachusetts elected to move on to

Boston and not participate in the parade scheduled for the next day, the Fourth of July.[14]

The parade started around 1100. The line of march began at 23rd Street and Madison Avenue. It continued up that avenue to 38th Street, where it turned left to Fifth Avenue. The march continued down the avenue to 14th Street and along the thoroughfare to Union Square. There, the paraders were formally reviewed by the mayor other dignitaries. Finally, the troops continued around the square past the Washington Monument, where individual units were marched off under command of their officers.[15]

The parade route was lined by thousands of cheering New Yorkers. The 69th was led by Lt. Colonel Smith, whose adjutant was Major Moroney. Well wishers cheered from windows and roof tops. Soldiers of the Irish Brigade were surprised by the crowd's enthusiasm.

The *New York Daily Tribune* reported: "Most of [the Irish Brigade veterans] appeared to be all but stunned by the character of the demonstration which their coming excited. The flags which the decimated regiments of the brigade bore, torn to tatters as they were by the lurid tempest of war were proof enough of the terrible scenes through which the heroes had passed, but evidence to the same effect were stamped in every ligament of their swarthy faces in every muscle of their brown horny hands and in every motion of their free swift stride...."[16]

The history of the homecoming wouldn't be complete without citing a humorous incident reported in the *New York Herald*:

An Incident

Only one fight occurred. It happened in this wise: As the procession was being dismissed on the eastern side of the square, a pretty, but tearful lady from the Emerald Isle, was wandering distractedly among the members of the Irish Brigade to find someone who could give her information of the last moments of her husband, of whose death she had been recently apprised. Suddenly, a brawny handsome fellow, approached her with open arms, when she turned as white as her pinafore and waved him back as though he was a ghost.

"Don't you know me Mavourneen? Don't you know your own Terrance?" asked the poor fellow looking considerably nonplussed. "Geo awa' wid ye! You're dead! You know you are," she exclaimed with quivering lips.

"Divil a bit of it Mavourneen!" he responded giving ample proof of the soundness of his assertion by folding her in his arms in a way that made every ones eyes water and kissing her in a way that made every ones lips water as well.

It was indeed her long absent Terrance, whom she had prematurely numbered with the dead.

"It was that villain Mike Flaherty towld me you was dead," sobbed the now joyous wife.

"Where is Mike?" asked her husband.

The unfortunate Mike happened to be in sight, and dropping his musket and "peeling" on the spot, the abused husband drubbed him thoroughly amid the cheers of his comrades.[17]

Later that night, about 600 soldiers and their guests attended a banquet in their honor. After the affair was concluded, Nugent rose and said, "Soldiers of the Irish Brigade, I call upon you to give three hearty cheers for the officers, soldiers and gentlemen who have provided for us the splendid collation you have just received."[18]

The veterans then marched out of the hall and into history. Following deactivation of the regiment, Nugent once again became active in affairs of the 69th New York State Militia and commanded the militia for a number of years in the interim between Appomatox and the onset of the Spanish American War.

Corporal Sam Clear, 116th Pennsylvania, provided a fitting epitaph for the Irish Brigade. The comment was written on the day his regiment was transferred to the Fourth Brigade of the First Division: "The old Irish Brigade is a thing of the past. There never was a better one pulled their triggers on the Johnnies."[19]

CHAPTER 7

Contribution of the Irish Brigade and 69th NYV

William F. Fox, the nineteenth-century authority on the fighting capabilities of Civil War units, stated that the Irish Brigade was "perhaps the best known of any brigade organization, it having made an unusual reputation for dash and gallantry. The remarkable precision of its evolutions under fire, its desperate attack on the impregnable wall at Marye's heights, its never failing promptness on every field and its long continuous service, made for it a name inseparable from the history of war...."[1]

Even its critics acknowledged the fighting qualities of the brigade. George Alfred Townsend, an English war correspondent who not unexpectedly had little use for the Irish, observed that "when anything absurd, forlorn, or desperate was to be attempted, the Irish Brigade was called upon."[2]

The brigade had more than 4,000 casualties during the course of the war, despite the fact that it never fielded more than 3,600 men at any one time. All five of its regiments, 63rd, 69th and 88th New York Volunteers, 28th Massachusetts and the 116th Pennsylvania, were on Fox's list of the 300 Union regiments that experienced the highest total losses as a result of combat.[3]

The 69th New York Volunteers was ranked sixth out of more than 2,000 Federal regiments, with respect to the number of its members who were killed or mortally wounded.[4]

The 69th New York Volunteers lost the most men in action, killed and wounded, of any of the over 300 regiments raised by New York State.[5] It is important to remember that at the First Bull Run, the 69th New York State Militia, the source of the brigade's officers and noncoms, suffered the second most casualties of the Federal regiments engaged.

The 69th New York Volunteers, on at least four occasions, sustained casualty rates that were greater than one third of its strength: Seven Days, 39 percent; Antietam, 62 percent; Fredericksburg, 54 percent; and Gettysburg, 33 percent. Peter Watson, in his *War on the Mind*, argues that a military unit is wrecked psychologically if it twice suffers casualties equivalent to one third of its strength. The 69th, in spite of its losses, soldiered on throughout the war and returned to New York City only after Lee's surrender at Appomattox.

It is interesting to note that during the war, two soldiers succumbed to disease for every one who died as a result of combat. For the Irish Brigade and the 69th New York Volunteers, that ratio was reversed, two died of wounds for every one who died of disease. Apparently, the brigade's soldiers were among the hardiest of the Federal army and had relatively fewer malingerers who shied away from combat.[6]

The success of the Irish Brigade in the Civil War did much to dispel the nation's doubts about the fidelity and fighting qualities of the Irish American soldier. Historian Paul Jones provides a fitting assessment: "No one who had ever fought side by side with the Irish, knowing at least that flank was secure, no one who saw the Brigade go into battle against all odds could have any doubt of the Irish-American's right to full citizenship."[7]

CHAPTER 8

World War I

The United States became a fledgling imperialistic world power in 1898, with the defeat of Spain and acquisition of the Philippines, Puerto Rico and Guam. By 1900, the United States, with a population of more than 75 million, was one of the leading economic powers in the world.

For several years prior to 1914, the major countries in Europe had been divided into two rival camps. One of these was the Triple Alliance, which consisted of Germany, Austria-Hungary and Italy. The other was the Triple Entente, which consisted of France, Russia and Great Britain.

On 20 June 1914, Archduke Francis Ferdinand, heir to the throne of the Austro-Hungarian Empire, and his wife Sophie were murdered in Sarajevo, the capital of Bosnia. Their killer was Gavrilo Princip, a young Serbian student in Bosnia, which at that time was a province of Austria. Princip belonged to Mlada Bosna (Young Bosnia), a radical group that considered the assassination "tyrannicide" for the common good. The student terrorist group was supported by the Black Hand, a pan–Serbian society with links to officials in Serbia's military intelligence.[1] In killing the Hapsburg royal couple, Princip imagined he was striking a blow to free Bosnia from Austrian domination.

Austria-Hungary saw the assassination as an affront to its status as a great power. More importantly, it provided an opportunity to neutralize Serbia, Vienna's most implacable foe in the Balkans. Since Russia was an ardent supporter of their Slavic neighbor, Austria-Hungary asked Germany, their ally, to back them in their show of force against Serbia. Kaiser Wilhelm II, eager to exercise his nation's growing political power, assured Franz Josef, the aged monarch of the Austro-Hungarian Empire, that he would support his empire if Russia came to Serbia's aid.

Emboldened by the kaiser, Austria-Hungary sent an ultimatum to Serbia. The message made a number of demands, including creation of a commission to investigate the assassination. Serbia was expected to comply within 48 hours. The general intent of the note was humiliation or rejection and justification for a punitive strike. Surprisingly, Serbia agreed to all of Austria-Hungary's requests except its key demand, formation of an investigatory committee. As a precaution, however, Serbia mobilized its army.

Austria-Hungary was not placated and on 28 July declared war on Serbia. As

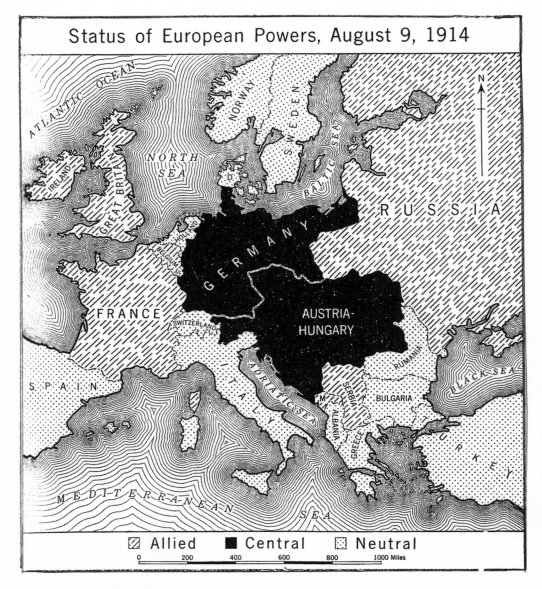

Status of European powers, 9 August 1914 (from Official Sources).

Emperor Franz Josef mobilized his army, Russia, the patron of the Slav states, began to activate its forces.

As far as the German General Staff was concerned, mobilization meant war. They were concerned that Russia and France, as allies, would attack the Fatherland on two fronts. Germany could not allow Russia to assemble its huge army without calling up its own troops. War by timetable had begun.

On 1 August, King George V of Great Britain, appealed to his cousin, the czar, to back down and demobilize his army. The momentum toward conflict, however, was unstoppable and by that evening, Russia and Germany were at war. On 3 August, Germany declared war on France, Russia's ally.

Germany's plan was to hold off the Russian army while its legions obtained a quick victory over the French. Its Schlieffen Plan called for the advance of German armies through Belgium to bypass formidable French defenses on the frontier. The major problem with the scheme was Belgium. Its monarch, King Albert, refused to let German troops move through his country. In 1839, Britain and Germany signed a treaty guaranteeing Belgian independence. When Germany invaded Belgium on 3 August, Great Britain honored its commitment and the next day declared war on the Teutonic aggressor. German Chancellor Bethmann-Hollweg lamented that Great Britain was going to war "just for a scrap of paper."[2]

The Ottoman Empire (later Turkey), signed a secret mutual defense treaty with Germany on 3 August. The Entente tried to get Turkey into their camp, but in late October, Turkey's naval forces bombarded Russian ports in the Black Sea. The Allies then declared war on the Ottoman Empire. The Great War was underway: the Central Powers—Germany, Austria-Hungary, Turkey and their colonies versus Britain, Russia, France, Belgium and their possessions.

1914

The German army swept through Belgium and into France. They defeated the main French armies in the Battle of the Frontiers and by late August were threatening Paris. The British Expeditionary Force (British Expeditionary Force), fighting against the German armies moving through Belgium, were driven back toward the English Channel. In the time frame 2 August to 14 September, the French, in the First Battle of the Marne, turned back the advancing German army. In the period 21 October to 17 November 1914, the British Expeditionary Force, in the First Battle of the Ypres, halted the German advance to the Channel. Both sides tried unsuccessfully to outflank the other. By the onset of winter, however, the adversaries faced each other from entrenched positions extending from Dixmuide, on the Belgian west, 460 miles southward to the French city of Belfort on the Swiss border. The resultant scar, which extended through France and Belgium, was the so-called "Western Front."

The Russian army mobilized more rapidly than the Germans anticipated and invaded East Prussia. The Boche high command panicked and sent some of its divisions eastward from Belgium. In the time frame 26 August to 14 September, General Paul Von Hindenburg, using Germany's superior rail system (based on studies of the American Civil War), crushed Russian armies in the vicinity of Tannenburg and the Masurian Lakes in East Prussia. The Russians suffered over 300,000 casualties. In Galicia, however, the czar's troops were more successful. Between 1 September to 3 October, the Russians at Lemberg inflicted 350,000 casualties on the Austro-Hungarian Army, but subsequent German successes in the vicinity of Warsaw and Lodz derailed the Russian steamroller.

Meanwhile, the Ottoman Empire was grappling with Allied forces in Mesopotamia, Palestine, Sinai and the mountains of Russia's Caucasus.

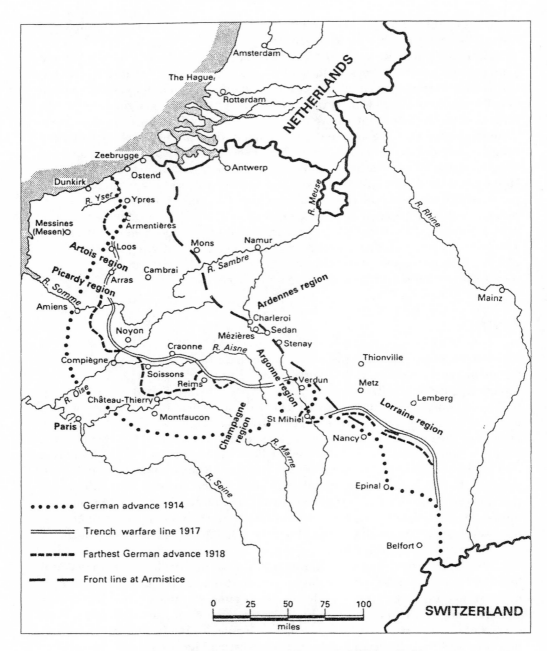

The Western Front (courtesy Sutton Publishing, Ltd.).

1915

On 22 April 1915, the Germans, using poison gas for first time in the war, attacked the British at Ypres. The Boche thrust failed to dislodge the British Expeditionary Force from their position on the left flank of the Western Front. Elsewhere on the line, fighting alternated between large scale assaults, trench raids and counterattacks.

On the Eastern Front, a powerful offensive was launched by the Central Powers. By October, the Russians were forced out of Galicia, Poland and Lithuania. On 14 October, Bulgaria joined the Central Powers. Later in the year, Bulgarian and German forces overran Serbia.

On 25 April, the Allies landed a force consisting primarily of Australian and New Zealand (ANZAC) troops, on the Gallipoli Peninsula. It was an attempt to capture Constantinople (now Istanbul) and knock Turkey out of the war. The attack was badly handled and another stalemate resulted. Near year's end, Britain was forced evacuate the peninsula.

In April, Italy secretly signed the Treaty of London, agreeing to join the Allies in exchange for territory in Europe and Africa. On 23 May, Italy declared war on Austria-Hungary. The Italians then launched a series of offensives against their erstwhile ally along their border in the southern Alps.

German forces in Cameroon and German East Africa surrendered to Allied troops in 1915. In that year, a Turkish attack on the Suez Canal was turned back.

On the high seas, Germany declared the waters around the British Isles to be a war zone. It warned that enemy merchant ships within the area would be attacked. On 7 May, a German submarine sank the British passenger liner *Lusitania* off the coast of Ireland. The death toll of 1,198 persons included 128 Americans.[3] The United States protested the sinking and Germany agreed to stop attacking neutral vessels and passenger ships.

1916

In February 1916, Germany opened the Battle of Verdun. General Erich von Falkenhayn, Chief of the German General Staff, ordered the attack on the fortress city. He believed the French would fight hard to retain the ancient citadel. Falkenhayn hoped to conduct a successful war of attrition against the French at Verdun, but both sides were caught up in the battle. The Germans never took the city. French and German casualties were approximately 362,000 and 336,000 men respectively. Falkenhayn lost some of his best troops in the struggle.[4]

British General Haig launched a huge offensive in the area of the Somme River in late June. His goal was to smash through the German lines near Bapaume. On July 1, after an artillery bombardment of about a week, the British infantry went over the top. On the first day of the assault, the British suffered 57,400 casualties, including 20,000 killed. Later at Flers, on 15 September, General Haig used tanks for the first time in the war. Only 18 of the 36 vehicles employed in the assault functioned properly and this first deployment of mechanized forces was only partially successful. Haig's offensive turned into another battle of attrition and he finally called off the slaughter on 18 November. His forces were still several miles from Bapaume, the main objective of the offensive. The Allies had made negligible gains at a cost of 415,000 British and 195,000 French casualties. Haig claimed

German losses to be 650,000 men, but recent research indicates his estimate to be greatly exaggerated. Enemy losses totaling about 237,000 men appears more likely.[5]

On the Eastern Front, General Alexi Brusilov's Russian troops attacked on a 70 mile wide front in Galicia. His armies captured over 400,000 prisoners and advanced as much as 60 miles. Brusilov's offensive was eventually halted by the arrival of German reinforcements. The Russians suffered over 1,000,000 casualties in the operation, losses that crippled the czar's army.[6]

The Italians, under General Luigi Cordova, launched a series of offensives along the Isonzo River in the Julian Alps. By years' end, Cordoba had failed to achieve a breakthrough toward Vienna and sustained over 600,000 casualties.[7]

In August, Romania, believing the Central Powers were losing the war, joined the Allies. Its price for entering the conflict was the Transylvanian and Banat regions in Hungary. Romanian forces invaded Transylvania but were soon turned back. By January 1917, Central Power forces had swept through Romania and captured Bucharest.

The greatest sea battle of the war occurred on 31 May and 1 June. The Battle of Jutland took place near the entrance to Skagerrak Strait in the North Sea. In the two day contest, the British lost three battle cruisers, three armored cruisers and eight destroyers. A total of 14 ships sank with 6,097 men killed. The Germans lost one battleship, one battle cruiser, four light cruisers and five destroyers. A total of 11 ships sank and 2,551 men were killed. Germany claimed a great victory but Great Britain still ruled the seas. The German High Seas Fleet remained inactive for the rest of the war. Meanwhile, German submarine fleets continued attacks on British shipping.[8]

Both sides used airplanes in the large scale offensives at Verdun and the Somme. Air battles became common, as each side tried to force the other from the sky. The Germans developed dirigibles as part of their bomber force. As early as 1915, they sent the airships and large airplanes to bomb London. The dirigibles, inflated with hydrogen gas, were readily set on fire by incendiary projectiles.

On Easter Sunday, about 2,500 militant members of Sinn Fein seized key buildings in Dublin and proclaimed Ireland's independence from Great Britain. The insurgents, fighting under the green, white and orange tricolor flag, were forced to surrender after six days of resistance. Few of the Irish population supported the "rising," but when British authorities executed most of its leaders, public opinion changed in favor of the Nationalists. An underground Irish Army was created and guerrilla warfare began against the British establishment.

1917

On 1 February 1917, Germany initiated unrestricted submarine warfare, announcing that its submarines would sink any vessel heading toward or standing out of Allied ports. Germany extended the war zone to the high seas. In March, several American merchant ships were torpedoed without warning. The next month, German U-boats sank 900,000 tons of Allied shipping, the all-time record for the war.

On 6 April, the United States declared war on Germany. It associated itself with the Allies, but did not sign a treaty of alliance with them. Principal reasons for the United States' entry into the conflict were Germany's policy of unrestricted submarine warfare and its secret attempt to create an anti–U.S. alliance with Mexico (the Zimmerman Telegram).

Although the United States was woefully unprepared for war, American soldiers, under General John J. Pershing, began arriving in France in late June and moving into the trenches by October.

On 16 April, French General Robert Nivelle launched an enormous offensive in the vicinity of the Aisne River. The attack was carried out on a 50 mile front between Soissons and Reims. The offensive was a disaster. The French achieved negligible gains and suffered enormous casualties. By 25 April, French losses exceeded 96,000. Unknown to the Germans, some regiments in the French army later mutinied. Most of the defiant soldiers would defend their trenches but they refused to attack. On 15 May, General Henri Phillipe Petain succeeded Nivelle. During the remainder of the year, Petan restored the army's morale. Thus, his forces were primarily engaged in defensive actions and limited attacks where success was virtually guaranteed.[9]

The British army, under General Haig, supported Nivelle's offensive with a large scale attack in the Arras sector. The Germans had withdrawn to a relatively shorter, more defensible line of trenches called the Hindenburg Line. Haig's advance was essentially unopposed. With the near collapse of the French army, the British were forced to keep pressure on the Germans. In early June, General Plummer conducted a successful attack in the Messines area of the front. Haig launched Third Ypres on 31 July. The campaign's objective was the capture of high ground in the vicinity of a Flanders village called Passchendale. The operation, which ended in early November, met with minimal success and cost the Allies in excess of 399,000 casualties. Haig claimed that the Germans had sustained over 400,000 casualties. Recent studies, however, indicate that number was grossly exaggerated, as were earlier figures for the Somme.[10]

On 20 November, after the great offensive in Flanders was concluded, Haig authorized a large scale tank attack at Cambrai. A total of 381 tanks, under the operational control of General Sir Julian Byng, attacked the German lines. There was no preliminary bombardment and the Germans were taken by surprise. The attack punched a six-mile-wide gap in the German lines. The initially successful thrust was not followed up. The Germans quickly sealed the breach and then counterattacked. Haig ordered a withdrawal on 4 December. The British sustained 43,000 casualties, the Germans 41,111 men, including 11,000 troops captured. The failed attack, however, demonstrated the war-fighting potential of armor.[11]

The Allies faced disaster on the Eastern Front. In March, the Russian people overthrew their monarchy, forcing Czar Nicholas II to abdicate. A provisional government under Alexander Kerensky continued the war and General Brusilov's armies advanced into the Carpathian Mountains. The Russian offensive was soon halted by a German counterattack. The Boche in turn menaced the Russian capital, Petrograd.

The Germans were determined to get Russia out of the war and defeat the

Allies on the Western Front before American armies made a difference. Vladimir Ilyich Lenin, the Bolshevik leader, was ferreted from exile in Zurich and transported to Petrograd via Sweden in the "famous sealed train." On 7 November, the Reds overthrew Kerensky's government. A short time later, Lenin ended hostilities with the Central Powers and began peace talks with the German government.

On their mountainous front, the Italian and Austro-Hungarian armies were evenly matched. In two years of bloody fighting, the Italian army had only moved about 10 miles into Austrian territory. On 24 October, however, at Caporetto, a village on the Isonzo River, German troops spearheaded an Austro-Hungarian offensive that shattered the Italian army. General Cardovo's forces retreated all the way to the Piave River, where, with the support of British and French troops, they halted the German advance, an advance which was then within striking distance of Venice. Italian losses included 10,000 killed, 30,000 wounded, 293,000 prisoners and 350,000 deserters.[12] Thereafter, the Italian government and people supported the war more enthusiastically and the army was in effect reborn.

1918

On 8 January 1918, President Woodrow Wilson announced his "Fourteen Points" as a basis for a postwar settlement. They included open covenants, removal of economic barriers, reduction of armaments and formation of an association of nations. His ideas gave hope to enemy peoples that a just peace settlement was possible and encouraged agitation for a cease fire.

In February, peace negotiations between Russia and Germany broke down. The Germans resumed battering the Russian army and soon forced Lenin's government to sign a humiliating treaty at Brest-Litovsk on 3 March. A few months later, Romania formally surrendered to the Central Powers. At that point, few would have predicted an Allied victory before year's end.

On 21 March, shortly before 0500, the most concentrated and devastating artillery bombardment of all time opened up from six thousand German guns along a 40 mile front on the Somme. Using the infiltrating tactics of Caporetto, German General Erich Ludendorff's troops soon captured approximately 160 square miles of territory. By 5 April, when the first phase of Ludendorff's offensive petered out, the British Expeditionary Force had sustained 164,000 casualties. The Germans had taken a total of 90,000 prisoners and almost 1,000 artillery pieces.[13]

General Ludendorff was deputy chief of staff to the German Second Army when the war broke out. He was credited with the rapid capture of the Belgian fortress at Liege and won acclaim for German victories on the Eastern Front. His influence on the Western Front dates from 29 August 1916, when he was appointed first quartermaster general of the German forces. General Paul von Hindenburg was essentially a figurehead and with the kaiser politically occupied, Ludendorff was *de facto* commander on the Western Front.

The ferocity of the German offensive forced the Allies to act together in a

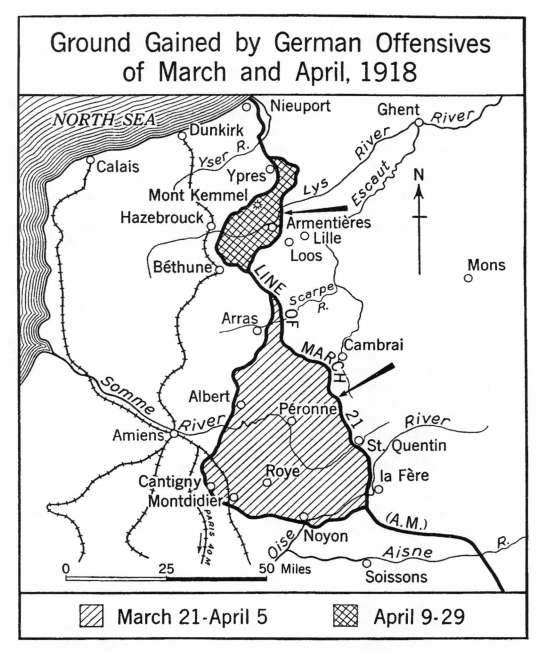

Ground Gained by German Offensives of March and April, 1918

NORTH SEA

Nieuport

Ghent

Dunkirk

Calais

Yser R.

Ypres

Mont Kemmel

Hazebrouck

Lys River

Escaut River

River

Armentières

Lille

Loos

N

Béthune

LINE OF

Scarpe R.

Mons

Arras

MARCH 21

Cambrai

Somme

Albert

Péronne

River

Amiens

St. Quentin

Roye

la Fère

Cantigny

Montdidier

PARIS 40 M.

(A.M.)

Oise

Noyon

Aisne R.

0   25   50 Miles

Soissons

▨ March 21-April 5   ▩ April 9-29

Ground gained by German offensives of March and April 1918 (from Official Sources).

more unified manner. Accordingly, on 3 April, General Foch was given authority for the "strategic direction" of all Allied armies. On 14 April was named supreme allied commander.

Foch had a diverse military background and quickly rose in rank during the early months of the war. By December 1914, he held power second only to Joffre, the original commander in chief of the French armies. When Joffre was sacked in December 1916, Foch fell with him. Foch was a military consultant for a year but was raised to chief of the general staff when Nivelle was dumped after his disastrous offensive of 1917.

On 9 April, General Ludendorff opened the second phase of his offensive. His armies now struck the British line in Flanders. His "Lys" operation pushed the British Expeditionary Force back, but by 29 April, with some help from the French, the drive was halted. During the month of April, the Germans sustained about 350,000 casualties, the British 305,000.[14] The slight edge in numbers held by the Germans at the beginning of the campaign was being rapidly eroded. General Pershing's army in France was now the size of Haig's British Expeditionary Force.

Ludendorff decided to make a thrust at Paris and force Foch to concentrate his forces in that area. Then, the Germans would open a final, all-out drive in Flanders that could possibly end with a British surrender on the coast.

At 0100 on 27 May, Ludendorff launched his "Aisne Offensive" (27 May to 6 June), the biggest push of the war. On that day, the Germans punched a 12 by 30 mile wide bulge in the French lines. It was the greatest one-day advance anywhere in four years. By the end of three days, the depth of the German thrust reached 30 miles. The Allies lost 650 guns, 2,000 machine guns, 60,000 prisoners and huge stores of supplies.[15] During this struggle, American counterattacks regained the French towns of Cantigny and Belleau Wood.

Ludendorff launched the fourth offensive of his 1918 campaign on 9 June. He intended to link the vulnerable Amiens Salient with his newly created Aisne-Marne Salient and thereby threaten Paris. The thrust ended on 14 June. The Germans captured six miles of territory before they were stopped. Ludendorff's forces suffered 35,000 casualties and the French 15,000.

Beginning in March 1918, the Germans had launched one offensive per month. Ludendorff planned to initiate his fifth such operation on 15 July. The attack's objective was the capture of Reims and enlargement of the salient around Chateau-Thierry by reaching the Marne at Epernay and Chalons. The German high command hoped to force French reserves to the defense of Paris. The French would then be unable to support the British Expeditionary Force in Flanders, Ludendorff's primary target.

The Germans selected Monday, 15 July, the day after Bastille Day, as the kickoff date for their attack. They assumed the French army would be somewhat debilitated as a result of its celebration of the national holiday.

The French high command, warned of the attack, was prepared to meet the threat. The German push was greeted by determined French and newly deployed American units, such as the 42nd Division. The Yanks weathered a fierce bombardment and then fought off the German attack. The 165th Infantry was prominent in the fighting. The Boche advance gained only four miles in some sectors and none in others. Ludendorff canceled the operation on Day Two of the offensive.

In four months, Ludendorff's troops had seized ten times the territory cap-

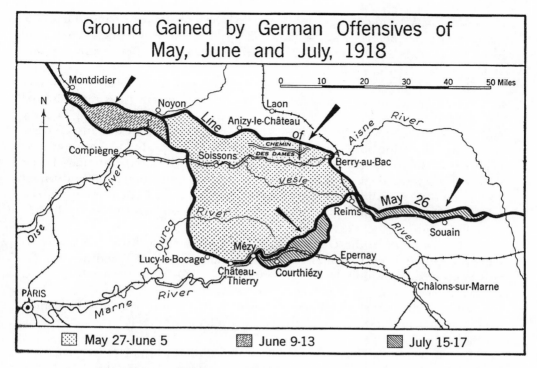

Ground Gained by German Offensives of May, June and July, 1918

Legend: May 27–June 5 | June 9-13 | July 15-17

Ground gained by German offensives of May, June and July 1918 (from Official Sources).

tured by the Allies during all of 1917, a year of continuous offensives in the west. His swift attacks seized 225,000 prisoners and 2,500 guns. The Germans inflicted some 448,000 and 490,000 casualties on the British and French respectively. German losses for this period approached 1 million men, including 125,000 dead and 100,000 missing. Pershing's divisions suffered 9,685 dead and wounded during the 120 day period.[16]

On 18 July, Foch mounted a massive counterattack with four French armies and 14 Allied divisions, including a number of American units. Strikes were directed at the salient generated by Ludendorff's Third Offensive. The assault was spearheaded by the French XX Corps, comprised of the American 1st and 2nd Divisions plus the 1st Moroccan Division. The XX Corps' attack, which was directed at Soissons, was supported by over 350 tanks. The thrust threatened German communications along the Soissons–Chateau Thierry Road, forcing the Germans to retreat toward a new line along the Vesle and Aisne rivers. Many historians consider Foch's counterattack of 18 July as "decisive" on the Western Front in 1918.[17]

The 42nd Division, on 27 July, was ordered to attack across the Ourcq River and to pursue German forces, which were on the north side of it and presumed to be rapidly retiring toward the Vesle River. The Boche were in fact withdrawing slowly and still strongly dug in on their side of the Ourcq. Nevertheless, the Rainbow Division, led at times by the 165th Infantry, hastened the Germans behind the Vesle. The Village of Sergy, one of the division's objectives, changed hands a number of times before it was secured on 29 July. The New Yorkers sustained heavy losses while eliminating machine gun nests fronting a Boche strong point at a site called Meurcy Farm.[18]

The Battle of Amiens was fought between 8 August and 3 September. It was the second Allied offensive of 1918. The operation's objective was reduction of the salient created by Ludendorff's March offensive. By 3 September, Haig's troops had forced the Germans back to the Hindenburg line. The Germans suffered 75,000 casualties, including 30,000 prisoners during the push. On 8 August, "the black day of the German army," per Ludendorff, the British Expeditionary Force punched a seven-mile-deep hole along a 15 mile front, taking 27,000 prisoners and some 400 guns.[19] The opening date of the British Expeditionary Force offensive, and not 16 July, is considered by Hart and other historians to be the turn of the tide on the Western Front.[20]

A key position in the German lines near the Somme River was Mont St. Quentin. On 30 August, elements of the Australian Corps attacked the supposedly impregnable position. By 2 September, Mont St. Quentin was firmly in Allied hands. The Germans lost 15,000 casualties, the Australians 3,000.

Between 21 August and 1 September, the Australians occupied Bapaume, while the New Zealand Division captured Grevillers, Avesnes-les- Bapaume, Faurevil and Fremicourt.

The St. Mihiel Salient was located southeast of Verdun. The Germans had held it since 1914. The protrusion interrupted direct French rail traffic from industrial areas into Paris. The American Army was given the task of reducing the salient. By late 1918, the Germans had planned to withdraw from the pocket. Before they got the operation underway, General Pershing launched his attack on 13 September. The assault was made by the newly created American First Army. I Corps, General Liggett commanding, was comprised of the 82nd, 90th, 5th and 2nd divisions, while IV Corps, General Dickman commanding, was comprised of the 1st, 42nd and 89th Divisions. The offensive, in which the 165th Infantry played a prominent part, was a tactical, logistical and operational success. The salient was reduced with the Germans and Americans suffering 20,000 and 7,000 casualties respectively. Almost two hundred square miles of French territory was liberated. Sixteen thousand enemy soldiers, 440 artillery pieces and 750 machine guns were captured. Pershing's first offensive was essentially a walk-over, but it was a very promising beginning for the green American army.[21]

In September 1918, the Allies launched a series of attacks along the Western Front. One of the operations was a gigantic pincer movement, intended to end the war before the close of 1918. The "Meuse River–Argonne Forest Offensive," directed at Mezieres and Sedan, began on 26 September. French armies attacked from the west and Pershing's divisions from the south, through the Argonne Forest where German defenses were 12 miles deep. The sector was commanded by Prince Freidrich Wihelm and General von Gallwitz. In the first five days, the French gained nine miles while the Americans progressed five miles along the Meuse Heights and two miles in the more difficult Argonne Forest. Between 26 September and 11 November, 22 American divisions and six French divisions, with

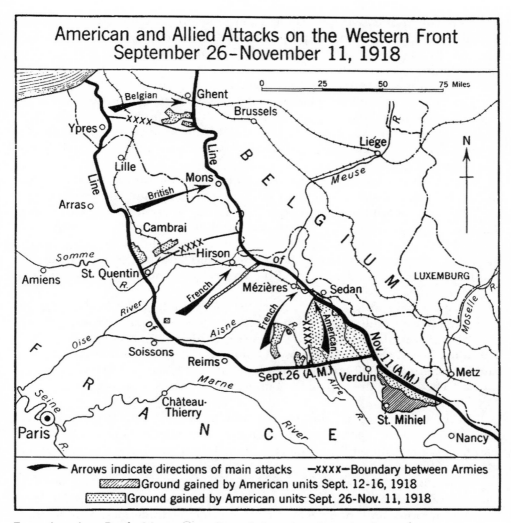

**American and Allied Attacks on the Western Front
September 26–November 11, 1918**

Arrows indicate directions of main attacks —XXXX—Boundary between Armies
Ground gained by American units Sept. 12-16, 1918
Ground gained by American units Sept. 26-Nov. 11, 1918

From American Battle Monuments Commission, *American Armies and
Battlefields in Europe*, Washington, D.C., 1938.

an approximate strength of 500,000 men, engaged 43 German divisions with an
approximate strength of 470,000 men.

Beginning on 4 October, the Americans won ground at a heavy cost in several frontal attacks, and by 1 November had broken the German lines in the
Argonne Forest. In the offensive, the Americans captured 26,000 prisoners and
almost 900 pieces of artillery. German and American casualties were approximately 100,000 and 117,000 men respectively.[22] The French attack, which began
on 4 October, reached the Aisne River by 30 October, a push of 20 miles. The
grinding, bloody advance was continued until the Armistice on 11 November. A
few days prior to the cease fire, the 165th Infantry reached Sedan, the historic
city on the Meuse River, while the French seized Montmedy.

Three other offensives were launched in September. On the 27th, the British Expeditionary Force's First and Third armies advanced toward Cambrai. Belgian and British troops in Flanders attacked toward Ghent on the 28th and the British Fourth and French First armies advanced toward Hiron on 29 September. Cambrai was captured on 4 October, with the Canadian Corps suffering more than 30,000 casualties. The British Fourth Army, which included the 27th and 30th American divisions plus the Australian Corps, broke through the Hindenburg Line near the Village of Le Catelet. American units, including the 107th Infantry (federalized Seventh New York Infantry, USNG) suffered heavy casualties.[23]

During the month of October, German forces facing the Allied thrusts conducted fighting retreats toward their border. Ludendorff and Hindenburg realized that only an armistice could save their dwindling armies. Early in the year, Austria-Hungary launched a huge drive to knock Italy out of the war. Floods and fierce resistance by General Armando Diaz's troops halted the advancing Austro-Hungarian forces in June. In October, General Diaz launched an offensive across the Piave River. The Italians severed the enemy army and then destroyed each segment in detail.

Allied forces from Salonika, Greece, broke through on the Bulgarian front in September. On the 29th of that month, Bulgaria signed an armistice with the Allies. British General Allenby's forces routed Turkish armies at Megiddo, Palestine, in early September. Subsequent mopping up operations in Palestine and Syria netted 75,000 prisoners of war at a cost of less than 5,000 Allied casualties.[24] The beleaguered Ottoman Empire agreed to an armistice on 30 October.

In the fall, the Hungarians, Czechs, Slovaks and Poles declared their independence from the Austro-Hungarian Empire. The fragile Habsburg monarchy had fallen apart and on 3 November it agreed to an armistice. Germany stood alone.

Sailors in the German High Seas Fleet at Kiel mutinied in late October. As the news of the event spread, revolts broke out in other parts of Germany. Mutinies occurred in other units of the German army. General Hindenburg feared a Bolshevik upheaval and informed the kaiser that he must seek an immediate armistice with the Allies. The kaiser appointed Prince Max of Baden chancellor, with the task of seeking an end to the war. General Ludendorff resigned on 26 October. The kaiser abdicated on 10 November and then exited the Fatherland to Doorn, Holland.

Armistice

In a drizzling rain at 0500 on 11 November, German delegates entered a railway car in Compiegne Forest and signed an armistice. General Foch ordered fighting to stop on all battlefields at 1100, thus ending World War I.

The terms of the Armistice, at French insistence, were harsh. The Germans were forced to:

1. Evacuate all occupied territory,
2. Surrender their arms and warships,
3. Withdraw all forces west of the Rhine River,
4. Return Allied prisoners, and
5. Permit Allied troops to occupy German territory.

The Allies established a six-mile neutral zone along the east bank of the river. British and Belgian forces occupied a bridgehead at Cologne, the Americans at Koblenz and the French in the vicinity of Mainz.

Social, political and financial costs of the war were staggering. The conflict cost more than $337 billion. Germany suffered 6,861,950 casualties including 2,037,000 dead and 4,207,028 wounded. Great Britain had 3,202,864 casualties, including over 921,000 dead and 2,090,212 wounded. France sustained 3,844,300 casualties with 1,398,000 dead and over 2,000,000 wounded. Italy suffered 2,055,000 casualties, including 578,000 dead. Russia's sustained 6,761,000 casualties with approximately 1,811,000 dead and 1,450,000 wounded. Austria-Hungary had 6,920,000 casualties with over 1,100,000 dead.[25]

The United States sustained the following losses for the period 6 April 1917 to the Armistice:

Combat deaths	52,513
Other Causes	63,195
Total Deaths	115,708
Non-mortal Wounds	204,002
Total Casualties	319,710[26]

Peace of Paris

The Allies signed separate peace treaties with Germany, Austria, Hungary, Turkey and Bulgaria. The pact with Germany was called The Treaty of Versailles. All five treaties comprised the Peace of Paris. The U.S. did not ratify the Treaty of Versailles but signed a separate pact with Germany.

The Treaty of Versailles was exceedingly harsh. Germany was held solely responsible for the war. It lost peripheral territory amounting to about 13 percent of its prewar area. The Reich lost 80 percent of its iron ore, 44 percent of its pig iron capacity and 38 percent of its steel production. Farm land, livestock and factory capacity were reduced by 17, 13 and 10 percent respectively. Germany lost all of its overseas colonies and foreign investments. The Navy was abolished and merchant fleet reduced in numbers. The size of its army was limited to that of Belgium. Finally, Germany was required to pay yearly reparations, amounts to be determined by a commission. In 1921, the figure was set at 132 billion gold marks or approximately $33 billion.[27]

The war's devastation and harsh peace treaty caused chaos in postwar Europe. Almost all of President Wilson's Fourteen Points were ignored. However, the League of Nations, Wilson's *cause célèbre*, was established. The U.S. did not become a member and the organization ultimately failed to prevent World War II.

Germany's constitutional monarchy was replaced by the Weimar Republic in 1919. It was a weak government and subverted by Adolf Hitler and his Nazi Party in 1934, with disastrous consequences for the world. Italy's economy was also ruined by participation in the war. In 1922, the constitutional monarchy of King Victor Emmanuel was replaced by a fascist dictatorship under Benito Mussolini, another problem for peace seeking countries. Russia's monarchy was replaced by a Bolshevik dictatorship under Lenin and then Josef Stalin, a huge calamity for the democratic peoples of the world. The Austro-Hungarian Empire collapsed after the war. Austria became a republic. The weakened country eventually reverted to an authoritarian form of government which was gobbled up by Nazi Germany in 1938. Hungary quickly went from a monarchy to a republic and then a Russian style dictatorship. By the end of 1919, it was a monarchy again with a regent instead of king. Romania remained a monarchy. Finally, Turkey, which was under the control of a reform party called the "Young Turks," eventually became a democratic republic.

In Ireland, Sinn Fein became the leading group in the fight for independence. By 1918, it had become Ireland's most important political party. The people elected 73 Sinn Fein members to the British Parliament in 1919. Instead of going to London, the delegates met in Dublin. There, they established a House of Deputies and declared Ireland a republic in January 1919. Revolution broke out throughout the country. Sinn Fein intensified its campaign of guerrilla warfare against establishment forces. In 1921, a war-weary British Government granted 26 of Ireland's 32 counties dominion status. The remaining six counties, where two-thirds of the inhabitants were Protestants, remained part of the United Kingdom as Northern Ireland. Eventually, in 1949, after years of civil strife and political intrigue, Ireland became an independent republic. One wonders if the founders of the 69th New York State Militia would have been satisfied with the new nation of 26 counties.

CHAPTER 9

America Enters the War

The news in 1914 that war had broken out in Europe astonished most Americans. Shortly thereafter, President Wilson stated his intent to keep the United States out of what had quickly become a worldwide conflict. Wilson declared that the United States would be "neutral in fact as well as in name."

There was strong anti-war sentiment in the United States during the first months. The country's two largest immigration groups, Irish and German-Americans, did not want their adopted country to enter the struggle. These people were not interested in fighting to save Great Britain or in shooting down relatives in the old country.

On 7 December 1915, even though he believed the U.S. would stay neutral, President Wilson presented to Congress a comprehensive plan for improving national defense. The president also toured the nation, urging military preparedness.

The National Defense Act was passed by Congress on 3 June 1916. It provided for the immediate expansion of the Regular Army to 175,000 men. Seven infantry and two cavalry divisions were authorized. Each division was provided with a signal battalion, one aero squadron, relatively larger medical detachments and administration and supply elements. The army was authorized annual increments of 11,450 officers and 223,580 enlisted men over a five year period. The militia, identified as the National Guard, was permitted expansion to 17,700 officers and 440,000 enlisted men. The act also established Reserve Officer Training programs at universities and military encampments. Finally, the bill contained provisions for government assistance in the conversion of peacetime industry to the production of wartime products.[1]

During the early part of 1916, Germany continued to sink unarmed ships. President Wilson, on 18 April, notified the kaiser's government that unless they quit their methods of submarine warfare, the United States would sever diplomatic relations. Germany reluctantly promised not to attack passenger ships and to give adequate warning to all other vessels their subs might seek to destroy. Following these concessions, tensions between the United States and Germany eased.

Wilson ran for a second term in 1916. The Democratic Convention coined the phrase, "He kept us out of war." The platform also favored, in addition to a number of progressive national initiatives, military preparedness and a world association of nations to secure peace based on national and individual rights. Wilson defeated his Republican opponent in a close election.

In January 1917, the British intercepted a telegram from Arthur Zimmerman, Secretary of Foreign Affairs to the German foreign minister in Mexico City. The message proposed that in the event of war between the United States and Germany, an alliance be formed between Mexico and Germany and that Mexico endeavor to persuade Japan to desert the Allies and align itself with the Central Powers. For that support, Germany would help Mexico "reconquer" Texas, New Mexico and Arizona.

The "Zimmerman Telegram," coupled with Pancho Villa's earlier border raids, inflamed public opinion against Germany.

In spite of potential problems with Mexico, Wilson recalled the Punitive Expedition. Federalized guard units were demobilized and in March 1916, the 69th New York marched down Fifth Avenue to a warm reception by New York City. Guardsman and welcoming New Yorkers would have scoffed at a prediction that in less than five months, a much larger regiment would march up Fifth Avenue on its way to France.

On 2 February 1917, Germany resumed unrestricted submarine warfare. It was a spectacular success which peaked in the month of April. The huge shipping toll included a number of U.S. vessels. By April 1917, nearly all of the American populace was against Germany. The country's attitude toward neutrality had changed from pacifism to bellicose war fever. This erosion of America's neutral stance is attributed to Germany's heavy-handed diplomacy during the war and clever Allied propaganda. Germany's attack on neutral Belgium, the sinking of the *Lusitania*, the first use of poison gas, the Zimmerman Telegram and then unrestricted submarine warfare provided the fuel needed by the Allies to generate blistering attacks on the kaiser and his countrymen.

On 2 April 1917, President Wilson addressed a special session of Congress. He enumerated Germany's hostile acts and advised that war be declared on that country. It was declared on 6 April. Diplomatic relations with Austria-Hungary were severed a few days later but war was not officially declared on that country until 7 December 1917.

Life in America changed from a leisurely pace to a feverish war effort. The country, however, was totally unprepared to enter the conflict. A selective service act, requiring all males between 21 and 30 years of age to register for the draft, was passed. A Committee on Public Information was established to make the Allied cause known in almost every city, town and village in the country. Prominent citizens urged Americans to buy "liberty bonds" and support the draft. A stern looking Uncle Sam appeared on Army recruiting posters announcing, "I Want You!"

Six major wartime agencies mobilized the country's economic and industrial systems for war. A War Industries Board under Bernard Baruch controlled war production. A Shipping Board struggled to build vessels faster than German submarines could sink them. A Food Administration urged Americans to save food. Billboards were covered with posters stating, "Food will win the war!" Meatless days were promoted. A Fuel Administration directed civilian use of gasoline. Finally, a War Trade Board controlled exports and imports.

Feelings against Germany became stronger as the war went on. Schools stopped offering courses in German language and literature. Those who criticized the war effort were suspected of working for the enemy. The Department of Justice received wide powers to investigate espionage. It was suspected that German saboteurs were responsible for an explosion at the Black Tom ammunition depot in Jersey City.

Nearly half of the country's male population, or approximately twenty-six million young men, were eligible for service. Of those, some 4,800,000 men were called into the armed forces. The U.S. Army received about four million men. The army's total strength at its highest point, the time of the Armistice, was 3,865,000 men, of which approximately 200,000 were officers.

The draft functioned smoothly and there were few protests. Unlike the Civil War, a drafted man could not hire a substitute. In addition, propaganda convinced most of the public that it was a just war. The draft riots of 1863 were not repeated.

It is interesting to note that 69 percent of the men called for induction were considered physically fit for service—a much higher percentage than that achieved by any of the Allies. The United States could have easily fielded an army of ten million men without calling up deferred or physically exempted elements of the population.[2]

On 9 March 1917, the Fighting 69th, escorted by its old comrade in arms, the Seventh New York Infantry, paraded down Fifth Avenue to 26th Street and then east to its armory on Lexington Avenue. More than 700 soldiers marched through cheering crowds. The band played patriotic tunes, including "Garryowen," the regiment's stirring marching song. The 69th New York was back from duty on the Mexican Border and soon to be mustered out of federal service. The throng of happy New Yorkers included numerous veterans of the old Irish Brigade. Undoubtedly, their thoughts included fading memories of the brigade's arrival in New York City following the end of the Civil War.

The regiment, when mustered out of federal service, numbered 783 guardsmen. Soon thereafter, for various reasons, the organization lost some 300 men. At that time, the required strength of a regular army regiment was 2,000 soldiers. When war with Germany became imminent, an intense effort was made to rapidly bring the regiment's roster up to fighting strength.

The 69th NY was interested in quality, not quantity. According to regimental chaplain Father Francis P. Duffy, there was no need to actively recruit volunteers. "The one bit of publicity we indulged in was to send round our machine gun trucks with the placard, 'Don't join the 69th unless you want to be among the first to go to France.'"[3]

It was a recruiting campaign of a special kind. In the words of the poet Joyce Kilmer, "It was desired to enlist strong, intelligent, decent living men whose sturdy Americanism was strengthened and vivified by their Celtic blood, men who would be worthy successors of those unforgotten patriots who at Bloody Ford and on Mayre's Heights earned the title of The Fighting Irish."[4]

Father Francis P. Duffy (courtesy of U.S. Army Military History Institute).

Volunteers were hand picked from Irish county societies and New York City Catholic athletic clubs. Martin J. Hogan was seventeen years old when he decided to "camouflage" his age and join up. He chose the old 69th, "because it and I were Irish."[5]

The Fighting 69th departs for Camp Mills, Long Island (courtesy Stackpole Books, Mechanicsburg, Pa., and Greenhill Books, London, England).

After Hogan passed his physical in the armory, he and four other relatively young men were assigned to Company K, Third Battalion. When Captain Hurley, the company commander, eyeballed the new recruits, he complained to the First Sergeant, "What are we getting now, sergeant, a Boy Scout outfit?"[6]

On 6 April 1917, when the president declared that a state of war existed between Germany and the United States, the 69th New York, anticipating federalization, was at full war strength. Every officer, non-com and private guardsman was participating in the unit's nightly drills with increased enthusiasm. They realized military combat on a European battlefield was in the not-too-distant future.

The National Guard was called into federal service on 25 July, and on 5 August the 69th New York was drafted into the regular army of the United States. Later in the month, New York City was electrified when it learned that the 69th NY was selected to join the Rainbow Division, which would be the first New York National Guard outfit to be sent abroad with the American Expeditionary Force.

The men of the regiment were informed of their incorporation into the Rainbow Division on 25 August, a hot Saturday afternoon. They were assembled in the armory following a divisional inspection in Central Park. Present were all three battalion commanders, Majors Donovan, Stacom and Moynahan plus eleven company commanders including Captains Anderson, McKenna and Kelly. The troops were informed by Lieutenant Colonel Reed of the great honor bestowed on the regiment by the War Department.

Most guardsmen realized that their regiment was selected to be in the vanguard of the American Expeditionary Force because of its outstanding performance on the Mexican border and not because of its past glories in the Civil War. It was unfortunate that Colonel William Haskell, the man most responsible for the regiment's praiseworthy service with the Punitive Expedition, was no longer in command of the 69th. He had been reassigned to a responsible position in the new national army.

Soon after the 69th New York was federalized, the U.S. Army increased the size of its regiments from 2,000 to 3,600 men. Colonel Charles Hine, the regiment's new commanding officer, was eager to recruit the required volunteers for the unit. The U.S. Army, however, wanted additional soldiers to come from other New York City organizations. Accordingly, one day in August, there arrived at the armory the first of the new increments, 335 men from the Seventh New York.

Every seventh man on the roster of the Seventh was designated for transfer to the 69th. The guardsmen assigned to the regiment were escorted to the doors of the armory by the rest of the Seventh New York. The new men were received enthusiastically. In the words of Albert L. Ettinger, one of the transferees, "The ceremony was unforgettable. As we entered, those Irishers of the 69th gave us a rousing roar of welcome. Men were up in the balcony and hanging from the rafters, and they cheered and cheered, because we were the first troops from other regiments in New York to make the transfer."[7]

On 20 August, the 69th New York, with a strength of 2,500 men, marched through New York City to the East River ferry landing in lower Manhattan. The troops crossed the river and then entrained for Camp Albert L. Mills, Mineola, Long Island.

CHAPTER 10

American Expeditionary Force

In early 1917, the United States considered itself a sea power, the equal of Great Britain. Germany and Russia were the land powers of the time. America went to war in 1917 to ensure freedom of the seas. Initially, President Wilson believed his government should cooperate with the British Navy and eliminate the German submarine menace. At that time, the president did not intend to deploy a large army in Europe. On 19 March, Colonel Edward M. House, President Wilson's military advisor, wrote, "No one looks with favor upon our raising a large army at the moment, believing it would be better if we permit volunteers to enlist in the Allied armies."[1]

House believed, as did many of Wilson's key advisors, that America should give naval aid and economic assistance to the Allies. Military help should be provided only as needed by the Allies.

When the United States entered the war, President Wilson came to realize that the weight of American political influence in the postwar world would be directly related to the contribution of the United States Army toward defeating Germany. Wilson's shift toward the creation and deployment of a large American Expeditionary Force (AEF), may have been influenced by Herbert Hoover, one of his principal advisors. In February 1917, Hoover stated, "Our terms of peace will probably run counter to most of the European proposals and our weight in accomplishment of our ideals will be greatly in proportion to the strength we can throw into the scale."[2]

President Wilson's Secretary of War was Newton D. Baker. Baker spent most of his life in municipal affairs, as a lawyer, a city solicitor and as mayor of Cleveland. Wilson and Baker selected Major General John J. Pershing as commander of the American Expeditionary Force. The army chief of staff (COS) at that time was Major General Hugh Scott. His assistant was Major General Tasker Bliss. Bliss became Chief of Staff in late September 1917. When he retired in December 1917, he was replaced by Major General John Biddle. Then Biddle was relieved by Major General Peyton March in March 1917.

March was a ruthlessly efficient officer who did an excellent job in bringing the War Department up to speed. Secretary of War Baker once said March was "arrogant, harsh, dictatorial and opinionated." Apparently he ruled by a reign of terror, "...riding rough-shod over everyone."[3]

Organization

The regular army of the United States in April 1917 consisted of 133,000 enlisted men and 9,000 officers. An additional 67,000 National Guard troops had been federalized for active duty on the Mexican Border. Many of these units, however, such as the 69th New York, had been demobilized and returned to their respective states. There were no units larger than a regiment, about 2,000 men, on active duty at that time. One machine gun company of six weapons was organic to each infantry regiment in 1916.

By July 1917, the Wilson administration was committed to the creation of a million man army. The plan to raise that force, the General Organization Project, stated: "It is evident that a force of about a million is the smallest unit which in modern war will be a complete, well balanced and independent fighting organization. It is taken as the force which may be expected to reach France in time for offensive in 1918 and as a unit and basis of organizations. Plans for the future should be based, especially with reference to manufacture of material, artillery, and aviation on three times this force, that is at least three million men. Such a program ... should be completed within two years...."[4]

The greatly expanded army was to be comprised of regular army divisions—numbered from 1 to 20, National Guard divisions—numbered from 26 to 42, and national army divisions numbered from 76 to 93. The national units were to be made up of volunteers and draftees. By war's end, 45 divisions were activated and 42 of them served in France.

General Pershing's military advisors recommended the size of American divisions be enlarged so as to improve their staying power. Accordingly, the War Department established the so-called "square division." It was composed of two 8,500 man brigades, one artillery brigade, a combat engineer regiment, three machine gun battalions plus signal and administrative units. Each infantry brigade consisted of two regiments. The square division was larger than a full size Union Army corps. The 28,000 man division was powerful (260 machine guns) but not as agile as contemporary British, French and German units.

Each regiment of the "square division" was organized as follows:

- Regiment: 3,600 men commanded by a colonel, three battalions of infantry and a machine gun company.
- Battalion: 1,000 men commanded by a major, four companies.
- Company: 250 men commanded by a captain, four platoons.
- Platoon: 58 men commanded by 1st or 2nd Lieutenant, basic infantry unit.[5]

42nd Division

The 42nd Division was Secretary Baker's personal creation. During the summer of 1916, he and Major Douglas MacArthur, then a staff officer in the War Department, decided to organize a division with units from all the states. Every locale in the country could then take pride in the fact that some of its own boys were among the first to go overseas. MacArthur suggested that National Guard divisions had surplus units which might be joined to form such a division. When Baker added that he wanted them visually to cover the United States, MacArthur reportedly replied, "In the make up and promise of the future of this division it resembles a rainbow."

A newspaper reporter picked up on MacArthur's descriptive phrase and identified the then-unnumbered division in a dispatch as the Rainbow. The sobriquet appealed to Baker and MacArthur, who then obtained an official designation, Rainbow Division, from the War Department.[6]

Brigadier General William A. Mann, who had been chief of the Militia Bureau, was the first commander of the 42nd Division. A West Point graduate, he saw active service during the Indian Insurrection of 1890, Spanish American War, Philippine Pacification Campaign of 1899 and Pershing's Punitive Expedition on the Mexican Border in 1916. When the Rainbow Division arrived in France, he quickly realized that it was being cannibalized. Equipment and clothing were taken from the unit and given to the 1st and 26th divisions, the first such units in France, which were experiencing supply difficulties. In addition, 33 of its finest officers, including Colonel Charles P. Summerall, who would become Chief of Staff of the post war Army, were pirated to other divisions or Pershing's headquarters. The Rainbow was on the verge of becoming a replacement division. General Mann and his Chief of Staff, MacArthur, used strong political support and influence with the secretary of war to save the division. The 41st Division became the replacement division and the Rainbow went on to become one of the best divisions in the American Expeditionary Force. Pershing believed Mann was a better politician than a general.[7]

Major General Charles T. Menoher relieved Mann as commander of the Rainbow in December 1917. Menoher, who graduated from West Point in 1886, was a classmate of General Pershing. He served in Manilla following the Spanish American War, returning to the States in 1901. He was a field artilleryman with minimal experience directing infantry under combat conditions. There were some on the American Expeditionary Force staff who doubted his ability to effectively lead the 42nd Division. Nevertheless, Pershing was sure of his friend's ability, case closed.[8]

The 42nd Division was organized at Camp Mills, Long Island, during the summer of 1917. Per Baker's orders, the division was comprised of National Guard units selected from each of 26 states and the District of Columbia. Most of the outfits had long-standing records of excellence and all had been previously inducted into federal service. Some of the organizations had been deployed on the Mexican Border as part of General Pershing's Punitive Expedition.

The Rainbow's four infantry regiments, the 165th, 166th, 167th and 168th, were expanded versions of the 69th New York, Fourth Ohio, Fourth Alabama and Fourth Iowa respectively. The division's three machine gun battalions (MGBs) were the 149th, 150th and 151st from Pennsylvania, Wisconsin and Georgia respectively. The 42nd Division had two light artillery regiments, the 149th and 151st Field Artillery from Illinois and Minnesota, one heavy (6 inch) artillery regiment, the 150th Field Artillery from Indiana, and a trench mortar battery (TMB), the 117th from Maryland. The engineer regiment was comprised of units from South

Carolina and California, while the engineer train was made up of guard units from North Carolina.

Other units assigned to the 42nd Division were: 117th Field Signal Battalion (Missouri), military police (Virginia), headquarters troop (Louisiania), ammunition train (Kansas), supply train (Texas) and sanitary train (District of Columbia and seven other states).

Medical units attached to the 42nd Division included 165th, 166th, 167th and 168th Ambulance Companies from New Jersey, Tennessee, Oklahoma and Michigan, respectively. Field hospitals were the 165th, 166th, 167th and 168th from District of Columbia, Nebraska, Oregon and Colorado respectively.

Fourth Ohio Infantry. The Ohio National Guard was demobilized at the close of the Civil War. During the winter of 1876, there was labor unrest throughout the country. The governor of Ohio, to protect private property, organized a regiment of infantry. That unit, the 14th Ohio, was periodically activated between 1877 and 1898 to maintain order.

When war was declared on Spain in 1898, the 14th Ohio offered its services to the government. The regiment was federalized in May 1898 and mustered into the national army as the Fourth Ohio. The unit saw action at Guayana, Puerto Rico, where the Ohioans fought a small engagement against Spanish troops. At the war's end, the Fourth Ohio returned to the United States and was mustered out of federal service in January 1899.

The regiment retained the designation Fourth Ohio following the Spanish American War. From 1906 to 1913, the unit was activated a number of times to maintain order during labor strikes. On 18 June 1916, President Wilson federalized the regiment for service on the Mexican border. By mid–August, the Fourth Ohio was operating along the Rio Grande. The regiment took part in the famous Las Cruces Hike, a gruelling march of about 77 miles, most of which was performed under desert-like conditions. The regiment's excellent performance on the border was the prime reason for its inclusion in the 42nd Division.[9]

Fourth Alabama. The Fourth Alabama was organized at Dalton, Georgia on 2 May 1861 and mustered into the Confederate Army at Lynchburg, Virginia, in May 1861. The Fourth Alabama fought at the First Bull Run and during the early stages of the battle suffered considerable losses in killed and wounded at the hands of the 69th New York State Militia. Later in the day, the regiment was part of the Confederate force holding Henry Hill that turned back the attack of Sherman's Brigade. Sherman's assault was made piecemeal, regiment by regiment. The 69th New York State Militia was the third and last of his units to charge up Henry Hill. This time, the Alabamians helped inflict heavy casualties on the Fighting Irish.

The Fourth Alabama fought at Seven Pines, Second Bull Run and Sharpsburg. The regiment was then incorporated into Law's Alabama Brigade, James Longstreet's First Corps, Army of Northern Virginia.

The 69th New York Volunteers and the Fourth Alabama fought on opposite sides at Fredericksburg, Gettysburg, Wilderness, Spotsylvania, Cold Harbor and the siege of Petersburg. During those battles, the regiments did not directly confront each other as they had during the opening action of the war.

The Fourth Infantry, Alabama National Guard, was organized in May 1911. The reborn regiment was mustered into federal service in Montgomery, Alabama on 18 June 1916. Many of the paternal ancestors of the outfit's officers and men served in the Confederate Fourth.

In October 1916, the Alabamians were on the Mexican border at Nogales, Arizona. The Fourth Alabama served approximately four months in Pershing's force. During that period of time, the guardsmen never came to grips with Pancho Villa's bandits. Their training, however, was rigorous and conducted under difficult conditions. When the regiment returned to Montgomery in March 1917, it was a hardened outfit, ready for further service.[10]

In 1917, the end of the Civil War was only 52 years in the nation's past. Alabama had been occupied by federal soldiers for nine years after Appomattox. Many Alabamians had negative opinions of Yankees. The 69th was one of the more famous regiments in the Army of the Potomac, the Union force that eventually compelled Lee's troops, including the Alabamians, to lay down their arms. It is understandable that the 165th Infantry would be a lightning rod for negative energy generated by Alabama's diehard Rebels.

Third Iowa. The Iowa National Guard was reorganized in 1892. Eight companies of the Fifth Iowa were combined with four companies of the old Third Iowa to form the new Third Iowa. One of the original companies served with distinction during the Civil War.

The regiment was federalized by President William McKinley in April 1898 and served in the Philippines until early November 1899 as the 51st Iowa Volunteers. There, the regiment fought against Philippine insurrectionists. The regiment was known as the 55th Iowa for a period of time, but in July 1915 was redesignated the Third Iowa Infantry.

The Third Iowa was federalized in the summer of 1916 and sent to the Mexican border in the fall of that year. The regiment served with distinction on the border. It was mustered out of federal service in February 1917.[11]

Organization of the Rainbow Division was finalized in early September. The 165th and 166th Infantries plus the 150th Machine Gun Battalion comprised the 83rd Infantry Brigade, commanded by Brigadier General Lenihan. The 167th and 168th Infantries plus the 151st Machine Gun Battalion formed the 84th Brigade, commanded by Brigadier General Brown.

Lenihan graduated from West Point in 1887. He fought in the Indian Wars and served in the Cuban Army of Occupation. He saw action during the Philippine Insurrection from 1899 to 1902 and was serving on the War College General Staff when assigned to the Rainbow.

During their stay at Camp Mills, the troops were trained in use of the rifle and bayonet, in addition to being conditioned via vigorous physical exercise and long marches. While at Camp Mills and in the neighboring town of Mineola, members of the 165th and 167th, opponents in the Civil War as the Fighting 69th and Fourth Alabama, renewed old acquaintances and participated in a number of brawls. Rivalry on drill fields and in local bars between the New York Irish, the Alabama Rebels and the two Midwestern regiments translated into beneficial competition in France.

Organization of the 42nd (Rainbow) Division

Organization	Original (State) Designation	Commanding Officers
42d Division.........	Composed of National Guard Units from 27 States.	Major Generals Mann, Menoher, Brigadier General MacArthur, Maj. Gen. Flagler.
83d Infantry Brigade.	Composed of National Guard Units from 4 States.	Brig. Gen. Lenihan; Col. Reilly, Brig. Gen. Caldwell.
165th Infantry......	69th N. Y. Inf................	Lt. Col. Reed, Colonels Hine, Barker, McCoy, Mitchell, Lt. Col. Dravo, Colonels Howland, Donovan.
166th Infantry......	4th Ohio Inf..................	Col. Hough
150th M.G. Battalion	Cos. 1, 2 and 3, 2nd Wis. Inf. and Co. I, 4th Pa. Inf............	Majors Hall, Smith, Capt. Graef, Maj. Calder.
84th Infantry Brigade	Composed of National Guard Units from 4 States.........	Brigadier Generals Brown, Caldwell, MacArthur.
167th Infantry......	4th Alabama Inf..............	Col. Screws.
168th Infantry......	3d Iowa Inf..................	Colonels Bennett, Tinley.
151st M.G. Battalion	Cos. B, C and F, 2d Ga. Inf. and Co. K, 4th Pa. Inf..........	Maj. (Lt. Col.) Winn.
67th F. A. Brigade....	Composed of National Guard Units from 5 States.........	Brigadier Generals Summerall, McKinstry, Gatley.
149th Field Artillery.	1st Ill. F. A...................	Col. Reilly.
150th Field Artillery.	1st Ind. F. A.................	Col. Tyndall.
151st Field Artillery..	1st Minn. F. A................	Col. Leach.
117th Trench Mortar Battery...........	3d and 4th Cos., Md. C. A. C.	Captains Gill, Carson, 1st Lt Greene, Capt. McCabe.
117th Ammunition Train.............	Kansas Ammunition Train	Lt. Col. Travis, Majors Frank Cushing, Lt. Col. Martin.
149th M. G. Battalion	Cos. L and M, 4th Pa. Inf......	Major Reitzel, Captains Godley, Peacock, Majors Mills, Frank, Caldwell, Palmer.
117th Engineers......	1st Bn. from South Carolina; 2nd Bn. from California.........	Colonels Kelly, Johnson.
117th Engr. Train...	N. C. Engr. Train............	Capt. Clowe, 1st Lt. Hines.
117th Field Signal Battalion..........	1st Field Bn., Missouri Signal Corps......	Majors Garrett, Smith.
117th Supply Train...	Texas Supply Train...........	Majors Devine, Becker
117th Military Police (42d M. P. Co.).....	1st and 2d Cos., Va. C. A. C. (2d Co., Va. C. A. C.)......	Majors Shannon, Battle, Potts, Worthington, Capt. Varney.
42d Hdqrs. Troop.....	2d La. Cavalry..............	Captains Taylor, Caldwell.

Table reproduced with permission from *A Doughboy with the Fighting 69th: A Remembrance of World War I* by Albert M. Ettinger and A. Churchill Ettinger, 1992.

165th Infantry

Shortly after the 69th's arrival at Camp Mills, reinforcements were received from the 23rd, 14th, 71st and 12th New York regiments. Most of the men were excellent additions. Some transferees, however, were obviously jettisoned from their previous organizations. The undesirable soldiers were quietly eased out of the regiment.

At Camp Mills, the New Yorkers became acclimated to their new status in the American Army, the 165th Infantry, 83rd Brigade, 42nd (Rainbow) Division. (The accompanying table presents the 165th's organization.)

Colonel Charles W. Hine replaced Haskell as commander of the regiment shortly after it was federalized for service in the Rainbow. Hine, a West Point graduate, served for a time as a lieutenant in the regular army. Later, he entered the railroad business and eventually became a respected leader in the industry. Hine reentered the service during the Spanish American War and was given the rank of major in the First District of Columbia Volunteer Regiment.

Lt. Colonel Reed was second in command. He was relieved by Lt. Colonel Harry D. Mitchell in early 1918. The 1st Battalion was led by Major William Donovan. He served in the New York Division on the Mexican border. There, Captain Donovan commanded Troop I of the First Cavalry. Following recall of the expedition, he was assigned to the New York Division's brigade staff. Shortly thereafter, he transferred to the 69th.

Major William Stacom led the 2nd Battalion. Stacom, a graduate of St. Francis Xavier College, joined the 69th as a private. When the regiment served on the border, Stacom commanded Company B. Colonel Haskell considered Stacom to be one of his best company commanders.

Major Timothy J. Moynahan commanded the 3rd Battalion. He had a military background and was an instructor of that discipline at several colleges. When the Rainbow went to France, he was the division's senior major.

Captain Alexander E. Anderson was a 69th man by heredity. His uncle, Colonel Duffy, commanded the regiment in 1898. Anderson enlisted in the unit as a private. He attended Officer's Candidate School and graduated with high honors. Anderson was a company commander when the regiment was federalized.

Captain James A. McKenna was a graduate of Fordham University and Harvard Law School. McKenna served eight years with the Seventh New York before joining the 69th in 1916. He was a lawyer in civilian life and, like Donovan, a well known athlete. His reason for leaving the silk stocking outfit was an opportunity for promotion in the 69th.

Captain Michael Kelly led Company F. Born in County Clare, Ireland, he served in the British Army and saw action in the Boer War. Later, he immigrated to New York City and became active in law enforcement, rising to second in command of the Aqueduct Police.

The 165th was the first unit of the 42nd Division to arrive at Camp Mills. The base was really an expanse of cleared farmland. Areas to be occupied by various units of the Rainbow were laid out by army engineers.

Initially, chow was poor. According to Private Ettinger, "Our only problem

Organization of 165th U.S. Infantry

165th (69th NY) Infantry
(3,600 Men)
Commanding Officers

Colonel Charles Hine
Colonel John Barker
Colonel Frank McCoy
Colonel Harry Mitchell
Colonel Charles Dravo
Colonel William Donovan

1st Battalion	Majors William Donovan Michael Kelly Merle-Smith	3rd Battalion	Majors Timothy Moynahan James McKenna Thomas Reilley
Company A	Captains George McAdie William Baldwin William Hutchinson	Company I	Captains Richard Ryan Michael Walsh
Company B	Captains Thomas Reilley John Clifford	Company K	Captains John Hurley Emil Guignon
Company C	Captains William Kennelly Herman Bootz	Company L	Captains Merle-Smith William Given
Company D	Captains James McKenna Edmond Connelly Oscar Buck	Company M	Captains Martin Meaney John Rowley
2nd Battalion	Majors William Stacom Alex Anderson Herman Bootz	Heaquarters Company	Captains Walter Powers Alex Anderson William McKenna
Company E	Captains Alex Anderson Charles Baker John Connors	Adjutants	Captains William Doyle Alex Anderson William McKenna Martin Meaney
Company F	Captains Michael Kelly Frank Marsh		
Company G	Captains James Archer John Prout Louis Stout		
Company H	Captains James Finn Kenneth Ogle		

Regiment Chaplin: Father (Major) Francis Duffy
Medical Department: Doctor (Major) George Lawrence
Supply Company: Captain John Mangan
Machine Gun Company: Captain R.B. De Lacour
Regiment Sergeant Major: Ambrose Steinert

SOURCE: Duffy, Father Francis P., *Father Duffy's Story*; Ettinger, Albert M. and Ettinger, A. Churchill. *A Doughboy with the Fighting 69th: A Rememberance of World War I.*

was the food, which was terrible. Inexperienced cooks served up boiled beans with gobs of pork fat one day and canned corn beef stew the next. Men soon sickened from the greasy pork and we were assaulted with an epidemic of boils...."[12]

During its early days in camp, the Alabamas were on friendly terms with the New York Irishers of its division. When the folks back home learned their regiment would be brigaded with descendants of 69th New York State Militia, they bombarded their soldiers with newspaper stories about Civil War confrontations with the New Yorkers.

The good natured rivalry between the 165th and 167th regiments turned to animosity. Fights broke out between groups of soldiers in the Hempstead and Mineola taverns, where the men relaxed after duty.

According to Ettinger, bad feelings between the New Yorkers and Alabamians were exacerbated by the arrival of the 15th NY, a black regiment. He wrote:

> Our boys from the 69th received those of the 15th New York as buddies. Not so the Alabamians. They resented Blacks coming into camp. Hell they resented us! The first thing you knew fights erupted all over the place, and the 69th guys usually stood up for the 15th men and fought alongside them against the Alabamians.
>
> It got so bad that the men of the 15th were required to turn in their ammunition. Not so the Fourth Alabamians. We thought it was unfair, so a number of us slipped ammunition to our fellow New Yorkers. They never forgot that, and once, when I visited with a unit of the 15th in France, some of the fellows thanked me for it.
>
> A riot nearly started when over a hundred fellows from Alabama attempted to invade a section of the 69th's camp intending to tear it down. I'm sure they believed they had sufficient provocation. Our language alone was not the most elegant. The Rainbow's military police, units from Virginia, drove them back with fixed bayonets, and one of the Alabamians was killed. It was hell to pay, but finally the officers of both regiments, and Father Duffy in particular, calmed down the situation.[13]

As it turned out, the warring regiments were not brigaded. The Irish were combined with the 166th Ohio while the Alabamians were joined with the 168th Infantry.

When the Rainbow Division left for France, the men of the New York and Alabama regiments were not good friends. Nevertheless, as the two units engaged the common enemy, they learned to respect each other.

Ettinger will have the last word on the matter: "However, as we got into combat, we came to appreciate each other and became good comrades, even though we were in different brigades. They usually fought on our right flank, or we would relieve one another, and we could always count on them. They were terrific fighters."[14]

As we know, General Pershing believed the most potent weapon in the war was an American soldier equipped with a bayonetted rifle. Accordingly, the men of the 165th received extensive training in the use of the bayonet. Joyce Kilmer observed, "Cold steel propelled by Irishmen was said to be what the Germans chiefly feared and every effort was made to make sure that the 69th should not, through lack of practice, be less skillful with the bayonet than were the Dublin

Fusiliers and the Connaught Rangers." (The Fusiliers and Rangers were regiments in the British Expeditionary Force.)[15]

Uniforms

American uniforms sometimes included the Sam Browne belt, an over-the-shoulder strap designed by a British officer of that name while stationed in India during the 1870s. Originally, it served a practical purpose—holding up the waist belt when it was heavily loaded with sword, revolver, binoculars and canteen. The strap was also worn on the dress uniform and eventually became the distinguishing mark of a British officer. General Pershing liked the belt's look and prescribed it for all American Expeditionary Force officers. Chief of Staff March believed the Sam Browne belt served no real purpose and was an extravagant waste of scarce leather. Pershing and Marsh disagreed over use of the item. Accordingly, officers in the American Expeditionary Force wore the belt and those that remained stateside did not. In time, the item became a symbol identifying officers who served in France.

Equipment

When WW I started, the Springfield 30–06 rifle (Model 1903) was the nation's standard service weapon. At that time, the rifle was out of production. By 1917, Winchester, Remington and Eddystone were producing Enfield 303 (Model 1914) rifles for the British. Shortly after the U.S. entered the war, the War Department realized that an enormous number of rifles would be required to equip the rapidly expanding American Army. It was decided to modify the design of the Enfield rifles being manufactured by American firms to accept the 30–06 rimless cartridge. Thereafter, Springfield and Enfield rifles used the same ammo. Most of the divisions organized after April 1917 were equipped with Enfield rifles. The First, Second, 26th and 42nd Divisions, however, went overseas carrying 30–06 Springfields.

During the war, the Springfield Armory resumed production of the Model 1903 and some American Expeditionary Force units were equipped with the weapon. Most doughboys preferred the Springfield over the Enfield. They considered the latter to be heavier, clumsier and less accurate than the American designed rifle. Nevertheless, both weapons were considered superior or at least the equal of any rifle used by other Great War belligerents.[16]

The American Expeditionary Force didn't have a satisfactory light machine gun in 1917 and during early 1918 used the French Chaucat automatic rifle. The weapon frequently jammed when used with American made ammo. The Browning automatic rifle (BAR) became available near the end of the war. The American weapon, which weighed 18 pounds and tended to jam when fired at its maximum rate, was preferred by the Doughboys.[17]

Initially, the American Expeditionary Force used 54 pound French Hotchkiss,

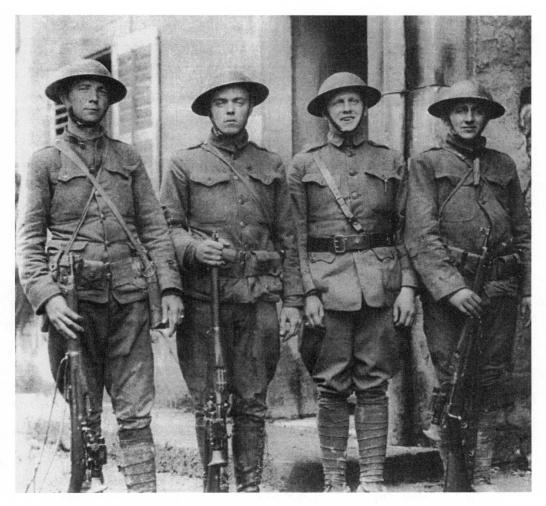

Rainbow Division Raiding Party. Four Rainbow Division soldiers are shown after a successful stint in No Man's Land. Their uniforms are typical of that worn by American troops in France. All are wearing British style steel helmets. The officer can be identified by his Sam Browne belt. The three enlisted men have telescopic sights on their rifles. (Courtesy Stackpole Books, Mechanicsburg, Pa. and Greenhill Books, London).

Model 1914 and 38 pound British Vickers, and Model 1915 (water cooled) machine guns. The Model 1915 weapon was preferred by advancing troops. Later in the war, the American Browning machine gun, Model 1917, became available. The water-cooled weapon, which weighed 36 pounds, could fire 500 rounds per minute with minimum jams. The American Expeditionary Force preferred the Browning because of its better reliability.[18]

The American Expeditionary Force staff opted for the French 155-millimeter (6 inch) cannon and 75 millimeter rapid firing field gun instead of corresponding U.S. manufactured artillery. Pershing's staff argued that the French weapons would provide the firepower required by the American Expeditionary

Force and, more importantly, would be more readily available than the American guns.[19]

In France, the American Expeditionary Force utilized French Renault tanks. U.S. aviators preferred the French Spad XIII. No American-designed airplanes saw action in France.

Training

General Pershing expected the War Department to establish the American Expeditionary Force's training program. The AEF was not prepared to provide necessary doctrine and looked to Pershing for guidance. His response was, "The rifle and the bayonet remain the supreme weapons of the infantry soldier and ... The ultimate success of the Army depends upon their proper use in open warfare."[20]

Pershing objected to Allied training methods. He believed their doctrine emphasized trench fighting rather than open warfare. Trench warfare, as the name implies, was oriented toward the taking and holding of trenches. According to an American Expeditionary Force combat memorandum, it was "marked by uniform formations, the regulation of space and time by higher command down to the smallest details, absence of scouts preceding the first wave, fixed distances and intervals between units and individuals, voluminous orders, careful rehearsal, little initiative on the part of the individual soldier...."[21]

Open warfare, as construed by Pershing, was "marked by scouts who precede the first wave, irregularity of formation, comparatively little regulation of space and time by the higher command, the greatest possible use of the infantry's own fire power to enable it to get forward, variable distances and intervals between units and individuals, use of every form of cover and accident of ground during the advance, brief orders, and the greatest possible use of individual initiative by all troops engaged in the action."[22]

In the author's opinion, "open warfare" was a blend of German infiltration procedures and western style Indian fighting.

Pershing sincerely believed that a self-confident soldier, skilled in the use of infantry weapons, could advance by bold maneuver against strongly held enemy positions. The general was convinced properly trained infantry could seize strongly defended German positions employing interlocking machine gun fire.

Many prominent military historians are amazed at Pershing's failure to realize that the modern machine gun dominated Western Front battlefields. Scholars familiar with Pershing's theories believe his insistence on so-called "open warfare" was an attempt to infuse and maintain an offensive spirit within the American Expeditionary Force. The general and many of his advisors were of the opinion that the French and British had lost their enthusiasm for attack. The American Expeditionary Force chief of training, Colonel Harold B. Fiske, wrote, "The French do not like the rifle, do not know how to use it, and their infantry is consequently too dependent upon powerful artillery support. Their infantry lacks aggressiveness and discipline. The British infantry lacks initiative and resource...."[23]

Fiske worked hard and did the best he could, but the exigencies of the Western Front during the early months of 1918 undermined the training of most American divisions. Pershing received permission from the Allies to use the Lorraine Sector for the assembly and training of the American Expeditionary Force. This quiet area was located southeast of Verdun and extended to the Swiss border.

American Expeditionary Force units were supposed to receive infantry training in the United States before being shipped to France. Pershing wanted marksmanship with the rifle emphasized. He insisted his men be proficient with the weapon at 600 yards. In addition, troops were to be schooled in the concepts of open warfare. Very little training, however, was devoted to the latter discipline. Allied instructors tended to emphasize techniques of trench warfare since they believed the machine gun prevented implementation of open warfare. In addition, there were no army training manuals spelling out the nuts and bolts of open warfare.

As it turned out, some soldiers received adequate training in the States, while other individuals were poorly instructed. With respect to the latter situation, a former infantry private, Edmund Seiser, remembered that he had not seen a rifle or a pistol until he reported to the 77th Division in France. Much to his chagrin, he was quickly sent to an advanced outpost.[24]

Plans were to accomplish training in France in three phases. The first phase consisted of familiarization with weapons being used in the theater, followed by division level tactical exercises in training areas. The second phase called for a one month tour of duty in the trenches, under French regimental command, by infantry battalions. During this training phase, American Expeditionary Force commanders were to be stationed with French and British units to observe operations under fire. The third phase consisted of division-level operations by combined arms of infantry, artillery and aviation. Following these exercises, each division was to go into the line, under its own commanders, as part of a French corps.

With respect to training in France, only the 1st Division, the initial such unit to arrive in France, went through the entire training program. The First, after coming out of the trenches in March 1918, underwent refresher training. Still, after a year of combat and training, American Expeditionary Force inspectors found the division to be "too trench oriented." Pershing considered the First Division to be the best such unit in the American Expeditionary Force. It contained the largest number of commissioned and non-commissioned regular army officers. If its training was considered insufficient, then that of the other divisions serving in France had to be even poorer.

The next three divisions arriving in France—the 26th, Rainbow and Second— did not receive the third phase of the prescribed training program. Instead, they were deployed to blunt Ludendorff's 1918 offensive. The divisions remained operationally committed throughout the war, in spite of Pershing's desire to disengage them for more instruction.

The American Expeditionary Force's first significant engagement was at Seicheprey in April 1918. By that time, the major protagonists on the Western Front had been fighting for almost four years. Obviously, their armies had far greater experience in modern warfare than did the upstart American Expeditionary Force. Most officers in the European military community considered American troops improperly trained for modern warfare. They were correct. However, the American soldiers were better trained than credited by the Allies.

CHAPTER 11

American Expeditionary Force Arrives in France

General Pershing and his entourage arrived in Paris in June 1917. His chief of staff was Colonel James G. Harboard. The qualities Pershing admired in Harboard revealed the traits the general valued most—unselfishness, resourcefulness, energy, and above all, loyalty.

In late July, Pershing received permission from the French high command to use the Lorraine Sector for the assembly and training of the American Expeditionary Force. The British needed to control northern areas of the Western Front to protect communications with the channel ports. The French wanted to dominate the central region of the line shielding Paris from attack. There were no complaints from the Allies when Pershing opted for the Lorraine Sector.

Lorraine possessed several advantages. First, the sector's supply lines were not dependent on channel ports, threatened by Ludendorff's offensives. Second, the area was not congested and was ideal for the buildup of the American Expeditionary Force. Third, Lorraine had excellent offensive possibilities since a strategic railroad plus coal and iron mines were located in German controlled areas near the front.[1]

Advance elements of the 1st Division, some 14,000 men, arrived in France on 26 June. Most of the soldiers were undisciplined. Regulars were kept back in the States serving as cadres for new divisions being organized.

In early July, Pershing and a detail from the 16th Infantry rendered honors at the grave of Lafayette. The French loved the spectacle, especially the words of Lieutenant Colonel Charles Stanton, an officer in the quartermaster corps, who exclaimed, "Lafayette, we are here!" That famous phrase has been incorrectly attributed to Pershing, who wished he had said it.[2]

The general established his headquarters at Chaumont in September 1917. The city was located some 150 miles east of Paris. Pershing's residence was in a large house on the outskirts of town.

He inspected the 1st Division in July, August, and in early September. On each occasion, the unit did not appear militarily impressive. He inspected the division again in early October. The commanding officer of the 1st Division flubbed the

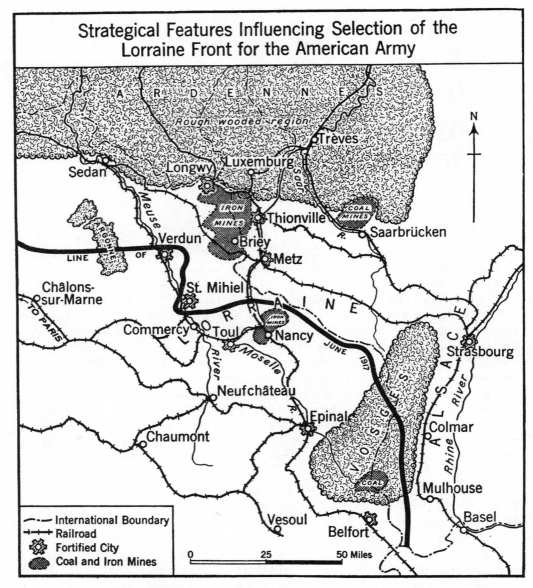

Strategical Features Influencing Selection of the
Lorraine Front for the American Army

Lorraine Front (from Official Sources).

From American Battle Monuments Commission, *American Armies and Battlefields in Europe*, Washington, D.C., 1938.

Lorraine Front (from Official Sources).

review's critique and Pershing decided to can him. At least one officer of the division impressed General Pershing, he was Captain George C. Marshall. Marshall rose steadily in army ranks and was a five star general in World War II.

On 21 October, American soldiers entered the trenches for the first time in the war. Each regiment of the 1st Division sent one of its battalions into the line for a ten day tour with corresponding French units. American captains controlled their companies but battalion and regimental commanders acted as observers.

The 1st sustained its initial casualties on 2 November, when a German raiding party surprised an American outpost. 1st Division losses included three killed, five wounded and 12 captured. German losses were two killed, seven wounded and one captured.[3]

By mid–November, there were four American divisions in France, the 1st, 2nd, 26th and 42nd. By late December, Pershing replaced the commanders of the 1st and 42nd divisions. Major General Robert L. Bullard was given command of the 1st and General Menoher the 42nd.

December was a miserable month for the American Expeditionary Force. The American troops were, in general, poorly clothed and supplied. Many men in Pershing's force likened that period of time to Washington's experience at Valley Forge during the Revolutionary War. Meanwhile, the Allies continued to put heavy pressure on Pershing to accept amalgamation.

Amalgamation is the combination of mercury with other metals to form alloys called amalgams. During World War I, the process meant incorporation of American soldiers into British or French divisions. Depending upon the Allied official recommending the procedure and the year of the war, the size of the American units to be integrated into Allied organizations ranged from small detachments to regiments.

Allied military leaders believed amalgamation made sense. They argued the procedure would be beneficial to the Americans as well as the British and French. In their opinion, raw recruits would train faster and better if they served with veterans. As a consequence, American casualties would be lower. Further, senior American Expeditionary Force staffs would not have to be created, permitting the force of American numbers to be quickly brought to bear on the enemy, and ending the war sooner. Finally, amalgamation would ease shipping problems since it would not be necessary to transport support troops from the U.S. to France. Support required for American divisions was estimated to be 45 percent of the American Expeditionary Force's strength in France.

The amalgamation question reared its ugly head early in the conflict, when General Bliss warned Secretary of War Baker that "When the war is over it may be a literal fact that the American flag may not have appeared anywhere on the line because our organizations will simply be parts of battalions and regiments of the Entente Allies. We might have a million men there and yet no American Army and no American Commander. Speaking frankly, I have received the impression from English and French officers that such is their deliberate desire."[4]

In January 1918, French observers reported that the four American divisions in France were in a dismal state with respect to training for modern warfare. The report predicted the Americans would have minimal impact on the fighting in 1918 and that by May 1919, the American Expeditionary Force would be able to deploy only 16 trained divisions. The overall situation looked very bleak for Pershing's American Expeditionary Force during the early months of 1918.

The 26th Division went into the line on 6 February, the 42nd on 21 February and the Second on 17 March. All three units were initially deployed in regimental and then battalion strength for training with the French in quiet sectors.

With the Russians essentially out of the war, the Allies realized that a strong German offensive was planned for the Western Front. Pershing was depressed: "Here we were," he said in his memoir, "likely to be confronted by the mightiest military offensive that the world had ever known and it looked as though we should be compelled to stand by almost helpless and see the Allies again suffer losses of hundreds of thousands of men in their struggle against defeat."[5]

42nd Division's Early Days in France

In mid–October, most of the Rainbow's units were transported by rail from Mineola to the Manhattan Ferry. The troops were moved across Manhattan Island and the Hudson River to the piers at Hoboken, New Jersey. There, the soldiers boarded five transports and on 18 October, the vessels stood out to sea. The ships were escorted by a cruiser, two destroyers and later a converted German raider. On the night of 29 October, first units of the 42nd Division arrived at St. Nazaire.

Most of the Rainbow were billeted in Vaucouleurs, an area within sight and sound of gun flashes and artillery explosions along the lines north of Toul. The artillery brigade, with the exception of the trench mortar battery, trained at Coetquidan. The latter unit trained at Fort de la Bonnelle near Langres. All of the above units rejoined the division before March 1918.[6]

Billets in Vaucouleurs, constructed by French Army engineers, were cramped, chilly, dark and not very clean. They were typical of housing provided by the French government for American Expeditionary Force troops during the war.

While in Vaucouleurs the division practiced target shooting. The soldiers also participated in long marches and other strenuous activities to harden them for front line service.

On 11 December, the division was ordered to La Fauche. The troops marched a distance of about 50 kilometers, through cold and blustery weather, in about two and a half days. The 168th Infantry and 149th Machine Gun Battalion, which had been delayed crossing the Atlantic, joined the rest of the division at La Fauche. Vigorous training was continued.

On 26 December, the 42nd Division was ordered to Training Area No. 7 at Rolampont, an area just south of Chaumont. The march was started over snow-covered roads through blizzard-like conditions. The soldiers wore the uniforms in which they paraded for Secretary Baker at Camp Mills the previous fall. Most of the troops had shoes that were falling apart The division hiked 75 miles in three days through the debilitating weather.

The Rainbow showed tenacity and endurance; it was ready for whatever the elements could throw at it. A soldier of the 166th Infantry, covered with snow and fighting to maintain his footing, summed up the march conditions, "Valley Forge—Hell!" he said, "there ain't no such animal."[7]

During the first two months of 1918, the division trained with two battalions of the 32nd French Regiment. In spite of the weather, the troops received instruction in trench warfare plus the use of hand grenades, machine guns and Stokes mortars.

On 16 February 1918, the division was moved by rail to the Luneville Sector of the Lorraine Front.

165th Infantry's Early Days in France

Secret orders to move out were finally received. Twice before, similar directives had arrived, but on each occasion they were canceled. On the night of 25 October 1917, Major Donovan led the 1st Battalion through the darkened camp to a train for transport to Montreal, Canada. There was little sleep on the special that night. Men of the battalion realized they were embarked on the adventure of their lives. For a good many of them it was to be the first and last escapade of their young lives.

Four days later, on the night of 25 October, the darkened ship *America* (formerly the *Amerika* of the Hamburg-American line), moved slowly out of New York Harbor. When the ship was out to sea, the khaki clad soldiers who had been massed below decks were allowed to go topside for a last look at their homeland. All that was visible was the fading lights of the Jersey shoreline. Most of men of the 2nd and 3rd battalions were excited to be on their way to France.[8]

The 1st Battalion sailed from Montreal to Liverpool on the *Tunisian*. The troops then traveled by train to Southhampton, crossed the English Channel and landed in Le Havre, France. From there, they went by train to the Champagne region detraining at Sauvoy on 15 November.[9]

Troops on the *America* had a smooth passage to France. Reportedly, men of the 2nd and 3rd battalions sang their way across the Atlantic.

Submarine lookout watches were manned by members of the regiment throughout the cruise. The guardsmen took the duty seriously. Early in the voyage, a watch officer approached a soldier scanning the dark horizon with a pair of Navy binoculars. He asked the watch stander what he was looking for. He got an appropriate response, "Looking fer somethin Oi don't wan ter foind."[10]

After a two week passage, the *America* arrived in Brest, France. The troops, however, were kept aboard ship for another week before they were allowed ashore. They were then loaded into freight cars, where they quickly learned the meaning of "40 Hommes–8 Chevaux" (40 Men or 8 Horses). Three days later, after traveling day and night under miserable conditions, the 2nd and 3rd battalions were united with Donovan's men at Sauvoy. On 13 December, the Regiment moved to the historic village of Grand. The site, with a population of about 600 people, was about a three day march from Chaumont.

The day after Christmas, the regiment began a long trek to Longeau, a small town south of Chaumont in the Rolampont Training Area. Three days later, during the afternoon of 29 December, the troops arrived at their destination. The hike was made under miserable conditions. The men of the 165th Infantry and the other regiments were poorly clothed, shod and fed. They endured considerable pain and privation during the march; many of the men would not survive.

Upon arrival at Longeau, most of the soldiers looked as though they had aged 20 years. It was a hardening experience.

The infamous march to Rolampont was observed by Major General Hunter Ligget, American Expeditionary Force Headquarters Chaumont. His report to Pershing on the Rainbow's performance was not flattering. A similar report to Menoher by the Division's Assistant Chief of Staff, Lt. Colonel William H. Hughes was particularly critical of the 165th Infantry. In his opinion, the Regiment's supply system was in disarray. Skimpy rations, lack of proper shoes and winter clothing caused the normally boisterous New Yorkers to become "...surly, insubordinate and out of hand."

General Menoher convened a board of officers to investigate the 165th's supply problems. The board's findings were not flattering to Colonel Hine.[11]

While the regiment was at Longeau, Colonel Hine was relieved by Colonel John W. Barker. Hine was given an important position in the railway service. His replacement graduated from the academy in 1909. He served in the Cuban Army of Occupation, the Philippines and on the Mexican border. Barker saw action on the frontier and took part in one of the last Indian fights at Leach Creek, MT. In 1913, he was assigned to a French infantry regiment for one year's duty as an observer.

He remained in France when the war broke out as a representative of the American army. When the American Expeditionary Force arrived in France, he joined Pershing's staff. Barker served in that capacity until personally selected by the general for command of the 165th Infantry.[12]

An attempt was made to provide the men of the 165th Infantry with British uniforms until appropriate American clothing could be brought to Longeau. The British Expeditionary Force garb did not go over well with the Irish Americans. A typical reaction was, "What the blazes do they mane by insultin min fightin for thim like this. I'd stand hangin' rather than put wan of thim rags on me back."[13]

A compromise was reached with Colonel Barker. The troops temporarily replaced their worn out shoes with British footwear and battered American Expeditionary Force uniforms with British Expeditionary Force clothing. The buttons on the British outfits, however, with the King's coat of arms, were replaced with those displaying American eagles.

Temporary billets in Longeau were dry, warm and comfortable. New barracks were built in village outskirts to house additional troops. Regimental training was intensified. Specialized platoons were organized. Competent soldiers were sent to schools. Hand grenades were supplied to the troops and the men were taught how to use them. The soldiers were issued steel helmets and two gas masks, one French and one English box respirator. The troops received training in the proper use of the equipment. According to Cochrane in *The 42nd Division Before Landres-et-St. Georges*, however, training with respect to gas warfare was limited and only 30 percent of the men went through a gas chamber.[14]

Americans were drilled in the use of the bayonet and Stokes mortars by British instructors. French combat veterans provided training in the use of hand grenades and the art of trench warfare. British Expeditionary Force instructors encouraged trainees to curse and shout obscenities while attacking with the bayonet. The

The troops were ready for trench
marched to Longeau, under orders
French troops at the front. At long
going into the trenches.

A section of the 165th N
ing their "Montana Hats

practice upset Father ⸻ ...ning ne could do to change that aspect of the training.

Hogan had the following to say about bayonet training, "There was incessant bayonet drill and this stood us in good stead in many a tight place later. The officers of our battalion [Shamrock] were especially insistent upon individual skill in this work; for they looked forward, not so much to trench hugging, as to persistent and irresistible 'grips' with the enemy. Therefore, hours and hours were spent in perfecting ourselves for hand to hand fighting. I have gone through the bayonet manual in this French village day after day until I nearly dropped from exhaustion. When I think of Baissey, I think of long point and butt stroke."[15]

The 165th Infantry organized its own intelligence section, the first in the 42nd Division. The unit contained scouts, observers, map makers and snipers. They became so expert in detecting and hindering the movement of the enemy that several times during future operations they were temporarily attached to divisional headquarters.

In early February, the 32nd Battalion of Chasseurs arrived at Longeau. The famous French unit provided excellent instructors for the regiment. Long hours of training in trench warfare prepared the troops for service that lay ahead. It was a proud day, when the Americans realized that they were better in rifle marksmanship and grenade throwing than the veteran French instructors.

From 7 to 13 February, the regiment took part in maneuvers in which it was opposed by the 166th Infantry. The operations took place in hilly countryside around Longeau. The exercise's ultimate objective was seizure and holding of a local town. The difficult tactical operation was successfully accomplished by the regiment in a timely manner.

warfare. On 16 February, the regiment o entrain for Luneville, for training with ast, the Rainbow Division, and the 165th, were

CHAPTER 12

American Divisions
Enter the Trenches

As stated earlier, the 1st Division entered the trenches in late October 1917. The 26th Division, a National Guard outfit from New England, the "Yankee Division," went into the line on 6 February 1918. The Rainbow and 2nd divisions followed on 21 February and 17 March respectively. As was the case for the 1st Division, the three units were deployed in battalion and then regimental strength in quiet sectors.

42nd Division in the Luneville Sector

Colonel MacArthur, who as Chief of Staff, reported directly to General Menoher, finalized his staff's organization while the 42nd was in Luneville. Colonel Frank Lawton, a Regular from the Quartermaster Corps was made G1, Personnel Officer. His primary function was providing continuing assessments of Division manpower. Major Noble Brandon Judah, a mid-western lawyer, served as G2, Intelligence Officer. His responsibilities included preparation and distribution of situation reports. Lt. Colonel William S. Hughes, a Regular, was G3, Operations Officer. As G3, he provided plans satisfying mission requirements based on data provided by the G1 and G3 Officers. Lawton also served as G4, Logistics Officer. There was no G5, Training Officer, the French were responsible for that task.

The 42nd Division was assigned to four very distinguished divisions of the 17th Army Corps for trench warfare training. The French corps, commanded by Major General Bassiliere, was then holding the Luneville and Baccarat sectors of the front. Rainbow regiments were distributed among French units as follows:

- •164th French Infantry Division, General Gaucher, Luneville Sector—165th Infantry and elements of the 149th and 150th Field Artillery.
- •14th French Infantry Division, General Phillipot, Luneville Sector—166th Infantry and elements of the 149th Field Artillery.
- •128th French Infantry Division, General Segonne, Baccarat Sector—167th

and 168th Infantries plus the 151st Field Artillery and 117th trench mortar battery.[1]

During the month of February, each American regiment staged large scale trench raids on the German lines. The enemy retaliated on the night of 2-3 March, attacking an outpost manned by a company of Iowans. The assault was preceded by a heavy bombardment. Men of the 168th fought well, German soldiers who managed to enter American Expeditionary Force trenches did not get out.

On the evening of 20 March, during the persistent shelling of the Forest de Parroy, the enemy saturated part of the line held by the 165th's Company K, with about 400 mustard gas and 7,000 high expolsives and shrapnel shells. It was a novel use of the poisonous agent since it was delivered with great rapidity interspersed with high explosives.

Captain Charles H. Gorrill, 42nd Division Gas Officer, reported two separate attacks on the evenings of 20 and 21 March. In the first, he stated that approximately 250 mustard gas shells mixed with an equal number of High Expolsives shells made direct hits on Company K trenches and dugouts. Gorrill reported 271 casualties, more than one man gassed per shell. He believed the casualties were primarily due to poor gas training. He said the men delayed in masking or later removed their protective gear too quickly. The latter action was performed on advice from French instructors who believed the agent was tear gas. Gorrill reported that neither officers nor men realized the dangerous persistency of mustard gas, especially under conditions of high humidity. He was concerned that no effort was made to evacuate the area.[2]

The next day, a repeat bombardment fell on the same trenches but the 42nd Division was already moving out of the sector. Only 20 Americans became gas victims. French casualties were not reported.

Lieutenant Colonel H.L. Gilchrist, medical director of the gas service, counted 542 casualties, 417 from the 165th Infantry alone, at base hospitals. Most of the wounded suffered from burns of the face and neck plus severe damage to the respiratory tract, apparently due to premature removal of their masks. Gilchrist's total is more likely since it is known that at least 180 gas victims were evacuated by the French. At the time of his report, Gorrill was probably unaware of the casualties evacuated by Gaucher's men.[3]

In any case, poor gas training not withstanding, the men of the old 69th withstood the gas attack with *sang froid*. The 42nd Division left the Luneville Sector enroute to the American Expeditionary Force training area. The division was scheduled for participation in tactical exercises dealing with German infiltration techniques, procedures successfully used by the enemy at Caporetto. A German breakthrough on the Somme, however, derailed the division's training program.

During the month in the trenches, the Rainbow sustained 893 casualties due to enemy action; killed—95 and wounded—798 men.[4]

165th Infantry in the Luneville Sector

Luneville, Loonyville to the troops, was in the Lorraine Sector of the front. The city was located near the lines between Nancy and Epinal. It was the largest

Casualties per Campaign

Sector	Killed	Wounded	Total
Lorraine [17 Feb–22 Mar]	95	798	893
Lorraine [29 Mar–21 Jun]	105	971	1,076
Champagne [3–20 Jul]	340	1,298	1,638
Aisne-Marne [21 Jul–6 Aug]	1,172	4,346	5,518
St. Mihiel [4 Sep–4 Oct]	294	913	1,207
Meuse-Argonne [5 Oct–1 Nov]	701	3,163	3,864
Meuse-Argonne [2–11 Nov]	83	307	390
	2,790	11,796	14,586

town in which the regiment had been quartered thus far in the war. Luneville featured the Stanislas Palace, a magnificent stone building located in the center of town. Regimental headquarters was established in the building, which was also used to lodge a few companies of infantry.

The Luneville area of the front was considered a "quiet sector." Trenches in these inactive zones were sometimes separated by distances approaching five kilometers. In quiet sectors, opposing troops were content to merely hold their trenches. Shots were seldom fired in anger.

The Rouge-Bouquet-Chaussailles area of the Luneville Sector was a particularly quiet zone. The subsector was heavily wooded and almost free of underbrush. It was there, early in the morning of 27 February, that elements of the 165th Infantry went into the line. Companies D and B of the 1st Battalion relieved corresponding units of the French 15th Chasseurs. To some New Yorkers in the 1st Battalion, the series of outposts joined by little ditches in the sylvan setting seemed a lot like Central Park.[5]

As shown in the accompanying map, Donovan's men held a section of line running between Rouge Bouquet and Parroy Forest. The 2nd and 3rd battalions were in reserve at Luneville and Moncel respectively. Positions of the 149th Field Artillery and 150th Machine Gun Battalion are also indicated. The 166th Infantry was located on the right of the New Yorkers near the hamlets of Blemery and Domjevin.

The Fighting Irish upped the ante in their subsector of the line. Rifle and machine gun fire from Allied-held trenches increased dramatically. American Expeditionary Force artillery began a desultory bombardment of the German lines. The enemy quickly realized that an aggressive organization had taken over the trenches on the other side of No Man's Land. By midnight of 27 February, the Chaussaille–Rouge Bouquet subsector was no longer a "quiet sector." In days following, combat between the Americans and Germans gradually increased.

A patrol from the Alabamas captured the division's first prisoners. That small coup was followed by successively larger scale raids by the 168th, 166th and then the 165th Infantry.

The Germans retaliated to the division's thrusts into their lines. During the period 2 to 3 March, the enemy raided an outpost held by two platoons of Iowans. The Americans were successful in beating back the German attack. The raid was followed by a heavy bombardment of a section of the line held by the 165th

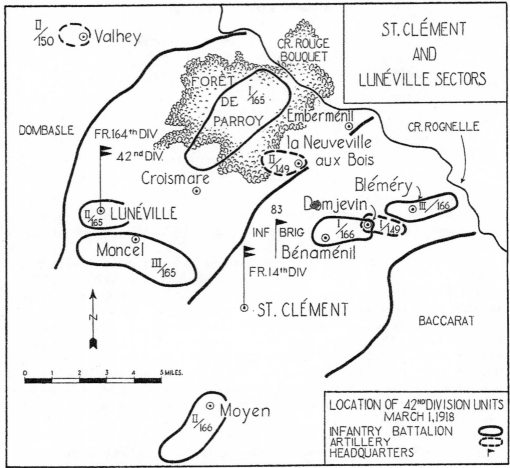

All Data from Official Sources.

This map depicts the 83rd Brigade's deployment in the Luneville and St. Clement sectors on 1 March 1918. (From official Sources).

Infantry in the Rouge Bouquet Forest on 7 March. Later on 20 March, the New Yorkers successfully raided a section of German trenches. The enemy responded to that thrust with a heavy gas attack on the regiment's positions in the area of the Rouge Bouquet Forest.

Rouge Bouquet

Early in the morning of 7 March, Company E relieved Company D in the Rouge Bouquet Forest. At 1600, the Germans began shelling the position with heavy aerial torpedoes called *Minenwerfers*. The huge missiles wobbled in flight over No Man's Land before crashing into the Allied lines. The torpedoes caused tremendous damage, creating large craters and huge clouds of earth and debris.

A minenwerfer landed squarely on an underground dugout located about 40 feet below the earth's surface. Twenty-two men were buried under piles of dirt and splintered timber. A working party was immediately organized and a frenzied effort made to release the soldiers from their living grave. The rescue team could hear their buried comrades' voices as they struggled to free themselves from the crushing rubble. Several times, a number of trapped men were almost out of the tomb, but the continuing bombardment caused them to slip below the heaving earth. Eventually, after a heroic effort of almost 24 hours, two living and three dead New Yorkers were extricated from the smoldering tomb. Five men escaped death in the bomb shelter but the bodies of 14 enlisted men and one officer were still buried under 40 feet of earth.[6]

It was finally considered unwise, in view of the continuing bombardment, to have additional men wounded in what was reluctantly recognized as a futile endeavor. Last rites of the Church were celebrated by Father Duffy at the disaster site. Later, an engraved tablet identifying the dead was placed over the tomb.

According to Corporal Alf Herman, survivor of the debacle, half of the men in the dugout died within the first 30 minutes of the explosion. Some he believed, may have lingered for days. The incident was a harrowing experience. Unfortunately, much worse was in store for the regiment.

First Trench Raid

On the evening of 20 March, Donovan's battalion launched the regiment's initial raid on German trenches.

Father Duffy reported an amusing incident that occurred before the raiding party went over the top. One of the soldiers in Company D had a little Irish flag fastened to the top of his rifle. An observer from another division protested against use of a foreign flag. After a short exchange, Captain Bootz, who was in charge of the operation, demanded, "What are you here for, anyway?"

"I'm an observer," was the response.

"Then climb a tree and observe, and let me run this raid."

Hernan Bootz was born in Germany. Four of his brothers fought for the kaiser. He was a non-commissioned officer in the regular army before he joined the 165th in Camp Mills. While there, he was commissioned second lieutenant, and given command of a platoon in Company C. During the long marches conducted by the regiment in January 1918, Bootz was an inspiration to his men. According to Father Duffy, "Lieutenant Henry Bootz came along at the rear of the infantry column to pick up stragglers. The most tired and dispirited got new strength from his strong heart. 'I think I'm going to die,' said one broken lad of eighteen. 'You can't die without my permission,' laughed the big lieutenant, 'and I don't intend to give it. I'll take your pack but you'll have to hike.'"[7]

The artillery preparation for the attack was intensive. The Germans suspected a trench raid was on the way and evacuated their forward lines. Not unexpectedly, the Americans quickly captured the targeted section of trench. The enemy then bombarded their previously evacuated positions. 1st Battalion raiders were also subjected to heavy machine gun fire. The New Yorkers, having achieved their objectives, fell back to their original positions. The attackers suffered additional casualties as they retired. The raid, however, was considered a success.[8]

Gas Attack

In addition to shelling the section of trench temporarily captured by the raiding party, the Germans suddenly began a heavy bombardment of Company K's positions in the Foret de Parroy. The area was blasted by fragmentation bombs and doused with mustard gas. The Americans exhibited good gas attack discipline but eventually had to remove their masks in order to properly defend their positions. A survivor of the attack reported,

> The men were prompt in putting on their masks as soon as the presence of gas was recognized, but it was found impossible to keep them on indefinitely and at the same time keep up the defense of the sector. Immediately after the bombardment, the entire company area reeked with the odor of mustard gas and the condition lasted for several days....
>
> By about midnight some of the men were sick as a result of the gas, and as the night wore one, one after another they began to feel its effects on their eyes, to cry, and gradually go blind....
>
> By dawn, the men were going blind one after another, and being ordered to the hospital.... Not a man lost his head or lay down on the job and not a man left for the hospital until he was stone blind, or ordered to go by an officer and a number of men were blinded while on post, while others stuck it out for so long that it was finally necessary to carry them on stretchers to the dressing stations; and this although all had been instructed that mustard gas was one of the most deadly gasses and that it caused blindness which lasted for months and was in many cases permanent.
>
> By ten o'clock in the morning fully two-thirds of the company had been blinded....[9]

A positive feature of the attack was the troop's excellent reaction to the gas attack. The threat of permanent blindness was ignored and not one man quit his post until properly relieved. The men of Company M showed equal courage in manfully relieving their blinded comrades in the gas-saturated trenches.

Combat often has its humorous occurrences, and one such event took place during the gas attack. Corporal Casey, K Company, related the following,

> We will never forget the night of March 20/21, 1918, when Company K, 165th Infantry received its baptism of mustard gas. About 6 PM March 20, we were in the front line in the Luneville Section. The gas alarm was given and everybody donned his mask with the exception of Private Jack Riordan, who was running around maskless offering five francs for a mask. There were no responses, he was getting frantic, death was staring him in the face. He finally increased the ante and offered five francs and a tall bottle of Cognac. Still there was no response. Everybody got on his feet looking for Riordan's mask. After a few minutes search, it was finally discovered in a shell hole and instantly clasped over Jack's map. Don't know what happened to the five francs but I sure could locate the empty cognac bottle if I ever get a chance to visit France. Private Riordan made the supreme sacrifice at Chateau Thierry.[10]

On a more serious note from Corporal Casey, "The next morning, about 4

AM, when the Boche quit shelling our positions, those of us who were lucky enough to be able to walk around, went through the trenches to find out what the casualties were. Men were lying all around wounded and unconscious and had to be taken to the rear. Captain Hurley and Major Moynahan were among those who had received more than their share of the gas. Men were detailed to carry them to the rear, but they refused to be taken until everybody who had in any way at all suffered from the gas and the shelling had been taken ahead of them."[11]

On 23 March, the regiment was ordered out of the Luneville Sector to Langres for rest and refitting.

The regiment sustained 457 casualties in the Luneville Sector, 30 killed and 427 wounded. The 69th received approximately 200 replacements following its stay in the Luneville Sector. Most of the men were poor immigrants who had worked in Pennsylvania coal mines and spoke very little English.[12]

42nd Division in the Baccarat Sector

On 1 April, the 42nd Division relieved the 128th French Infantry Division and took over the Baccarat Sector. The French division was needed to blunt a Ludendorff offensive then in progress. The Rainbow Division was the second such American Expeditionary Force unit to enter the line and the first to man a full, two brigade front. The 83rd and 84th Brigades held the left and right of the sub-sector respectively.

Soon after the Division entered the trenches, its troops gained control of No Man's Land. Before long the Germans abandoned a good part of their front line.

The Americans raided the German lines and the latter retaliated. In one raid, a small but very bold patrol of the 165th Infantry surprised and captured an entire enemy outpost at the hamlet of Ancerviller. In response to another raid, a battalion of Iowans were bombarded with explosive shells and poison gas which included mustard gas, phosgene and arsene. The 168th beat back the attack and that of a similar nature some ten days later. After those raids, the Iowans developed hatred and contempt for their German adversaries.

On 21 June, the 61st French Division and the 77th American Division relieved the Rainbow Division. The 42nd Division had held the Baccarat Sector for an unbroken stretch of 82 days. The division suffered 1,076 casualties; killed—105 men (including 45 men mortally wounded) and wounded—971 men.[13] As a result of its service, the outfit was somewhat jaded and glad to be out of the trenches. Nevertheless, it was eager to participate in the fight against Ludendorff's latest offensive.

Colonel McCoy Relieves Colonel Barker

Colonel Frank McCoy, Secretary of the General Staff, relieved Colonel Barker in May. McCoy was told by General Pershing, "I have selected you myself for that particular regiment."[14]

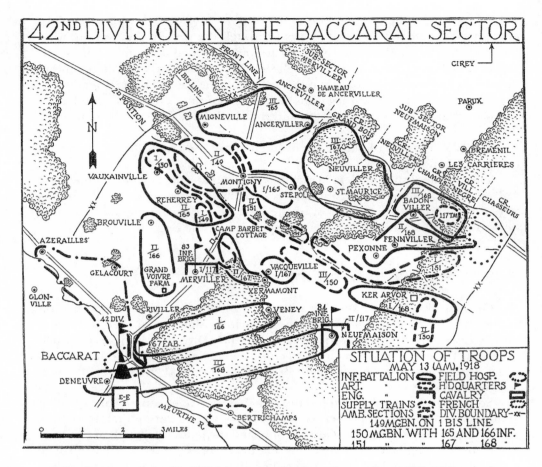

Deployment of the 42nd Division in the Baccarat Sector (from Official Sources).

Colonel Billy Haskell, who had commanded the 69th New York on the Mexican border, had hoped to regain command of his old regiment. Pershing was adamant; McCoy was to lead the 165th Infantry, case closed once again.

McCoy served with distinction during the Spanish American War and was wounded in the engagement at Kettle Hill. Later, he fought against Moros in the Philippine Islands. He was one of the promising young officers assigned to Pershing's staff in France, the so-called Chaumont Circle.

McCoy described the 69th as follows:

> The Regiment was over ninety percent Roman Catholic Irish. A very large number were actually born in Ireland; for instance in John Prout's company there were over forty, including himself from Tipperary.
> The lieutenant colonel of the Regiment, Mitchell, was a regular like myself and there was a sprinkling throughout the line companies of officers and men from such fine regiments as the Seventh and 12th NY and, like Donovan, from the First New York Cavalry. There were also a few officers who had been old line non-coms of the Regular Army, such as Captain Mickey Walsh of the Head-

quarters Company, who had served fourteen years as top sergeant of the Fifth Cavalry, and Captain Henry Bootz who had been one of the senior sergeants of the 13th Cavalry, as well as Lieutenant Dowling and several others who had had non-com service in the Regular Army. There was, too, a flavor of Jews from the East Side, and I must say they added very much to the interest and value of the Regiment. But, first, last and all time, the Regiment was truly and magnificently New York Irish and its real leader, spiritually and otherwise, was Father Francis Duffy. I always told him that he ought to be colonel of the Regiment, but that I wasn't ready to go to Blois or Hades just yet.

"Now, Colonel, don't make fun of your priest. I'll be saving you from Hades yet," was his reply.[15]

According to Father Duffy, the men of the regiment quickly held their new commanding officer in high regard. "It is a delight to go to mess with McCoy's stimulating wit," the chaplain recorded in his diary, "and to discuss, the various aspects of war and life with all sorts of interesting people—Bishops, diplomats, soldiers and correspondents who drift in from afar, drawn by the magnetism of our colonel."[16]

McCoy was just what the bellicose New Yorkers needed. Shortly after he assumed command he suggested that his officers "enjoy this war—its the only war most of them can hope to have."[17]

Shortly before McCoy's arrival, Lieutenant Colonel Reed was relieved by Lieutenant Colonel Harry Mitchell. Later, Majors Stacom and Moynahan of the 2nd and 3rd battalions were replaced by Captains Anderson and McKenna respectively. The former officers were promoted and transferred to other commands in the American Expeditionary Force. The regiment had then lost three colonels, one lieutenant colonel and two battalion commanders to what was considered more important assignments in the rapidly expanding American war machine.

165th Infantry in the Baccarat Sector

In the closing days of March 1917, the 165th Infantry was assigned to the Baccarat Sector in the Lorraine Region of the front. That part of the line was named for Baccarat, a small town of about 151,000 people, located in the fertile valley of the Meurthe River. Before the war, the place possessed a well known glass factory. Baccarat was captured by the Germans in 1914 and then retaken by the French Army later in that year. The town was gutted by the retiring enemy, who fired the place in reprisal for real or imagined French acts of sabotage.

The 165th was placed in reserve when the Rainbow Division took over the sector, since its 3rd Battalion was considerably under strength. Company K had one officer and three enlisted men ready for duty while Company M was at half strength. Most of the absent soldiers were recovering from temporary mustard gas blindness.

The regiment entered the lines on 25 April, near the French town of Ancerviller. By then, most of the Shamrock's gas victims had returned to duty. Baccarat, like the Luneville Sector, was a relatively quiet area of the front. The New Yorkers and the rest of the Rainbow Division increased the tempo of the fighting in the sector. The regiments gained control of No Man's Land and raided deep into the German lines. As in the Luneville Sector, the Boche responded with equal intensity.

During the regiment's stay in the Baccarat Sector, Father Duffy was made senior chaplain of the division. Colonel McCoy, not satisfied with Duffy's new position, wanted his chaplain promoted to the rank of major. Father Duffy was then a first lieutenant. The result of his appeal to Colonel MacArthur, Division Chief of Staff, was later relayed to Duffy by McCoy, who reported the following exchange with a twinkle in his eyes: "Now if my chaplain is to be senior chaplain of the Division it is not right that he should remain a First Lieutenant. He ought to be a Major at least."

MacArthur replied, "Now, McCoy, if I were you, I would not bring up the question of rank of Father Duffy, for I had serious thoughts of making him Colonel of the 165th instead of you."

"You are a dangerous man, Father Duffy," continued McCoy, "and I warn you, you won't last long around here."[18]

In early June, Spanish influenza hit the 42nd Division and soon a large number of men were hospitalized. The fever caused by the flu was debilitating but not usually life threatening. When the flu led to pneumonia, however, stricken soldiers often died. The 165th Infantry like its parent, the 69th New York Volunteers, was a particularly hardy group. Men of the regiment were more resistant to Spanish Flu as well as measles, scarlet fever and diphtheria than those in the Division's other regiments. City boys had a distinct advantage over farm boys when it came to fighting off contagious diseases.

On 19 June, the 165th was relieved by elements of the 77th Division. The latter unit, representing the new national army, was comprised of draftees from New York City. Columns of the regiment filed by those of the 77th Division on a moonlit road in Lorraine. As the two units passed each other they engaged in good natured badgering.

"We're going up to finish the job you fellows couldn't do."

"Look out for the Heinies or you'll all be eating sauerkraut in a prison camp before the month is out."

"What are you givin us," shouted Mike Donaldson of the 165th, "we was over here killin Dutchmen before they pulled your names out of the hat."

"Well, thank God," came the response, "we didn't have to get drunk to join the army."[19]

On 23 June, the regiment boarded troop trains for movement to the Champagne region of the front, where Ludendorff's forces were battering the Allied lines.

Battle losses sustained by the regiment in the Baccarat Sector were light—three killed and eight wounded.[20]

Before leaving the sector, the regiment received 300 first class replacements from Fort Devens, Massachusetts. Equally good soldiers were also received from Kentucky-Tennessee and Texas-Oklahoma National Guard organizations. A good many men from the latter unit were American Indians.

CHAPTER 13

Ludendorff's Offensives of 1918

The expected German offensive started at 0440 on 21 March. Seventy-one divisions hit 26 British divisions. When the push was over on 5 April, the British had sustained 164,000 casualties and lost 90,000 prisoners, 200 tanks, 1,000 guns, 4,000 machine guns, 200,000 rifles and 70,000 tons of ammunition. It was almost another Caporetto.

Faced with catastrophe, France and Great Britain requested the United States ship only infantry and machine-gun units overseas. President Wilson and Secretary of Defense Baker agreed to provide the troops. Pershing opposed the request. With a preponderance of American soldiers in Europe, Pershing would have no choice but to allow them to be fed piecemeal into the Allied ranks as crisis followed crisis.

The 1st Division was ordered from Lorraine to the Picardy Front in early April. The unit was not engaged, however, since the German drive was by then halted. The 2nd, 26th and 42nd divisions relieved French divisions in quiet sectors. The only Americans to see action during Ludendorff's first offensive were two engineer companies serving with the British Expeditionary Force. They sustained 78 casualties.

Ludendorff launched his second offensive on 9 April. It was directed at Haig's army astride the Lys River. The attack again caught the British Expeditionary Force off guard. A few days later, General Haig issued his famous "backs to the wall" statement. For a while, the situation appeared grim, but by 29 April, Ludendorff's second offensive petered out. The British Expeditionary Force again lost considerable territory but eventually managed to establish a stable defensive front.

During the Lys offensive, Pershing's four divisions were in the line in quiet sectors of the French front. The 26th Division held the Seicheprey section of the line, which was south of the St. Mihiel salient. On 20 April, the Germans launched a large scale raid on the division. Two companies of the 102nd Regiment were overwhelmed in a wild, confusing melee. Total American casualties were 669: 81 killed, 187 wounded, 214 gassed and 187 missing. It was the largest U.S. action in the war to that date. Major General Clarence Edwards claimed his division had given more than it got. Pershing was not so sure. He believed the rank and file of the 26th performed well but that their officers made a poor showing. It must be noted that Pershing had a low opinion of National Guard units, especially their officers. The Seicheprey affair seemed to support Allied contentions that the men of the American Expeditionary Force were better than their officers. Another argument for amalgamation.[1]

Cantigny

By the end of May, the U.S. had been in the war for almost 14 months and had 650,000 officers and men in Europe. The Seicheprey affair was the biggest action that the Americans had participated in. Now, the American Expeditionary Force was scheduled to make an attack on Cantigny, a little village northwest of Montdidier. It was located near the high tide mark of the Germans March offensive.

The 28th Infantry Regiment, 1st Division, was selected for the attack. The assault was meticulously planned and carefully rehearsed. The French provided more than 350 pieces of field artillery. numerous trench mortars, twelve heavy tanks and air cover. The advance was launched on the morning of 28 May and was very successful. Cantigny was captured and casualties were light. Within a short period of time, however, the Germans began to counterattack. The attacks were beaten back but at a heavy cost in casualties.

Ludendorff launched his third offensive along Chemin des Dames and soon menaced Paris. In response to the emergency, the French transferred their artillery and airplanes supporting the Cantigny attack to the threatened area. The 28th Infantry took a pounding for three days but managed to repulse all German counterattacks. The American Expeditionary Force unit was relieved by the French 16th Infantry Regiment during the night of 30-31 May. What had cost 50 casualties to take required over 1,000 casualties to hold.

Pershing was elated over the success at Cantigny. His troops had seized and held a place the French had taken twice but lost twice. An American war correspondent pointed out the real significance of Cantigny: "Compared with the giant struggle going on elsewhere, it was just a little outburst."[2]

Chemin des Dames

Ludendorff's third offensive was a diversionary action. He hoped to draw British reserves away from his real target, the British Expeditionary Force in the north. The German attack at Chemin des Dames, a hitherto quiet section, caught the French totally by surprise.

Within three days, the Germans had advanced 30 miles, captured 650 guns, 2,000 machine guns, 60,000 prisoners and vast stores of ammunition, supplies and rolling stock. By 30 May, the Germans were at the Marne River.

French and British reserves were far away and it would take from three to four days for them to get to where they were needed. Two U.S. divisions were within reach of the advancing Germans; the 2nd and 3rd divisions. They were quickly rushed into the breach. Meanwhile, the 1st Division at Cantigny extended its front northward to permit a French division to enter the fray. Colonel Marshall organized the 1st Division non-combatants into two scratch battalions. One of Marshall's subordinates gave the newly created combat units their marching orders, "You are to die east of the railroad. That is all the orders you need."[3]

The thrown together battalions held their ground.

Chateau-Thierry

On 30 May, the 3rd Division was ordered toward Chateau-Thierry, a city on the Marne River. The first unit of the division to arrive on the scene was a motorized machine gun battalion. The infantry arrived the next day. 3rd Division troops blew up the principal bridge over the Marne River and deployed along the river to the east for about 10 miles. Subsequently, the Yanks repulsed all German attempts to cross the Marne. General Pershing was pleased with the performance of the division.[4] Detractors of the American Expeditionary Force maintained that the German thrust was an exploratory attack and not a massive assault.[5]

The 2nd Division was hurriedly moved by trucks to positions west of Chateau-Thierry. On the way to the front, they encountered demoralized French units heading the opposite way. On 1 June, the 2nd Division deployed across the Paris-Metz highway. Two French divisions on their front retreated through the American positions. The 2nd was the first Allied unit to stand before Ludendorff's Third Offensive. Not only did they halt the German onslaught, but the soldiers of the American division moved forward.[6]

The stand of the 2nd Division had a rejuvenating effect on the battered Allied armies. General Foch believed the American action had practically saved Paris.

Belleau Wood and Vaux

Belleau Wood was a rugged, heavily forested, rocky site located on the front between the 2nd Division and the Germans. A defender's dream, it was skillfully strengthened by mutually supported machine gun nests.

On 6 June, the Division's Marine Brigade attacked the German strong point. During the assault, Sergeant Dan Daly exhorted his men with an order that will be forever remembered by Marines, "Come on, you sons of bitches. Do you want to live forever?"[7]

On that first day of the battle, the Marines suffered 1,087 casualties. The Leathernecks drove the last Germans out of the woods on 26 June. For nineteen days, they slugged it out with four German divisions, two of which were rated among the better units in Ludendorff's army. The cost of the battle was high, over 5,000 casualties, more than 50 percent of the Marine Brigade.[8]

While the Leathenecks were fighting at Belleau Wood, the Army Brigade of the 2nd Division fought equally hard and captured the town of Vaux. The Germans were impressed with the American soldiers of the Second Division. A German intelligence officer wrote the following on 17 June, "The individual soldiers are very good. They are healthy, vigorous and physically well developed.... The troops are fresh and full of straight forward confidence. A remark by one of the prisoners is indicative of their spirit: 'We kill or get killed.'"[9]

Realignment of American Expeditionary Force

In late June, General Foch requested that five of the ten American divisions assigned to the British Expeditionary Force be transferred to the French. Foch wanted those divisions to relieve corresponding French units currently serving in relatively quiet sectors. Accordingly, the 35th, 77th, 82nd, 4th and 28th divisions were transferred out of the British zone. The last two divisions were sent to the vicinity of Chateau-Thierry. General Pershing then had the nucleus of an American army concentrated near the Marne Salient; the 2nd, 3rd, 26th, and 42nd divisions plus the two units transferred from the British Expeditionary Force.

Pershing wanted Foch to designate part of the Western Front as an American sector. He needed a large part of the line in which to create an American army. Pershing preferred the Lorraine Sector for reasons already discussed. General Foch, on the other hand, suggested a sector nearer the Marne Salient, a part of the line from Reims to the Argonne Forest.

Before the Americans could take over a sector of the line, however, they would have to respond to the exigencies of another German offensive.

CHAPTER 14

Champagne Defensive

Ludendorff launched his fifth offensive on 15 July. In 1918, Bastille Day occurred on a Sunday, so the French were expected to party into Monday and be vulnerable to a surprise attack. The offensive was initiated to enlarge the Marne Salient by seizing Epernay and Chalons-sur-Marne. Ludendorff hoped to draw French reserves from the north so that he could deliver his *coup de main* on the British Expeditionary Force in Flanders.

At 2400 on 14 July, German guns opened up on Allied positions and at 0400 on 15 July, the Boche infantry began to attack. General Gouraud's Fourth French Army east of Reims was ready for the assault and hammered the advancing Germans. West of Reims, the Fifth and Sixth French armies were badly mauled and the Germans crossed the Marne to a depth of five miles.

East of Reims, the 42nd Division played a major part in turning back Ludendorff's shock troops. According to Father Duffy, "The whole sky seemed to be torn apart with sound…. Approximately 5,500 German and Allied guns were trying to destroy each other. The fighting was ferocious."[1]

On 15 June, trenches manned by the 2nd and 3rd battalions of the 165th Infantry were penetrated on seven occasions by the hard charging Boche. On each occasion, they were driven out by the New Yorkers, who fought like wildcats. Later in the day at 1800, the Germans made an eighth, all-out assault of the American Expeditionary Force lines. That attack was also beaten back.

Fighting in the American sectors was violent. Colonel Douglas MacArthur was deeply disturbed by what he saw at the front. He recorded descriptive phrases in his memoirs, "The vision of those writhing bodies [Germans] hanging from the barbed wire…." and "The stench of dead flesh…."[2]

West of Reims, the 3rd Division, serving with the Sixth French Army, fought courageously and beat back the German attackers. For its gallantry, the division earned the sobriquet "The Rock of the Marne."

On 17 July, Ludendorff called off the attack. The 42nd and 3rd divisions contributed in a large way toward blunting what turned out to be Germany's last offensive of the war. The two divisions paid a stiff price in killed and wounded for their part in the Champagne Defensive.

42nd Division in Champagne Sector

The Rainbow Division was about to be tested. It was going into the line to meet the Fifth Ludendorff Offensive, which the French believed would start on 15 July. The division had served about five months on the Lorraine Front and received its baptism of fire. It had successfully withstood hostile artillery fire averaging 500 shells daily, punishing gas attacks and enemy trench raids. The 42nd Division had also launched a series of successful large scale attacks. The unit had suffered 1,969 battle casualties. Only seven soldiers had been captured. The men of the Rainbow Division were confident they could handle anything the Boche hurled at them. This confidence was demonstrated by the following observation of an Irishman in the 165th Infantry, "Why would I be afraid of thim? They're just Dootchmen, ain't they? And I never seen any four Dootchmen that I couldn't lick."[3]

The Rainbow arrived at Camp Chalons on the night of 28-29 July. The division travelled by train and then executed a punishing 35 kilometer march to reach the sector in the Champagne Region commanded by French General Gouraud, French Fourth Army.

Most of the Americans disliked the Champagne area of France. The ground was chalky, almost white. The limited foliage consisted of gnarled scrubby trees, patchy foliage, and heather. The area was brightened somewhat by fields of poppy. The chalky ground, however, permitted the construction of strong trenches and deep dugouts.

The Rainbow Division was scheduled to train with the Fifth French Army for a counterattack on the Germans north of the Marne River. Ludendorff's Fifth Offensive forced the Allies to abandon their planned assault. Instead, on 4 July, the division was placed under the command of General Gouraud, whose force was being readied to meet the anticipated Ludendorff offensive.

On 5 July, the Rainbow took over defensive positions in the rear of sectors held by the 170th and 13th French divisions. That area of the line was very quiet since defenses on both sides of No Man's Land were formidable. The French high command, however, was expecting an all-out attack in the area. General Gouraud, in anticipation of the pending offensive, planned to withdraw nearly all of his French and American troops from the front lines. The maneuver was to be performed at the "eleventh hour." The French general was counting on the veracity of information previously obtained from German prisoners.

Gourard ordered units of the Rainbow Division to man the intermediate line alongside elements of the French army. The 2nd and 3rd battalions of the 165th were among the troops awaiting the German onslaught. The remainder of the division was located in the second line.

The 3rd Battalion of the 165th was located on the left flank of the division in the intermediate trench line. The 3rd Battalion of the 166th Infantry was positioned on the right flank of the New Yorkers. The 2nd battalions of the Alabama and Iowa regiments manned the remainder of the positions in the American held sectors. One of the sacrifice posts was held by Ohioans.

The German bombardment began as expected at 0010 15 July. Fifteen min-

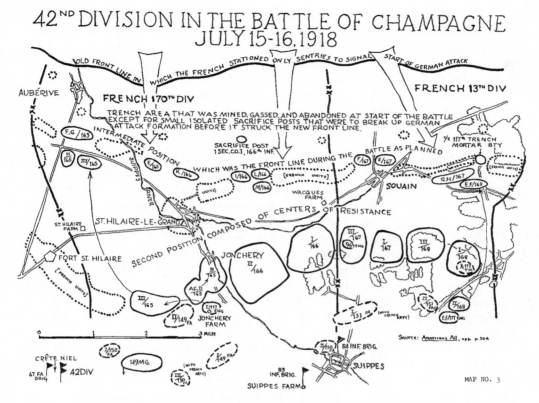

Deployment of the 42nd Division in the Champagne sector, 15 July 1918 (from Official Sources).

utes later, French artillery opened fire on the German trenches, hoping to catch shock troops massing for attack. At 0350, again as expected, the Germans launched a rolling barrage and the assault infantry went over the top. The Germans hammered the Allied lines for ten hours but could not advance beyond the intermediate line. Then the attacks petered out. Ludendorff's assaults in Gouraud's sector had failed.

The division sustained 1,638 casualties; killed—340 men (including 74 mortally wounded), and wounded—1,298 men.[4] The only soldiers captured were from the Ohioans in the sacrifice post. Most of the division's losses occurred on the first day of the offensive.

The Rainbow Division took pride in helping smash Ludendorff's fifth, and as it turned out, final offensive. None of the two dozen unlucky Ohioans assigned to the doomed sacrifice post were heard from again until after the armistice. Then, several men who had been captured were returned to their regiment.

165th Infantry in the Champagne Sector

The regiment was only a few days out of Baccarat when it was suddenly ordered aboard trains and moved west. They moved throughout the night, were detrained at daybreak, and then marched to a billeting area southwest of Chalons. The regiment relaxed and prepared for another training period. While at mess the next night, the unit was ordered to move out quickly for nearby Camp de Chalons. The troops made a rapid march and reached the assigned area sometime after midnight. The operation was performed smoothly. According to Colonel McCoy, "The whole of a war strength division moved through the narrow, dark streets of the ancient town past the moon-lit cathedral, without confusion, or as much jamming as usually takes place during a St. Patrick's Day Parade in New York."[5]

The regiment was just about quartered in Camp de Chalons when orders came to participate in a night attack against the Chateau-Thierry salient south of Reims. Troopers were boarding trucks for the attack when orders were again changed. Instead, the 165th was sent to the eastern side of Camp de Chalons. The 42nd Division was then part of the Fourth French Army under General Gouraud. The New Yorkers went into the line alongside a battalion of Chasseurs Alpines commanded by Colonel Arnoux.

On the night of 14-15 July, Companies F and G held the extreme left of the Esperance Sector. Company H was in support while Company E was positioned in the approximate center of the intermediate line. The latter unit was separated from the rest of the Second Battalion by elements of the French 17th Infantry Division.

The appearance and bearing of General Gouraud inspired confidence in the division's rank and file. The red-bearded general had alert eyes and wore his gold braided kepi at a jaunty angle. Gouraud, the youngest general in the French Army, had an empty sleeve and a game leg from wounds suffered in the Argonne Forest and later in the Dardanelles. Although still recovering from his injuries, he continued to serve on active duty. He was an example of courage and determination to the French and American forces.

General Gouraud gave a pep talk to his troops. The key phrase in his address was, "No man shall look to the rear, none shall yield a step."[6] Major Anderson, inspired by the French general, gave the following order to the Second Battalion as they awaited the German onslaught, "Fight it out where you are!"[7]

During the afternoon of 14 July, Colonel Arnoux, who was in immediate command of the Esperance Sector, inspected positions manned by Company G. The colonel was satisfied with the disposition of machine guns and automatic rifles. His inspection complete, he returned to his command post. A short time later, the company commander received a message from Arnoux. It ordered the American officer to arm dependable non-commissioned officers and to station them behind the intermediate line. These men were to shoot any soldiers who ran away from the front. When the American captain read the order, he became infuriated and said, "The French colonel must think that my men are a pack of cowards, I am going to see him."

The American asked the Arnoux to cancel the order. The French officer countered that it was standard practice in his army to issue such instructions The young captain persisted in his request, expressing his confidence that his men wouldn't run. The colonel relented and retracted the shameful order.[8]

The German attack started at midnight, as expected. Father Duffy described the onslaught as follows: "It was 12:04 midnight by my watch when it began. No crescendo business about it. Just one sudden crash like an avalanche; but an avalanche that was to keep crashing for five hours. The whole sky seemed to be torn apart with sound—the roaring B-o-o-o-m-p of the discharge and the gradual menacing W-h-e-e-E-E-Z of traveling projectiles and the nerve wracking W-h-a-n-g-g of bursts. Not that we could tell them apart. They are all mingled in one deafening combination of screech and roar, and they all seem to be bursting just outside...."⁹

Unfortunately, a detail of 80 men from Company H was sent out on a wiring detail around 2000. The soldiers were working with picks and shovels in an area between the front line trenches and intermediate positions when the German barrage started. Company H suffered 84 casualties (20 killed and 64 wounded) that day. Most of those lost were part of the ill-fated working party.¹⁰

Shortly after 0430, the German artillery ceased firing and minutes later the Boche infantry went over the top. Shock troops attacked 2nd Battalion positions *en masse.* Principal weapons were grenades; potato mashers for those in the front ranks and rifle grenades for those in the rear. The assault broke on the edge of the trench after a brief man-to-man struggle.

The Germans made five attempts on Anderson's positions. Some were made using infiltration techniques. In a number of instances, the Boche entered the American trenches but they never got out.

During the first German attack, the enemy penetrated the trench line where the Mourmelon-Auberive Road crossed the ancient road leading to St. Hilaire le Grande. The well-trained shock troops concentrated at what they sensed was a weak spot in the Allied line. The Boche were threatening to overrun positions held by a Company G platoon. The unit's lieutenant realized the Germans had numbers he couldn't stop with his available fire power. He made a quick decision and launched a desperate bayonet attack. His men climbed out of their trenches and drove the Germans back. The Americans regained the critical position with minimal losses.

During the lull following the failed first German attack, McKenna's battalion was ordered into the intermediate line in support of the French 116th Infantry.

The Germans resumed their attack on the morning of 16 July. A battalion of shock troops assaulted a defensive position manned by Company F. For a while the situation was serious, but resistance organized by Lieutenant Young turned back the Germans. Parties of German soldiers entered Company F trenches and were only dislodged by vicious hand-to-hand fighting. Lieutenant Young was killed in the melee. The men of the 165th fought heroically.

The deeds of Corporal John Finnegan are representative of the fight made by the men of the Second Battalion. Here is an excerpt from Father Duffy's story:

> Corporal John Finnegan had been wounded in the leg the day before [15 July]. He tied a bandage around the wound and stayed where he was. He was with Lieutenant Young when that leader was killed and ran to avenge him. A shell burst near him and he was in the air, falling senseless and deaf. I saw him in the First Aid Station a little way back, where he had been carried. The lads

Regimental Losses per Campaign

Regiment	Campaign Dates	Esperence-Sovain Sector and Champagne-Marne Defensive			Aisne-Marne Offensive			St. Mihiel Offensive and Essey-Pannes Sector				Meuse-Argonne Offensive						Totals	
		July 3–14	July 15–18	July 19–20	July 21–24	July 25 –Aug. 3	Aug. 4–6	Sept. 4–11	Sept. 12–16	Sept. 17– Oct. 1	Oct. 2–4	Oct. 5–11	Oct. 12–19	Oct. 20– Nov. 1	Nov. 2–4	Nov. 5–7	Nov. 8–11		
165	W	7	212	0	3	1,026	7	2	125	39	1	24	819	96	4	50	36	2451	
	DW	1	10	0	1	64	0	0	12	4	0	4	57	9	1	4	3	170	3,179
	K	0	47	0	0	256	1	0	35	5	0	5	180	15	1	13	0	558	
166	W	5	273	1	0	643	4	1	93	25	0	12	393	64	8	47	15	1584	
	DW	0	11	1	1	54	0	0	8	9	0	0	34	7	0	3	1	129	1,969
	K	0	37	7	0	117	0	0	23	3	0	0	44	8	0	17	0	256	
167	W	5	357	0	1	1,020	2	0	153	58	0	7	554	27	3	43	9	2239	
	DW	1	13	0	2	59	0	0	16	3	0	0	36	0	0	5	3	138	2,862
	K	0	69	0	0	261	0	0	44	7	0	0	81	8	2	12	1	485	
168	W	7	205	0	0	1,103	4	2	206	81	0	62	566	48	1	2	2	2289	
	DW	0	24	0	0	63	0	1	22	7	0	2	53	0	0	0	2	174	2,867
	K	0	58	1	0	183	0	0	52	9	0	4	90	6	1	0	0	404	

Data Source: 42nd Division Summary of Operations in the World War, American Battle Monuments Commission, U.S. Government Printing Office, 1944.

there had ripped up his breeches to re-bandage his earlier wound. He was just coming to. They told me he was shell shocked. "Shell shocked nothing," I said. "A shell could kill John Finnegan, but it could not break his nerves." Just then he got sight of me. "There's nawthin the matter with me, Father, excepting I'm deaf. They got the Lootenant [Young] and I haven't squared it with thim yet. I'm goin back." I told him he must stay where he was at least till I returned from the Battle Dressing Station, which was 500 yards down the old Roman Road....

It was a good while before I got back to the First Aid Station in the trenches and John Finnegan was gone. They had kept him for some time by telling him he was to wait for me. But after a rush of business they found John sitting up with a shoe lace in his hand. "Give me a knife," he said, "I want to make holes to sew up my pants. Johnny Walker had mine and he wouldn't lend it." "Lie down and be still." "All right," said Finnegan, "I have the tools God gave me." He bent his head over the ripped up breeches and with his teeth tore a few holes at intervals in the hanging flaps. He carefully laced them up with the shoe string, humming the while, "The Low Back Car." Then he got up. "Where's me gun?" "You are to wait for Father Duffy. He wants to see you." "Father Duffy did all for me I need, and he'd be the last man to keep a well man out of a fight. I'm feeling fine and I want me gun. I going back." He spied a stray rifle and seized it. "Keep out of my way now, I don't want to fight with the Irish except for fun. This is business." So wounded, bruised, half deaf, John Finnegan returned to battle. Immortal poems have been written of lesser men.[11]

The first German attack on 16 July was launched at 0430. It concentrated on the Esperance Sector. As we know, the attack was repulsed with a significant contribution by the 2nd Battalion, 165th Infantry. During the rest of the morning, the Germans continued to attack but on a much wider front. All onslaughts were turned back with considerable loss. The Germans launched their final attack during the afternoon. The recipients of the onslaught were units of the French 17th Division and the Third Battalion, 166th Infantry. This final attack was also stopped cold.

German airplanes controlled the skies over the Esperance Sector during the battle of Champagne. Father Duffy described the action as follows: "The German planes for two days had complete mastery. They circled over our heads in the trenches, front and rear. They chased automobiles and wagons down the road. You could not go along a trench without some evil bird spitting machine gun bullets at you. I doubt if they ever hit anybody. It must be hard to shoot from an aeroplane. After the first day they ceased to be terrifying—in war one quickly learns the theory of chances—but the experience was always irritating, as if some malicious small boy was insulting one. And they must certainly have taken note of everything we did. Well it was no comfort to them...."[12]

Colonel McCoy's after-action report sums up the battle succinctly:

Fortunately, for us in the regimental reserve position, most of the enemy's heavy artillery went over our heads like freight trains and the gas shelling took place mostly in the lower ground along the Suippes [River], while Anderson and his noble battalion put up a great fight in the front lines. Time and time again the Germans got into his lines, but not one of them ever left, and at the end of the attack the 2nd Battalion, though battered and suffering from heavy losses, retained their spirit and morale. Anderson's battalion put up such a fight that General Gouraud visited it on the battle ground the third day, and then and there decorated many and praised the entire unit. The following day he visited us again; assembled the officers and gave a most interesting account of the attack from the point of view of the Army headquarters. He told what had taken place on either side of the Division; made us feel very much a part of the great repulse of the last German attack, and directed that the story of these greatest of days in the annals of the Fourth Army be passed down to every soldier in our commands.[13]

The regiment sustained 277 casualties during the Champagne Defensive: 58 killed (including 11 mortally wounded) and 219 wounded.

CHAPTER 15

Aisne-Marne Offensive

As soon as Ludendorff's fifth offensive bogged down, General Foch moved to eliminate the Marne Salient. He delivered a blow between Soissons and Chateau-Thierry which compelled the Germans south of the Marne River to retreat north or risk being cut off and captured. The retreating Germans took up defensive positions on the Ourcq River, near the center of their remaining salient. The Germans were then driven out of their defensive positions by attacks of the 42nd, 3rd, 28th and 32nd dvisions and units of the French Army.

The series of attacks described above combined with the fighting on the Vesle River, to which the Germans retreated after the Battle of the Ourcq, constitute the "Aisne-Marne Offensive." That offensive combined with the "Champagne Defensive" of 15 and 16 July make up the two phases of the "Second Battle of the Marne."[1]

In the opinion of Henry J. Reilly and other historians of the Great War, the "Second Battle of the Marne" was the turning point of the conflict. Reilly states,

> The Second Battle of the Marne is the decisive battle of the Great War of 1914–1918, from the time the Russians dropped out of the war in 1917 until the Armistice. Therefore, it is one of the decisive battles in the history of the world.
> The following are the reasons why it is a decisive battle:
> First, because when it began, the Germans had the initiative as they had had throughout 1918. That is they could strike when and where they pleased while all the Allies could do was to wait, while wondering where the blow would come and whether or not they could stop it. When the battle was over this was exactly reversed. The Allies now had the initiative.
> The second reason was that when the battle began the German High Command believed it had the numbers necessary first to successfully carry through their attack and second when they had exploited their victory to the fullest possible extent to turn on the British once more and strike them a crushing blow. Thus they planned to win the war.
> Before the battle was over the American and French attacks on the Germans in the Marne salient came so near breaking through their line that they had to call off the planned attack upon the British in order to send the reserves they had intended to use to the help of their hard pressed troops in that salient.[2]

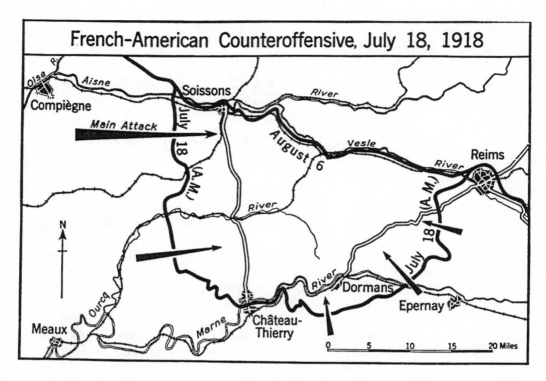

French and American counteroffensive, 18 July 1918 (from Official Sources).

Soissons

The attack near Soissons on 18 July was spearheaded by the French XX Corps. The corps consisted of the American 1st and 2nd divisions on either flank of the 1st Moroccan Division. The 2nd Division was then commanded by Major General Charles P. Summerall, a relentless, hard driving and efficient officer whom Pershing considered his best commander.

The attacking divisions, which were led by nearly 400 tanks, followed a rolling barrage. At the end of the first day, the 1st Division had advanced about three and half miles, the Moroccans slightly more and the 2nd Division about four and half miles. The advance of the Second was the most for any of the attacking divisions.

The 2nd Division was used up by the night of 19 July. In two days, the division had advanced seven miles, captured nearly 3,000 Germans, 75 artillery pieces and hundreds of machine guns. American casualties in killed and wounded were about 5,000 men.[3]

Summerall continued to drive the 1st Division until it was relieved on the night of 21 July. It had severed the Soissons-Paris Railroad and the Soissons–Chateau-Thierry highway. The unit captured nearly 3,400 Germans and 75 guns. Casualties in killed and wounded exceeded 7,300 men. Summerall forced his division forward in spite of mounting casualty lists. When one of his battalion commanders reported that he had stopped, Sommerall fired back the following response, "You may have paused for reorganization. If you ever send another message with the word stopped in it, you will be sent to the rear for reclassification."[4]

The general would get more ruthless as the war progressed.

With the principal railroad and highway into the salient severed, Ludendorff was forced to evacuate part of the Marne Salient. His forces then took up defensive positions on the Ourcq River.

Ourcq River

The Germans' withdrawal from the salient was by no means hasty. Ludendorff needed time to remove the huge store of war materials in the area. For two weeks, the Boche moved slowly backwards under pressure from the French Army and the 42nd, 3rd, 28th and 32nd American divisions. The Marne Salient continued to deflate like a huge gas bag letting out its vapors. The Germans retreated skillfully and made the advancing Allies pay a stiff price for hard won gains.

A cemetery was converted into a stretch of strong points by unceremoniously ejecting the dead from their resting places and using the empty chambers as dugouts. A critical hill in the area was girdled with multiple belts of machine gun nests.

The 42nd Division captured the village of Sergy on the north side of the Ourcq River for good on 29 July. Control of the village had changed hands eleven times prior to that date. Colonel Douglas MacArthur came across the dead of the Sergy contest and made the following observation, "We tumbled over them. There must have been at least 2,000 of those sprawled bodies…. The stench was suffocating. Not a tree was standing. The moans and cries of wounded men sounded everywhere."[5]

German strong points at Croix Rouge Farm and Meurcy Farm were captured by regiments of the 42nd Division, the 167th and the 165th Infantries. Members of the 165th sobbed when they came out of the line and encountered their dead comrades, stacked like cord wood on the hill slopes around the farm.

By 6 August, the Marne Salient was eliminated. German and Allied armies faced each other across the Vesle River, along an essentially linear front from Soissons east to Reims.

What the Americans lacked in experience, they more than made up for in elan. General Walther Reinhardt, Chief of Staff of the Seventh Army, which had opposed the Americans commented, "They may not look so good, but hell, how they can fight."[6]

General Pershing was extremely proud of the American Expeditionary Force's performance in the Second Battle of the Marne. He issued the following commendatory order on 28 August, 1918:

> G. H. Q.
> American Expeditionary Forces
> General Orders
> No. 143

France, August 28, 1918

It fills me with pride to record in General Orders a tribute to the service and achievement of the First and Third Corps, comprising the 1st, 2nd, 3rd, 4th, 26th, 28th, 32nd, and 42nd Divisions of the American Expeditionary Forces.

You come to the battlefield at the crucial hour of the Allied cause. For almost four years the most formidable army the world had as yet seen had pressed its invasion of France and stood threatening its capital. At no time had that army been more powerful or menacing than when on July 15th, it struck again to destroy in one great battle the brave men opposed to it and to enforce its brutal will upon the world and civilization.

Three days later in conjunction with our Allies, you counter-attacked. The Allied armies gained a brilliant victory that marks the turning point of the war. You did more than give our brave Allies the support to which as a nation our faith was pledged. You proved that our altruism, our pacific spirit, our sense of justice have not blunted our courage or virility. You have shown that American initiative and energy are as justly won the unstinted praise of our Allies and the eternal gratitude of our countrymen.

We have paid for our success in the lives of many of our brave comrades. We shall cherish their memory always, and claim for our history and literature, their bravery, achievement and sacrifice.

John J. Pershing,
General, Commanding in Chief
Official:
Robert C. Davis,
Adjutant General[7]

42nd Division on the Ourcq River

On 18 July, the 42nd Division was ordered toward the Chateau-Thierry battlefield. During transit, the Rainbow Division received replacements for the 124 officers and 3,425 men killed and wounded since its arrival in France.

The division reached the vicinity of Epieds and Verdilly, an area about five miles from Chateau-Thierry on 25 July. The 84th Brigade took over the front manned by the 26th Division. The 83rd Brigade relieved the 167th, 164th and 51st French Infantry divisions and somewhat later the 52nd French Infantry Division. The relief was performed in less then 24 hours. Terrain in front of the 83rd Brigade was the heavily defended Foret de Fere. Beyond the forest at the base of steep hills crested by the Foret de Nesles was the Ourcq River. The key to the German defense in the area was the Croix Rouge Farm. The position featured a large number of interlocking machine gun nests. Its loss would threaten the German pocket between the Marne and Vesle rivers.

The Battle of the Ourcq, insofar as the Rainbow Division was concerned, can be separated into three parts. The first phase occurred from 25 to 27 July. Actions during this phase of the battle were based on the French Army's erroneous assumption that the Germans were retreating. What resulted was a series of hurried, uncoordinated attacks on an enemy making a stand on the north bank of the Ourcq River.

The second phase of the battle occurred from 28 July to 1 August. The 42nd

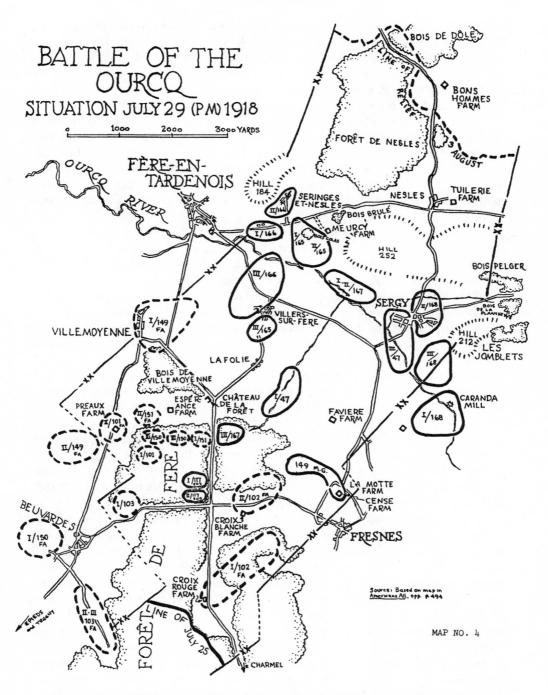

Deployment of the 42nd Division on the Ourcq River (from Official Sources).

Division mounted continuous, dogged attacks on German strong points on the Ourcq River defensive line. The Rainbow's front extended from Hill 184 on the left to Sergy on the right. Assaults were continued in spite of heavy losses until all Boche positions were carried. The last phase of the battle took place on 2 and 3 August, when the Rainbow's infantry pursued the retreating Germans for some five miles and the division's engineers a slight distance further.[8]

At 1730 on 26 July, less than 24 hours after the Rainbow Division relieved the three French divisions, it attacked Croix Rouge Farm. Two battalions of the 167th Infantry, with battalions of New Yorkers and Iowans on the left and right flanks, captured the German strong point via a bayonet attack. The New Yorkers and Alabamas then cleared the Foret de Fere. Early in the morning of 28 July, the 165th Infantry pushed a battalion of troops across the Ourcq River in spite of murderous machine gun fire.[9]

On the morning of 29 July, the 166th Infantry with the New Yorkers on its right and a fresh French division on its left, captured Hill 184 and then Seringes et Nesles. Later the French took possession of Fere-en-Tardenois. The 165th Infantry took Bois Colas and then a key position, Meurcy Farm.[10]

The 42nd Division maintained its bridgehead across the Ourcq in spite of heavy artillery fire on its exposed right flank. During this period of time, the division was struggling with the Fourth Prussian Guards Division commanded by the kaiser's son, the 201st, 10th Landwehr and Sixth Bavarian divisions, units ordered to hold their positions at all costs.

On the morning of 2 August, the Rainbow continued its attack on the German lines. The enemy, however, had retreated precipitously during the night. Within two hours the 42nd Division had cleared the Foret de Nesles. The division was relieved during the night of 2-3 August.

The Rainbow, in eight days, had accomplished one of the greatest advances recorded up to that point in the war. It advanced 18 kilometers against fierce enemy resistance and forced German abandonment of a key defensive position.[11]

The division sustained 5,518 casualties; killed—1,172 (including 266 mortally wounded) and wounded—4,346 men.[12]

The high losses sustained by the 42nd Division on the Ourcq River were said by Cochrane and others to have occurred largely because the unit was sent into action with minimal knowledge of enemy positions. Troops were not properly deployed in the battle zone. Supports and reserves were bunched up and subject to sudden concentrations of enemy fire. Battalions advanced in textbook formation, "bullheadedly assaulting machine gun strong points," instead of advancing on them by short rushes, crawling and infiltration. Apparently, the troops had not yet learned that accurate rifle fire was more effective than hastily delivered automatice fire. Machine gun officers believed that instead of dispersing their guns among the assaulting troops, they ought to have been positioned on the heights of the Ourcq, where they could have concentrated their fire on selected enemy strong points above the river. Artillery officers realized that shell fire concentrated on assault objectives would have been more effective than creeping barrages preceding attacking infantry.

Total losses to date were 9,125 men. The Rainbow Division had lost more than one third of its original fighting strength to battlefield casualties.

In early August, Brigadier General Brown, 84th Brigade, was relieved of his command by General Pershing. During the fighting on the Ourcq River, he made frequent requests that his brigade be taken out of the line. His unit had performed magnificently but under the stress of heavy losses he had shown signs of weakness. An inquiry indicated that he panicked during the bloody campaign. Brown had graduated in the top third of his class at West Point but he failed the test of battle in France. He was demoted to colonel, at which rank he retired from the army in 1923. He was replaced by Colonel Douglas MacArthur, who was thereafter promoted to brigadier general.

From 11 to 17 August, the Rainbow proceeded to the Lorraine Valley. Up to that period of time, the unit had evacuated a total of sick equal to the number of wounded men sent to the rear as a result of combat operations. The Rainbow Division was allowed to recuperate its strength at a rest area in the agricultural region. There, the division received reinforcements and new equipment while its soldiers drilled in "open warfare" procedures.

The latest batch of reinforcements, a levy of 5,614 men, arrived late in August, making a total of 10,272 men in two months. Colonel Donovan later stated that for the St. Mihiel operation, 65 percent of his men and 75 percent of the officers in the 1st Battalion were new and almost wholly untrained. During the St. Mihiel and Argonne offensives, replacements arrived who were civilian 30 days earlier and had been in France a mere nine days.

On 30 August, operational control of the 42nd Division was transferred to the IV Corps, General Dickman commanding.

165th Infantry on the Ourcq River

On 27 July, while at Epieds, the 42nd Division was ordered to cross the Ourcq and pursue German forces on the north side of the river, presumed to be in full retreat. Colonel McCoy, the senior officer present, ordered all three of his battalions to move out. The 166th Infantry advanced on the left of the New York regiment. McCoy directed Colonel Screws to support his right flank with battalions from the Alabama regiment. The advancing units moved ahead as quickly as possible and by nightfall, the New Yorkers reached the Ourcq. The 3rd Battalion was in the center of the line at Villers-Sur-Fere with the 1st and 2nd battalions on its right and left flanks respectively.

At midnight orders were issued for a general attack across the Ourcq River before dawn. Individual brigade commanders were ordered to attack ASAP, whether or not their flanks were supported. General Headquarters wanted the Germans prevented from digging in on the heights above the river.

Colonel McCoy decided to attack with his 3rd Battalion, supported by the 1st Battalion on the right. The 2nd Battalion was to be in reserve. Major McKenna and his company commanders were awakened and apprised of the planned assault. They informed McCoy that the river crossings were strongly defended and an assault without artillery support was a "forlorn hope," desperate and difficult. Colonel McCoy informed General Headquarters of the situation on his front and was told the attack must be made immediately even if it meant sacrifice of his command.

Company commanders, in spite of being awakened in the middle of the night, executed the assault with speed and courage. The Boche were surprised, river crossings were forced, machine gun nests captured and other defensive detachments taken with minimum American casualties. The battle of the Ourcq, however, was just beginning.

Colonel McCoy's description of the struggle is as concise as it is inspiring,

> I shall not go into the details of the next four days and nights of terrific battle, which tried out the Regiment from colonel to private, but I shall say that the Regiment put up one of the great fights of the war against a Prussian Guards Division. Though in a salient on the north bank of the river, sometimes nearly surrounded, it gradually pushed forward to the Bois de Colas where Donovan, with his great 1st Battalion, holding on by its teeth, bore the brunt of battle. Gradually, by the use of cover, he pushed forward until at the end of four days' fierce fighting his lines were extended along the north edge of the Bois Brule. In close support were Anderson's battalion and what was left of the 3rd Battalion, whose commander, Major McKenna, was killed, whose three front line captains were wounded, but whose survivors under Captain Martin Meaney went through to the bitter end. The losses of this one Regiment in the battle of the Ourcq were about the same as the whole American Army's losses in the Santiago Campaign—222 killed and 1700 plus wounded. I should not state these losses with pride, were it not for the fact that the Regiment was made the spear-head of the entire army and pushed forward by a most explicit order as a forlorn hope, against a whole German division. Despite its great performance for four days and nights on the battlefield, the Regiment took up the pursuit and followed the enemy toward the Vesle until it was relieved by Bolles' Regiment of the 4th Regular Division, though a Division staff officer [Judah], at the time, had reported that the 165th Infantry was still able to continue the pursuit.
>
> On being withdrawn from the pursuit the Regiment was ordered to the woods between the Ferme de l'Esperance and the Croix Rouge Farm, where it stayed in bivouac for some days. Needless to say, it was a sad Regiment which realized the loss of friends, brothers and comrades, who were necessarily buried by their own comrades on the battlefield. Father Duffy, as always, stood us in good stead, encouraged the brave, and helped me to cheer and restir the Regiment for its next campaign. On the day the Regiment marched to the rear, Father Duffy set up his altar on a wagon and preached a fiery and stirring sermon to the whole Regiment, which was formed in a square around him.
>
> Several days later the Regiment marched into Chateau-Thierry with colors flying and the band playing the "Wearin' of the Green'." The Army Commander, General Degoutte, with his staff, reviewed the Regiment in the ancient square in front of Army Headquarters, and highly complimented it, not only on its splendid performance in battle, but on its fine appearance so soon thereafter.
>
> The battle on the Ourcq was full of incident and will always be the proudest remembrance of every man in the 165th Infantry who took part in it.
>
> In looking back over more than forty years of service in all parts of the world and in many different commands, in both our own and foreign armies, I can find no regiment quite like it. There are no soldiers more loyal and devoted and heart warming in remembrance. There are no officers that stand out more vividly as happy warriors than those I served with in that Regiment; men like Donovan, the bravest of the brave, McKenna, Anderson, Merle-Smith, Hurley,

Martin Meaney, Basil Elmer, Baker, Spencer, George McAdie, young Ollie Ames, Captain Mickey Walsh, Captain Henry Bootz, Wheeler, Kane, Joyce Kilmer and the shepherd of them all, Father Duffy.[13]

3rd Battalion Story

At 0030 on 27 July, the battalion was dumped from *camions* (motor trucks) into woods near Epieds. Major McKenna was informed by French officers that the battalion was near the front. Later in the morning, McKenna was ordered to move toward the Ourcq River. Company L under Captain Merle-Smith spearheaded the advance. The battalion moved forward against relatively light resistance, primarily sniper fire. McKenna's men reached Villers-Sur-Fere by dark. The place was a scene of indescribable confusion. The Germans had abandoned the village in a hurry. Corpses, dead horses and the debris of war lay everywhere. Movement was impeded by miles of tangled telephone wire. Companies L and K (Captain Hurley) pushed on to the river's edge. In American parlance, the Ourcq was more like a large stream. Companies I (Captain Ryan) and M (Captain Meaney) remained in and about Villers-Sur-Fere. Merle-Smith's and Hurley's men exchanged fire with Germans on the other side of the inky Ourcq.

Later that night, Colonel McCoy arrived at Villers-Sur-Fere and informed McKenna and his officers that the regiment was ordered to attack immediately. Since the 3rd Battalion was the only unit near the Ourcq River, it must go it alone. It was to be a bayonet attack in the dark. Major McKenna and his lieutenants realized that the planned assault was a desperate undertaking and said so to their colonel. Nevertheless, they had to attack at once. The corps chief of staff, Colonel Henry Stimson (later Secretary of State under President Herbert Hoover), who was at the meeting, finalized the discussion: "Orders are orders."[14]

The plan of attack called for companies I and L to attack and seize the high ground on the north side of the river. Company K was to support their attack and then assault and carry Meurcy Farm. Company M, with Colonel McCoy, was in reserve near Villers-Sur-Fere. The 1st Battalion (Major Donovan) would support the attack by moving up on the right flank of the 3rd Battalion.

The advance got underway at daybreak. The troops moved out toward the river, which was about 30 feet wide. The men of companies I and L waded across the Ourcq under scattered enemy fire. Men started to drop. The troops reached the north bank of the stream and quickly overran small detachments of Germans and at least five machine gun nests. The machine gunners fought bravely, firing their weapons to the last moment, expecting and getting no quarter. The advancing line moved up a hill against increasing German resistance, which included enfilading fire from the Bois Colas and high ground at Sergy. The hill slopes were becoming littered with khaki clad figures, many of them writhing in pain. Men were dropping in ever increasing numbers but the New Yorkers pressed on.

Martin Hogan, then a corporal, described the attack,

> Men plunged to earth to the right and left of me. Almost at every stride some comrade fell stumbling forward lifeless, or falling to [catch his] wind and rock for a while through the first disordering sting of a fatal wound. Others just

slipped down and lay low and still, too badly wounded and spent to go on with the advance. I saw these incidents, little nightmare incidents, flashed upon the screen of my vision in jumbled, jerky fashion, and I ran on feeling that the whole thing was just a dream, stopping to aim and fire as some chance gray uniform showed, and then blindly running on.

    I was winded, so were we all, but on such a field and at such a time one never seems to notice things like that. The mind is detached from the work of the field and the actions of the body are automatic, going on and on. It is a good thing, when the fight goes warm, that one can't think too much.[15]

Company K's objective was Meurcy Farm consisting of a main dwelling and a number of outbuildings. The structures were connected by a stone wall which formed a large courtyard. The farm was dominated by wooded, relatively higher ground at Bois Colas, Hill 184 near Seringes et Nesles and Bois Brule.

Although outnumbered, platoons from companies K and L quickly captured Meurcy Farm. Later, the Germans counterattacked and overwhelmed the 3rd Battalion defenders. On 29 July, men of the 1st Battalion recaptured the farm but did not occupy it. Officers of the 42nd Division learned it was better to control the perimeter of a captured strongpoint than to occupy a position which was probably registered by enemy artillery.

Sergeant McKenney of Company L, who was instrumental in seizing the farm, was wounded during the attack. He was captured when the Germans regained the position. McKenney was in bad shape and remained in German hospitals until sent to Switzerland by the Red Cross near the war's end. He was eventually sent home but died of his wounds in September 1919.

Companies I and L sustained heavy losses but managed to reach their objective, the crest of high ground on the north bank of the river. By this time both company commanders were wounded, Merle-Smith in the right arm and Ryan more seriously in the leg. The troops were subjected to withering machine gun fire from German positions on their front and right flank. All the New Yorkers could do was dig in and hold on until friendly troops came up on their right or until they were relieved.

Captain Merle-Smith's account of the fighting follows:

    The damaging fire was coming from our left and right, the source was completely invisible but yet a sheaf of bullets through the young wheat. A man crouches to run forward. He is shot through the legs, drops to his knees, is hit in the legs and arm, down flat and is again hit in the head. A bullet cuts my coat on the back of my shoulder but barely scratches. The men of my headquarters group are all hit but one, a terrible feeling of helplessness because there seems no one to fight against and it is the officers responsibility to pick the targets and reduce the enemy fire by your own. 180 degrees of emptiness. We fire on every possible bit of cover but it seemed pretty futile there were so many."[16]

German airplanes flew over the 3rd Battalion positions and helped register Boche artillery. Soon accurate artillery fire was added to the murderous machine gun bursts raking Major McKenna's advanced positions. It was approaching noon. Half of the Shamrock Battalion was out of action. Of Company K's five lieutenants, three were dead and one was wounded. All of Company I's officers were casualties.

Captain Meaney sent reinforcements from Company M to fill in the thinning line held by their buddies bordering Meurcy Farm and adjacent high ground. Finally, around noon, the 3rd Battalion was ordered to withdraw through Donovan's men.

According to Father Duffy, "The survivors were a sorry remnant of the splendid battalion that had so gallantly swept across the Ourcq that morning. But they had carried out a soldier's task.

"Their's not to reason why, their's but to do or die."[17]

Sometime after the attack was launched, the order was countermanded by headquarters. Major McKenna tried to recall his men but it was too late. The troops would be slaughtered recrossing the Ourcq with nothing gained for their sacrifice. He left his command post with Company M to find Colonel McCoy. McKenna was killed by shellfire before he reached the colonel. Captain Hurley informed the other company commanders of McKenna's death. Hurley was seriously wounded attempting to reach McCoy. The colonel, aware of the 3rd Battalion's dilemma, ordered Donovan's Battalion across the river. Following relief, the Shamrocks retired to Villers-Sur-Fere.

Corporal Hogan reported an amusing incident involving a captured German officer,

> Some of the men roused a German captain along the line. He was an unmannerly old spartan, and insisted upon being annoying and rough even after surrendering. At last, however, he was subdued by a short tempered Irishman. This officer thought his rank gave him the unusual privilege of twitting his victorious enemy about his shortcomings during the heat of continuing battle. He set out to encourage [discourage?] us with sneering remarks. He outdid himself to express in rotten English his supreme contempt for America and everything American for the benefit of his captors. Finally, he turned to his guard and said,
>
> "You Americans think you're going to win this war, don't you?"
>
> "Yes," answered his Irish guard, "and you think you're going to the hospital, don't you?" and he gave him a punch in the jaw that almost knocked him west.[18]

The 3rd Battalion relieved Donovan's Battalion early in the morning of 1 August and renewed its fight against the then-withdrawing Germans. At 0400 on 2 August, American patrols reported no enemy resistance. The 3rd Battalion hustled through the Foret de Nesles, maintaining contact with friendly units of its flanks. Contact with the enemy was finally made near the town of Morevil en Dole.

The 4th Division was about to relieve the 42nd and Colonel MacArthur wanted the Rainbow to make one last effort to bloody the nose of the retreating Boche. Father Duffy described what followed:

> He [MacArthur] called on one regiment, and then another, for a further advance. Their commanders said truthfully that the men were utterly fatigued and unable to go forward another step. "It's up to you, McCoy," said the Chief of Staff. Our Colonel called Captain Meaney, now in command of what was left of the Third Battalion.

"Captain Meaney, a battalion is wanted to go ahead and gain contact with the enemy; you may report on the condition of your men."

"My men are few and they are tired, sir, but they are willing to go anywhere they are ordered, and they will consider an order to advance as a compliment," was the manly response.

As the brave and gallant few swung jauntily to their position at the head of the Division, Mac Arthur commented, "By God, McCoy, it takes the Irish when you want a hard thing done."

The Battalion located the enemy and took up the fight with them, but already the 4th Division was coming up and the orders for relief were issued.[19]

1st Battalion Story

Major Donovan's Battalion crossed the Ourcq River sometime around 1030 on 28 July. By noon, the 3rd Battalion was relieved by Companies A, B and C. Company D fought all that morning with the Shamrocks and one of its platoons participated in earlier fighting at Meurcy Farm. The unit suffered casualties and was supposed to be relieved. Company D's commanding officer, Captain Connelly, talked Donovan into allowing his men to remain in the fight.

Donovan didn't try to retain all the ground seized by the 3rd Battalion. His men took up positions enabling them to make the Boche pay heavily should they counter attack. In addition, the New Yorkers were in a good position to move forward again.

During the night of 28-29 July, plans for a renewed assault were finalized. The 165th was to sweep the valley, advancing beyond Bois Colas and Meurcy Farm. The 2nd Battalion was to support the 1st on the right.

Further left, the Ohios were to advance on the right of French troops and seize the village of Seringes et Nesles. The 84th Brigade was to move up on the right of the 165th Infantry.

The 1st Battalion attacked at first light. It was aligned as follows: Company D was on the left in support of Company C (Bootz) which was in the van on the left side of a brook that meandered through the valley. Company A (Lieutenant Baldwin) was in the lead on the right side of the brook, supported by Company B, (Reilley) Company C was to clear out Bois Colas while Company A seized Meurcy Farm.

When the attack started, the troops moved forward in dense clusters, suitable for an attack following a rolling barrage. The battalion, however, was advancing without artillery support. Donovan quickly gave his company commanders the following order,

> I insisted that the company commanders send their men forward as we used to do in the old days, which is, one, two or three at a time, moving fast, and when they have advanced a few yards to flop. This gives the machine gunners a small target to fire at, and the smaller the target and the less time we could present it, the better we would be. Then, covering this advance, I had our own machine gunners open in the general direction of where I heard the Boche machine gun fire and then put with each machine gun, snipers to pick off the Boche personnel. With that system working, we went up the valley. It was more difficult on the hill slopes because there we had to charge machine gun nests with resultant losses. One sergeant took a platoon against a machine gun nest.

He had 29 men when started and when he reached the gun, he had four. But he took it and the seven men who were serving the gun. We took very few prisoners. The men when they saw the Germans serving machine guns against us, firing until the last minute, then throwing up their hands crying "Kamerad" became just lustful for German blood. I do not blame them.[20]

The 1st Battalion's attack was successful, Bois Colas and Meurcy Farm were carried. While they moved forward, German aircraft flew over Donovan's men. They identified targets for Boche artillery which laid down an effective barrage on the 1st Battalion. Donovan's men dug in for the night. According to Wild Bill, "We had done it with rifles, machine guns and bayonets and against artillery and machine guns—one machine gun to every four men."[21]

It was a victory for General Pershing's concept of open warfare by American soldiers armed with a rifle and bayonet.

The battalion held on during the night of 29-30 July under German artillery fire and sweeping machine gun bursts. During the afternoon of 30 July, German fire on Donovan's positions in Bois Colas and Meurcy Farm intensified. The fighting consisted of platoon size attacks and counterattacks by the Americans and the Boche. All but one of Donovan's headquarters staff were wounded. His sergeant major was also down, and his replacement, Joyce Kilmer, was killed, shot through the head.

Donovan had ordered Sergeant Kilmer and two others to reconnoiter enemy positions bordering Bois Colas. The patrol advanced about a 100 yards when Kilmer was shot in the head and chest. He died instantly. His comrades marked the spot where he lay and then completed their mission. The next day, they brought his body back to the C.P. He was buried a short time later. Kilmer's grave was initially marked by a wooden stake bearing his identification tags and somewhat later by a wooden cross.

One of Sergeant Kilmer's buddies suggested that his obituary be the poem he dedicated to the regiment's first dead.

> Comrades true,
> Born Anew,
> Peace to you.
> Your souls
> Will Be
> Where heroes are
> And your memory shine
> Like the morning star.
> Brave and dear,
> Shield us here,
> Farewell.[22]

Donovan himself was wounded in the hand and heel. In addition, he had shrapnel embedded in one of his legs. His wounds, however, were not serious. In his own words, "I guess I have been born to be hanged."[23]

During the night of 30-31 July, the troops were finally fed, in spite of a fierce German bombardment which lashed roads and woods with shrapnel and high explosives.

The battalion was ordered to hold on to its positions in the salient during the daylight hours of 31 July. The rest of the Rainbow was ordered to advance and come abreast of the New Yorkers. In the meantime, the 1st Battalion managed to seize Bois Brule. German aircraft continued to hover the American positions. During the day they strafed troops and acted as artillery spotters. At night, the planes dropped aerial bombs.

Early in the morning of 1 August the 1st Battalion was relieved by the 3rd Battalion. The relief was effected at 0230. Donovan's men made their weary way back to Villers-Sur-Fere.

At 0600, Donovan was roused from a refreshing three hour sleep by Lt. Colonel Mitchell. The major was informed that the Germans were pulling out and that the 3rd Battalion was sending out patrols. Donovan roused his company commanders, all second lieutenants, and got the battalion moving again. The troops advanced over ground they had previously seized from the Germans. Reported Major Donovan, "We went over the field on which we had fought and while we found our dead, we found five Germans for every one of us."[24]

He continued, "To those people who are inclined to write a general indictment of German-Americans, I would like to point out a little knoll where a certain machine gun platoon from a state in the middle west was wiped out. And when you look at the identification tags of the men who lay dead about their guns all facing the front, you see nothing but names as German as those of the enemy across from them."[25]

Days later, the battalion was assembled in a wood waiting transport to a rear area. It was a wet, miserable night. An animal-drawn wagon train was also assembled in the damp woods. A major general and his staff arrived and took possession of the position. The animals were drawing flies, so the general ordered the train to move out of the woods. Major Donovan tells the rest of the story,

> A Major General named Cameron, and who is a father of one of Dave Dunbar's lieutenants who had just arrived and taken possession, ordered the train away. An Irishman named Gilhooley, who did not know that his man was a General who was talking and perhaps would not have cared if he did know said, "this is a hell of a note, we go and capture this place and you guys come and live in it."
>
> The General rated him roundly and said there were too damn many flies around there now without bringing in a lot of animals in the yard, and Gilhooley answered, "Flies is it? If it is flies you want, go up on the hillside and you will see thousands of them feasting on the blood of our men!"
>
> The General said nothing more. The train stayed in the chateau yard that night.[26]

Sergeant Richard W. O'Neil of Company D won a Congressional Medal of Honor on 30 July. The citation read: In advance of an assaulting line, he attacked a detachment of about 25 of the enemy. In the ensuing hand-to-hand encounter he sustained pistol wounds, but heroically continued in the advance, during which he received additional wounds; but with great physical effort, he remained in active command of his detachment. Being again wounded he was forced by weakness and loss of blood to be evacuated, but instead insisted upon being taken first to the battalion commander in order to transmit to him valuable information relative to enemy positions and the disposition of our men."[27]

Following is the account of Captain Jacobson, a French liaison officer attached to Colonel McCoy's headquarters staff. During the attack on Bois Colas, he volunteered to carry a telephone wire beyond the advance of the infantry to the edge of the woods. From there he could direct fire on Bois Brule from which the 1st Battalion was receiving intense machine gun fire.

> After our reconnaissances in Villers-Sur-Fere, strewn with American bodies, and bombarded without relaxation by the Germans' heavy artillery, I had the good fortune to be able to admire the extreme courage of a small detachment of American infantrymen and artillerymen, who, after having crossed the Ourcq, carried through a very courageous operation in the little Colas Wood on the north bank of the river.
>
> The problem was to drive the Germans out of their strongly organized position in the Bois Brule to the north of the Bois Colas, from which they vigorously shot up the American troops with their machine guns.
>
> Because of the form of the terrain, the Bois Brule could not be seen from the artillery observatories. It was only possible to adjust the artillery fire from the northern edge of the Bois Colas. A small group, including Lieutenant Corbett, decided to establish an observatory there, at a few dozen meters from the enemy. This was done with the help of infantry soldiers of the 165th New York, and under an extremely violent fire. Twice this group was on the point of being captured by the enemy who had commenced to encircle the Bois Colas. However, the New York infantrymen stopped them. Thanks to the establishment of this post of observation, an accurate fire was brought down by our artillery on the Bois Brule. This fire so tore up that wood that the Germans left alive had to evacuate it and retreat to the Foret de Nesles.[28]

2nd Battalion Story

On 26 July, Anderson's battalion was unloaded from *camions* near woods south of Epieds. The next day, the unit, which was in reserve status, set up camp in woods near Villers-Sur-Fere.

At 0430 on 28 July, Lt. Colonel Mitchell showed up unexpectedly at the 2nd's headquarters. He informed Anderson that at 0445, his unit must execute a bayonet attack across the Ourcq on the 3rd Battalion's left flank. Anderson read the extraordinary order under a blanket by candlelight.

Anderson roused his company commanders who in turn got the troops up and on their way. The battalion reached the river by 0600. There, Anderson received a message from Colonel McCoy ordering him to halt. The 2nd Battalion was receiving artillery fire as well as machine gun fire from the enemy on the other side of the Ourcq. Anderson told the messenger, "Hell, I can't stop now."[29]

As Anderson's leading companies crossed the river, they suffered a large number of casualties. When the battalion reached the other side of the Ourcq, the major received a second message from McCoy again telling him to halt. Anderson's men were receiving increasingly heavy fire from the Germans on the high ground overlooking the river. It was no place to stop. He instructed his company commanders to continue the advance while he went back to Villers-Sur-Fere to explain the situation to McCoy.

Anderson found Colonel McCoy in the village, which was being pounded by artillery fire. The colonel agreed with Anderson's assessment of the situation and told him, "All right, use your own judgment."[30]

Anderson hurried back to his men, who were advancing toward the summit of Hill 156, a German strong point near Bois Colas. The battalion suffered heavy losses but gained the ridge. There, Anderson's men were stopped cold. The troops were receiving fire from machine gun nests located in Fontaine-Sous-Pierre, Seringes et Nesles, Bois Colas and Meurcy Farm. Anderson's men dug in. Later in the morning, the situation on the battalion's left flank was eased somewhat when French troops carried Fontaine-Sous-Pierre.

The 2nd and 3rd battalions were holding hills separated by the valley containing Meurcy Farm. The Battalion, like the 3rd, was stuck out into the German lines like a goose ready to be plucked. The Second Battalion, its flanks unsupported, was ordered back to the north shore of the Ourcq. Thereafter, the unit supported the advance of the 1st Battalion.

On 29 July, Anderson's men helped the 1st Battalion capture Bois Colas and Meurcy Farm. Echeloned to the right of Donovan's troops, the 2nd later assisted in clearing Bois Brule.

Aftermath

Following the Battle of the Ourcq River, the regiment licked its wounds in Foret de Fere. It was in reserve status until relieved by elements of the 77th Division on 11 August.

According to Father Duffy, the area was a dirty, dank and unwholesome spot made worse by daily rain. The troops were sleeping in holes in the ground or in tents. About 60 percent of them had diarrhea and everyone was crawling with cooties.

The depressing environment of Foret de Fere was exacerbated by the gloomy task of burying dead comrades. During the period 21 July to 7 August 1918, the regiment sustained 1,358 casualties: killed—322 men (including 65 mortally wounded) and wounded—1,036 men. Total battlefield casualties from 1 March to 7 August were 2,103 men.

Ignoring temporary and permanent reductions due to sickness, which approached the magnitude of battlefield casualties, and assuming an original strength of 3,600 men, the regiment had then sustained losses approaching 58.4 percent of its original numbers.

Assuming a pre-battle strength of 2,800 men, the regiment was dealt a heavy blow on the Ourcq, suffering 48.5 percent casualties. In comparison, the Irish Brigade sustained 61.8 percent casualties on the Antietam.

In spite of his heart-wrenching duties in Foret de Fere, Father Duffy managed to recall a number of humorous incidents that occurred during the battle.

> The most striking incident I heard described took place in Company D as they were waiting in the streets of Villers-Sur-Fere about three o'clock in the morning of the 28th. The Germans were raking the streets with high explosives and shrapnel and men were falling, hit by the flying pieces. The most trying moment in battle is going into action under shell fire especially at night....

Company D was going through all this, and for the time being, was without officers.... Two corporals, Patrick MacDonough and John Gibbon, had been working hard, giving first aid to the wounded, and they began to worry about the possible effect of the shelling on the men. So they went up to the line to look for some person in higher authority.

They found no officer but they did find Sergeant Tom O'Malley sitting against a stone wall, sucking philosophically at his pipe, as if the wall were at the side of a stone fence in his native Connemara. Now the sight of Tom O'Malley breeds confidence in the heart of every soldier in Company D.

"Where's the officers, Tom?"

"Oi don't know where th' hell they are," says Tom between puffs of his pipe and in the slow soft speech of the West Coast Irish, "If ye were in camp and ye didn't want to se thim, ye'd be thrippin over thim. But now whin ye want t'know what ye got to do in a foight ye can't foind wan of thim."

"Well Tom, we'll elect you captain and you take charge of the men until some of the officers get back, or they may be getting out of hand."

"No, lads, oi don't fancy meself in a Sam Browne belt. Dick O'Neil here is a noice young fellah, so we'll elect Dick captain and o'll make ye fellahs do what he tells ye."

So Sergeant O'Neil, a youth of twenty-one, took charge of the situation, got the men together in small groups under their non-coms, and in places of comparative safety and had them ready when Lieutenant Cook came back from the conference to issue orders to cross the Ourcq.

It is something that we call typically American that a number of men under stress and in an emergency like this, should get together, choose their own leaders and obey them implicitly for the common good.[31]

A second humorous incident follows.

I overheard a conversation in the woods which gave me a good story on Major Donovan. The majority of his battalion have always looked on him as the greatest man in the world. But a certain number were resentful and complaining on account of the hard physical drilling he has continually given them just to stay in condition for just the sort of thing they had to go through last week. As a result of watching him through six days of battle—his coolness, cheerfulness, resourcefulness—there is now no limit to their admiration of him. What I overheard was a partial conversion of the last dissenter. He still had a grouch about what he had been put through the last year, and three other fellows were pounding him about Donovan's greatness. Finally he said grudgingly,

"Well, I'll say this: Wild Bill is a son of a _____, but he's a game one."

When I told it to Donovan, he laughed and said, "Well Father when I'm gone write it as my epitaph."[32]

The third humorous story involved the Ourcq River and John Finnegan.

We joked with (the French liaison officer) Rerat about the size of French rivers. I told him that one of our soldiers (Jack Finnegan) lay badly wounded near the (Ourcq) river and I offered him a pull at my canteen. Raising himself on one elbow and throwing out his arm in a Sir Philip Sydney fashion, he exclaimed, "Give it to the Ourcq, it needs it more than I do." Unfortunately, Finnegan later died of his wounds.[33]

On 28 July, Frank Gardella of the regiment's machine gun company performed a spectacular feat of arms: "Two enemy airplanes were flying parallel to the American infantry lines and pouring machine gun bullets into them, driving everyone to cover. Sergeant Gardella, noting the situation, rushed to his machine gun and took aim at the upper of the two machines. Although he was constantly subject to a storm of bullets from the planes and from enemy snipers on the ground, he nevertheless coolly sighted his gun and riddled the upper plane, causing it to collapse and fall in flames. In falling it struck the lower plane and brought it to earth also. For his coolness and bravery he was awarded the Distinguished Service Cross.[34]

During the night of 23 September, a large shell made a direct hit on a shelter in which Sergeant Gardella and his comrades were sleeping. Gardella was killed instantly and three of his four comrades were seriously wounded. Per the fortunes of war, one occupant of the dugout was only slightly bruised.

During the Battle of the Ourcq River, President Teddy Roosevelt's son Quentin was shot down in a battle over a sector held by the 32nd Division. Colonel McCoy had been Roosevelt's military aide and knew Quentin as a boy. He decided to pay his respects to the fallen aviator. The colonel and Father Duffy drove to the grave site with a marker. When they got there, the two officers were surprised to discover the Germans had identified Quentin's grave with a cross fashioned from parts of his plane. McCoy and Duffy did not disturb the German marker. In Father Duffy's words, "It is a fitting that enemy and friend alike should pay tribute to heroism."[35]

The New Yorkers were getting restless and longed to get out of the debilitating Foret de Fere. Father Duffy, while making his rounds, came upon some Alabamas that felt the same way the Fighting Sixty-Ninth did about their miserable surroundings. One of them asked if

> "the government hadn't othah soldiehs than the Fohty-Second Division?" I answered, "Well, if they're using you so much, it is your own fault?"
> "How is it ouah fault?" demanded my friend, and twenty pairs of eyes asked the same question.
> "It's your fault all right; the trouble with you fellows is that your too blamed good."
> It was true, the 167th Infantry was proving itself to be a first class fighting outfit.[36]

Of course, the 69th knew that all too well.

Father Duffy celebrated a mass for the regiment's dead. The key point of his homily was, "Greater love than this no man hath than he lay down his life for his friends."

After church services, the regiment marched out of Foret de Fere, buoyed by the sounds of "Garry Owen." They had suffered grievous losses but they had whipped a first class German opponent; their heads were held high.

Two days later the regiment marched through Chateau-Thierry in a similar manner. Their military bearing did not go unnoticed. Father Duffy recorded, "Colonel McCoy came to mess with a smile of pride on his face telling us he had encountered an old friend, a regular army officer who had said to him, 'What is that outfit that passed here a little while ago? It is the finest looking lot of infantry I have seen in France.' 'That is the 165th Infantry, more widely known to fame as the 69th New York, and I am proud to say that I command it.'"[37]

Color Guard, 165th New York, 7 September 1918. Color Sergeant William Sheahan, third soldier from left, was killed during the Meuse-Argonne Offensive. (Courtesy of U.S. Army Military History Institute).

In late August the regiment was encamped in the Neufchateau district for rest and rehabilitation. There, the 165th received 500 replacements from the 81st Division.

Colonel Mitchell Relieves Colonel McCoy

Shortly after the Battle of the Ourcq, Colonel McCoy was promoted to the rank of brigadier general and given command of the 63rd Brigade, 33rd Division. The regiment's company commanders agreed that Lt. Colonel Harry Mitchell should replace McCoy. McCoy supported Mitchell's advancement. Mitchell was promoted to colonel and given command of the regiment prior to the St. Mihiel Offensive. Donovan then became the Regiment's Lt. Colonel. He was seriously considered for the 165th's colonelcy. He argued against his promotion and pressured McCoy to support Mitchell's advancement.

CHAPTER 16

St. Mihiel Offensive

Following the successful Aisne-Marne counteroffensive, General Foch proposed eliminating two key German salients, the Somne and St. Mihiel, which threatened the Paris-Amiens and Paris-Nancy railway networks respectively. Reduction of the latter bulge was assigned to the American Army.

On 10 August, the American Army became a reality, with General Pershing as its field commander. At that time, there were 33 American divisions in France (see map). Later in August, Pershing managed to get Haig to release the 33rd, 78th and 80th divisions, which had been serving with the British Expeditionary Force. The British managed to retain two divisions, the 27th and 30th, for the remainder of the war.

During the latter part of August, Pershing's staff worked on plans for an offensive against the St. Mihiel salient. On 30 August, however, General Foch arrived at Pershing's headquarters and threw a wrench into the American Army's plans. Foch proposed a de-emphasis of the St. Mihiel Operation in favor of the American Army's participation in a French offensive directed at the capture of Mezieres on the Meuse River. One unpleasant aspect of Foch's operation would be fragmentation of Pershing's newly formed army.

Pershing and Foch engaged in a heated debate over strategy for well over two hours. The meeting ended in a deadlock.

Foch: "I must insist upon the arrangement."

Pershing: "Marshall Foch, you may insist all you please, but I decline absolutely to agree to your plan. While our army will fight wherever you may decide, it will not fight except as an independent American Army."[1]

On 2 September, Marshall Foch and Pershing came to an agreement. Pershing's army would reduce the salient but would not exploit breakthroughs in the German lines. Instead, he would disengage and move most of his army some 60 miles to the east for a major offensive in the Meuse-Argonne Forest. In addition, Pershing consented to the Americans manning an additional 48 miles of front, all the way to the Argonne Forest.[2]

In order to maintain an independent American Army, Pershing was forced to bite off a lot more than he could chew.

The St. Mihiel salient was approximately 25 miles wide at its base from Hau-

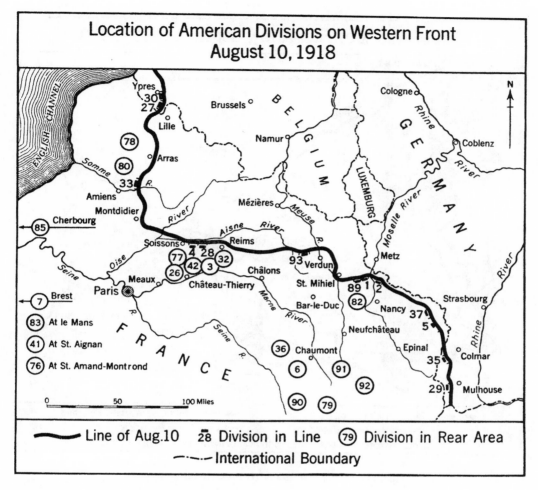

Location of American Divisions on Western Front
August 10, 1918

Line of Aug. 10   ②⃘8̲ Division in Line   ⑦9 Division in Rear Area
International Boundary

Location of American divisions on the western front, August 1918 (from Official Sources).

diomont and Pont-a-Mousson and 16 miles deep from its apex at St. Mihiel. It was held by the Germans for nearly four years and had formidable defensive works. The French made two strong but futile attacks on the salient during 1915. In September 1918, the bulge was manned by second and third class German troops.

Pershing's staff directed 550,000 American and 110,000 French troops into positions around the salient. The soldiers moved at night with great difficulty since rainy weather made the muddy roads almost impassable. A member of the 42nd Division recalled that the only vehicles making their usual speed were airplanes.

Pershing's order of battle was:

- South face of salient (from left to right)—U.S. I Corps (Hunter Liggett); 82nd, 90th, 5th and 2nd divisions, plus U.S. IV Corps. (Joseph T. Dickman); 89th, 42nd and 1st divisions.

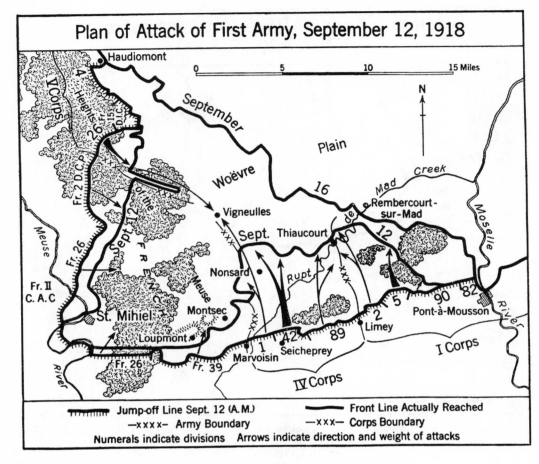

St. Mihiel plan of attack (from Official Sources).

- Apex of salient—French II Corps.
- West face of salient—U.S. V Corps (George H. Cameron); 26th and 4th divisions, plus French 15th Colonial Division.

The attack was to be spearheaded by the 1st and 42nd divisions supported by about 270 light tanks.

At 0100 on 12 September, thousands of guns opened up on the German positions and four hours later, Allied troops went over the top.

The advance went well, especially on the south face where the 1st, 2nd and 42nd divisions moved ahead rapidly. Major "Wild Bill" Donovan urged his Irish men on, "Get forward there! What the hell do you think this is, a wake?"[3]

At 0615 on 13 September, American troops from both sides of the salient met at Vigneulles. The main road out of the salient was cut. By 16 September, the bulge was eliminated. Pershing's offensive had cost the Germans 450 guns and 16,000 prisoners. Allied casualties totaled 7,000 men. The operation returned 200 square miles of territory to France, restored the Paris-Nancy Railroad, opened river boat transport on the Meuse and protected the right flank of the First Army in its later offensive in the Meuse-Argonne Sector. Most importantly, Pershing's elimination of the salient demonstrated that the American Army could successfully handle an operation of some magnitude.[4]

Pershing received considerable praise from the Allies following his victory at St. Mihiel. The Germans, on the other hand, downplayed the victory, claiming that Ludendorff planned to evacuate the salient anyway and that his troops retired in good order to previously prepared positions. Nevertheless, the American Army, in less than 48 hours, had wiped out a salient long held by the Germans that had been unsuccessfully attacked by the French on two occasions.

Lt. Colonel William J. Donovan in fighting trim after St. Mihiel (courtesy of U.S. Army Military Institute).

42nd Division at St. Mihiel

The Rainbow Division reached Seicheprey, in the vicinity of St. Mihiel, after traveling about 100 kilometers in ten days. Initially, the troops marched at night, hiding from German observation planes during the day. Near the end of the trek, movement was made in broad daylight. The Rainbow's destination, the wet and soggy Foret de la Reine, was reached on 10 September. Woods near Seicheprey was the assembly site for the American Expeditionary Force attack on the salient.

The 42nd Division left the forest on the night of 11 September and by midnight was in its jump-off position. All four infantry regiments were in the line. At 0100, American Expeditionary Force artillery started to bombard the German positions. At 0500, the rolling barrage began and the American First Army went over the top. The troops swept forward and quickly overcame stoutly defended

German strong points. By noon, the Rainbow had achieved its goals for Day One and its final objectives early in the morning of 13 September. The 165th Infantry pushed at least two kilometers beyond the division's objective line. From that position, the fortress city of Metz was only 20 miles away and appeared vulnerable. Pershing, however, had promised Foch that the American First Army would only reduce the St. Mihiel Salient.[5]

The Rainbow Division settled in against the retirement position of the German Army, which eventually became a section of the Hindenburg Line. The 84th Brigade occupied the division's sector of the Allied line for about two weeks and was then relieved by the 83rd Brigade. Both outfits worked hard establishing strong defensive positions in their section of the line. On the night of September 30–October 1, the Rainbow Division was relieved by the 89th Division.

Total casualties for the St. Mihiel Offensive and subsequent in the Essey-Pannes Sector until 30 September were 1,207 men: killed—294 men (including 91 mortally wounded) and wounded—913 men.

Total casualties for the division were then 10,332 men. Assuming an initial strength of 27,000 men, battlefield casualties had exceeded 38.2 percent of the division's original fighting strength. On 30 September, the division was withdrawn from the Essey-Pannes Sector and, after five nights of slogging through cold, penetrating mud, arrived at Bois de Montfaucon on the vicinity of the Meuse-Argonne Front.

165th Infantry at St. Mihiel

The 42nd Division moved out with the 83rd and the 84th Brigades on the left and right respectively. The regiments relative positions were the same as on the Ourcq River—from left to right, Ohioans, New Yorkers, Alabamas and Iowans. Each regiment had one battalion in the front line and another in the second line. The remaining battalion was in reserve.

The regiment moved into its jump-off position, north of Seicheprey, on the night of 11-12 September. The 1st Battalion was in the front line with Lt. Colonel Donovan in command. He was not willing to let his newly achieved rank hinder an opportunity to lead his battalion into one more fight. Picked men of the 2nd Battalion followed close behind the lead unit to mop up bypassed German strong points. The 3rd Battalion was in reserve.

American guns opened up at 0100 on 12 September. The fire was deliberate. There was minimal response from the German artillery. At 0500, the troops went over the top behind a rolling barrage, a smoke screen and tanks. According to Father Duffy, "...Tanks advanced with our infantry crawling like iron clad hippopotami over the wire in front to make a passageway...."[6]

Donovan's men swept forward. Machine gun nests were encountered in the German second line. They were quickly silenced. St. Baussant was taken with the aid of the tanks.

The Germans made a stand at the village of Maizerais. Again their resistance was quickly overcome. Donovan recorded, "The difficult thing was the maintenance of order and organization. In many ways it is more difficult in easy victory than when stiff resistance is encountered. Men would gather around prisoners, they would seek out Boche property, curiously gaze about, and the attack would lose momentum. Other units would drift over into our sector. I was the ranking officer of the entire Division on the front line and I went cursing up and down the line getting men into positions. One tried to assert his rights as an American citizen but I physically convinced him that his only right was to keep up forward."[7]

By the evening of 12 September, the 1st Battalion was in defensive positions just south of Bois de Thiaucourt, the 2nd was about 1,000 yards in the rear of Donovan's unit. The 3rd Battalion was located near the Village of Pannes.

At 0600 the next day, the 1st Battalion resumed its advance and by 0900 had seized St. Benoit. The 2nd was again slightly to the rear of the Donovan's men. The Shamrocks were in reserve at Sebastopol Farm. Orders were received to establish a defensive line around Hassavant Farm and along the edge of Bois de La Grande Souche. Patrols were pushed out through the Bois des Haudronville Bas. The objectives of the 165th had been achieved.

Father Duffy described an incident at St. Benoit:

> When our fellows reached St. Benoit they found that the Germans had started a fire in the Chateau, but it was quickly extinguished. The church too, had been set on fire and was beyond saving. When Jim Barry of Company C saw it blazing he shouted, "Glory be to God, those devils have burnt the church. Let's see what we can save out of it."
>
> With Tierney and Boyle and others he ran into the burning building and carried out statues and candelabra which they deposited carefully outside. Having finished their pious work they began to remember that they were hungry. Barry took from his musette bag some German potatoes which he had stored there in place of grenades that could be used up in action, and said, "Well we have done what we could, and now we've got a good fire here, and might as well use it."
>
> They stuck the potatoes on the ends of their bayonets and roasted them in the embers. Just then another party came along with some bottled beer that they had salvaged from the Germans' supplies in Pannes, so they picnicked merrily in the square in front of the blazing temple.[8]

From 14 to 17 September, the 165th Infantry maintained its defensive positions in the vicinity of Hassavant Farm. Patrols were sent out night and day. Prisoners were taken and losses sustained. On 17 September, the regiment was relieved by the Alabamas The New Yorkers went into reserve status near the Village of La Marche. The place consisted of a large farm, some stone buildings and a few shacks. The troops had plenty of provisions, most of which were captured from the Germans.

On 27 September, the 2nd Battalion replaced the Iowans in a section of line near Marimbois Farm. Elements of the 89th Division relieved the regiment 30 September and shortly thereafter, the 42nd Division was ordered to Montfaucon in the Meuse-Argonne Sector. The town had been taken by the American Expeditionary Force in the opening stages of the Meuse-Argonne Offensive.

Montfaucon was about 60 miles west of St. Mihiel, so most of the troops were transported by bus or truck. The vehicles were driven by Vietnamese from French

Patrol, 165th New York, in Hazavant, France, September 1918 (courtesy of U.S. Army Military Institute).

Indo China. According to Ettinger, "They were a crazy bunch, who drove those trucks like madmen, wrecked a couple on the way, and scared the hell out of us."[9]

Father Duffy, rather insensitively, described the Asian drivers as "....sun burned almond-eyed, square-cheeked Chinks...."[10]

Sadly, the French government charged the U.S. a per head fee for transporting American soldiers to the front.[11] The New Yorkers were at their assigned destination by 5 October.

At Montfaucon, the regiment's camp was buzzing with rumors of a pending armistice. Officers of the regiment knew the rumors were true but realized the German war machine would have to suffer a few more serious knocks before the Boche high command would begin serious peace negotiations. Colonel Mitchell, Donovan and the battalion commanders were concerned the armistice rumors might degrade the troops' fighting spirit. They realized no soldier in his right mind wanted to assault machine gun nests on what might be the last day of the war.

Mitchell asked Father Duffy to go among the men and determine the effect of the rumors had on their combat readiness. One of the first men he spoke to was First Sergeant Mulholland. The New Yorker's response to the chaplin's questions pretty much typified the regiment's feelings at that time, "Of course I would like to see the war over, but not while the old Regiment is back here in army corps reserve. I want to see this war end with the 69th right out in the front line, going strong."[12]

The regiment sustained 223 casualties during the period 4 September to 4 October 1918; 56 men were killed (including 16 mortally wounded men) and 167 were wounded.

CHAPTER 17

Meuse-Argonne Offensive

The Meuse-Argonne Sector was arguably the most strategically important area on the Western Front. Supply of German forces in northern France was primarily dependent on two great railroad networks. One passed through Liege in the north, the other through Thionville in the south. The most important section of the southern line ran between Carignan, Sedan and Mezzieres, over which, it was said, some 250 trains routinely passed each day. Severing the railroad, for example at Sedan, would create an unacceptable burden on the remaining artery through Liege.[1]

Foch designated two armies for the Meuse-Argonne offensive. Pershing's American First Army would attack east of the Argonne Forest and the French Fourth Army would attack west of the forest. The two armies were to drive toward the northwest and cut the Thionville-Lille Railroad in the vicinity of Sedan-Mezieres.

The terrain over which the American Army had to move provided its defenders with Hellish advantages. It was bordered on the east by the non-fordable Meuse River and on the west by the nearly impenetrable Argonne Forest. The 20 mile wide tunnel between the river and forest was split by a spine of high ground about 13 miles long, which created two narrow defiles through which an attacking army would be funneled. The resultant passages were dominated by German artillery located on hills in the Argonne Forest, the heights of the Meuse River and high points on the central spine such as Montfaucon.

The Germans improved natural defenses of the region by adding an elaborate system of mutually supporting trenches, concrete dugouts, fortified strong points and interlocking machine gun nests. All defensive positions were fronted with thick swirls of barbed wire. The Germans had three successive lines of defense named after Wagnerian witches; Giselhen, Kriemhilde and Freya.[2]

Opening Moves, 26 September

Pershing had committed his most experienced divisions to the St. Mihiel Offensive. He was forced to use relatively untried divisions in the opening assault

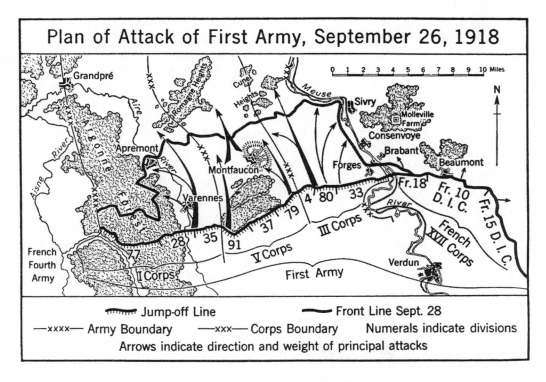

Meuse-Argonne plan of attack, 26 September 1918 (from Official Sources).

in the Meuse-Argonne Sector. One of his more veteran units, the 77th Division, had recently received 4,000 completely green soldiers, some of whom had never handled a rifle. To make matters worse, four of Pershing's nine divisions lacked organic artillery.

Getting attacking units to their jump-off positions was a nightmare since there were just three roads into the sector. The French Second Army which vacated the front lines, used one artery and Pershing's assembling troops the other two. The enormity of the transportation problem may be understood when it is realized that about one thousand trucks were required to move one American division. Imagine nine divisions and their equipment moving along two badly maintained roads in darkness under sporadic artillery fire.[3]

Replacement of the French Second Army by Pershing's nine divisions was coordinated by Colonel George C. Marshall of the 1st Division. As a result of his brilliant effort, the American First Army rapidly extended its front westward from the St. Mihiel Sector and eastward to the Argonne Forest, about ninety-four miles or about one third of the active front from the North Sea to the Moselle River. The huge, surreptitious movement was performed in slightly less than two weeks.

Pershing hoped to smash through the German lines and then advance more than ten miles within the first 24 hours of his attack. By the end of day two, he needed to have his lead divisions through the main German defensive live, the Kriemhilde Stellung. After the second day of the attack, Ludendorff would be able to reinforce his positions and the American offensive would bog down into another battle of attrition.

On the night of 25 September, Pershing's three corps were aligned for attack. At 2330, almost 4,000 Allied guns, of all calibers, began bombarding the German lines. The firing continued until 0530 the next day, when the infantry went over the top. Troops following the rolling barrage were supported by almost 200 light tanks and about 850 airplanes.

The attacking Americans quickly broke through the German lines, but in the words of Colonel Marshall, the advancing units soon became "disorganized or confused to a remarkable degree...."[4]

Historian Allan R. Millett, who also studied the operation, aptly remarked that within 24 hours, the Meuse-Argonne Campaign "turned from a sprint to a slugging match."[5]

The American Army resumed the attack on 27 September. The Germans employed an elastic style of defense similar to that used by the French against Luddendorff's thrusts. They fought with tenacity and by 29 September, the American advance was brought to a standstill. As a result of inexperience and incompetence, First Army was mired in a nightmarish logistical traffic jam. Only airplanes and carrier pigeons were able to carry out their assignments.

Renewed Attack, 4 October

Foch was aggravated by the American First Army's failure to move and strongly suggested to Pershing "that your attacks start without delay and that once begun, they be continued without any interruptions such as those which have just arisen."[6]

Pershing was outraged. He believed Foch had overstepped his authority. Later, the generalisimo sent a mollifying note to the American general which eased the latter's ire. Nevertheless, by 4 October, General Pershing had reorganized his army and was ready to advance once again.

Four inexperienced divisions (35th, 91st, 37th and 79th) were replaced with three veteran units, the 1st, 32nd and 3rd divisions. The individual divisions were ordered to advance independently without stopping at predetermined objectives.

The First Army attacked at 0500, without a preliminary bombardment. The Germans, however, were not surprised. They had used the four day lull in fighting to bring in fresh divisions and strengthen their defenses.

The attack was initially successful but then it too bogged down. Once again, American and German troops slugged it out for small, local advantages in position.

By 10 October, I Corps had cleared the Argonne Forest, V Corps was at Bois de Romagne, III Corps was approaching the Cunel Heights and the French XXVII Corps was in a pocket short of the heights. The American Army had reached the Kriemhilde Stellung at many points, but nowhere had the German line been pierced.

During the fighting between 4 and 10 October, two famous incidents occurred. In one, a detachment of the 77th Division, since called the "Lost Bat-

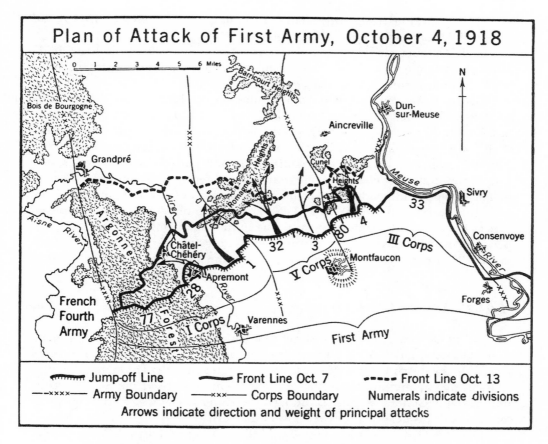

Meuse-Argonne plan of attack, 4 October 1918 (from Official Sources).

talion," was surrounded in the Argonne Forest for a number of days and then rescued. In the other escapade, Sergeant Alvin York (82nd Division), a former con-
scientious objector, single handedly killed 28 Germans and captured another 132
of the enemy (including a major and two lieutenants) plus 35 machine guns.[7]

The attacks were not going well and casualties were piling up. One American Expeditionary Force division moving up to the front suffered nearly 5,000
casualties from German artillery without firing a shot in retaliation. The 1st Division, an attacking force of 12,000 men then commanded by Summerall, sustained
about 10,000 casualties, many of whom were left on the field.[8]

Rexmond Cochrane evaluated the impact of gas warfare on the performance
of the American Expeditionary Force. He believed the enemy's use of gas during
the Meuse-Argonne Offensive was one of the reasons for the marginal performance of the attacking divisions. Cochrane's thoughts on the effectiveness of German gas warfare are summed up in this statement: "It was said that around
mid–October gas evacuations real, suspected or feigned reached something like
42 percent of the troops engaged in battle, as a general average in the American
Expeditionary Force. Clearly, it was the enemy's continous use of gas that pro-

duced the enormous losses and exhausted condition of the men that Army found so harmful, both as fact and verbal expression."[9]

By 12 October, the First Army's second attempt at cracking the Kriemhilde Stellung had petered out. General Pershing was depressed and nearly undone, but like Grant before Petersburg, he continued to fight.

George C. Marshall believed that Pershing's determination to soldier on while his beloved American Army was being blasted by friend and foe (with adverse communiques and machine gun fire) was the highlight of his wartime service. Marshall's words succinctly describe the plight of the beleaguered general, "With distressingly heavy casualties, disorganized and only partially trained troops, supply problems of every character due to the devastated zone so hurriedly crossed, inclement and cold weather, flu, stubborn resistance by the enemy on one of the strongest positions on the Western Front, pessimism on all sides and the pleadings to halt the battle made by many of the influential members of the army, you persisted in your determination to force the fighting over all difficulties and objections.... Nothing in your leadership throughout the war was comparable to this."[10]

Third Assault, 14 October

On 12 October, General Pershing reorganized the American Expeditionary Force by creating two armies. Those divisions on the Meuse-Argonne Front comprised the First Army under Major General Hunter Liggett. The remaining divisions in the vicinity of the old St. Mihiel Salient comprised the Second Army under Major General Robert L. Bullard. Pershing became Army Group Commander with his headquarters at Ligny-en-Barrois.

Liggett's First Army was composed of the I, III and V corps. I Corps, Joseph T. Dickman commanding, consisted of the 77th and 82nd divisions. III Corps, John L. Hines commanding, consisted of the 3rd, 4th and 5th divisions, and V Corps, Charles P. Summerall commanding, consisted of the 32nd and 42nd divisions.

Pershing hoped the 42nd and 5th divisions would drive deep salients on either side of the Bois de Romagne and pinch off Cote Dame Marie, one of the linchpins in the Kriemhilde Stellung.

The three German corps facing Liggett's First Army were nearing exhaustion. Their reserves were long since committed or weakened. The Germans, however, were far from ready to give up their defensive positions. The Boche manning the Kriemhilde Stellung realized they held the hinge of the German line on the Western Front. The pivot that made it possible for the northern armies to gradually yield ground to the French and British without endangering their lines of communications or avenues of retreat.

Terrain in the area continued to be difficult, providing defenders with formidable advantages. Nature's impediments were intensified by clever German fortifications. The foreboding landscape was littered with mangled corpses and debris of battle.

First Army attacked on 14 October. As usual, the weather was miserable. Many of Pershing's men were poorly clothed and suffered accordingly. The attack went

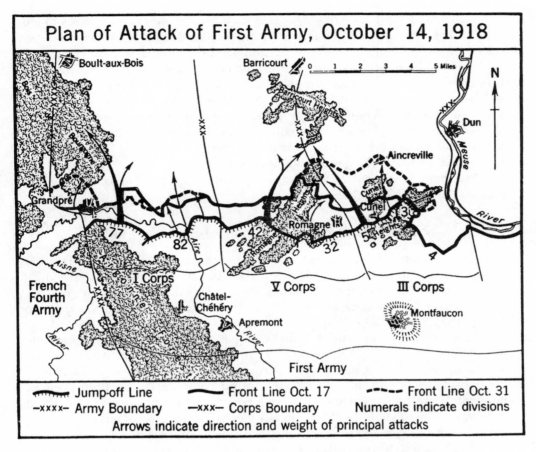

Plan of Attack of First Army, October 14, 1918

Meuse-Argonne plan of attack, 14 October 1918 (from Official Sources).

poorly. The Germans continued to fight stubbornly. Their artillery smothered both attacking and support troops with artillery and gas. Bloody day followed bloody day with the Germans exacting a heavy price as they fell back.

On 16 October, the 32nd and 42nd divisions took Cote Dame Marie and Cote de Chatillon respectively, strong points in the Kriemhilde Stellung. Casualties were enormous and way out of proportion to the ground gained. Those division commanders who did not achieve results were sacked. General officers canned included Beaumont E. Buck—3rd Division, George H. Cameron—4th Division, John E. McMahon—5th Division and Clarence R. Edwards—26th Division. Surviving officers were those who drove their subordinates. The night before the 42nd Division captured Cote de Chatillon, Summerall sacked Brigadier General Lenihan of the Division's 83rd Brigade and Colonel Harry Mitchell of the 165th Infantry. It was produce or else, in the Meuse-Argonne Sector.

After the First Army broke through the Kriemhilde Stellung, General Liggett decided his troops needed a breather. His artillery was essentially immobilized and his infantry regiments were depleted and dog tired. For almost two weeks,

Liggett allowed the First Army to regain its strength. He only ordered limited attacks that were intended to gain advantageous ground and certain to be successful. Worn out units such as the 4th and 32nd divisions were relieved.

Marshal Foch, at a Supreme War Council conference on 25 October, stated his opinion that the German Army was beaten. He had called the meeting to discuss the terms of an armistice when the Germans finally realized they were whipped. During the conference, Pershing commented that the Germans should be forced to surrender unconditionally. Without realizing it, he became involved in political issues outside of his domain. An angry Secretary of War Baker recommended chastising him with a letter of reprimand.

President Woodrow Wilson, however, realizing the war was almost over, advised Baker to let Pershing off the hook.

42nd Division at Landres-et-St. Georges

On 11 October, after a week in the Montfaucon Woods, the 42nd Division received orders to relieve the 1st Division. The Rainbow was also transferred to V Corps, General Summerall commanding. The 1st Division had fought hard in the pass between the Argonne Forest and the Romagne Heights and was then up against the Kriemhilde Stellung.

The 42nd Division was worn down by fatigue, hunger, wet and cold. Its morale was further compromised by rumors of an imminent armistice. Word reached Rainbow Division Headquarters on 13 October that President Wilson had arranged peace discussions with the enemy based on his Fourteen Points. Rumors of an impending armistice reached the troops. A typical comment expressed by enlisted men was, "Why the hell should we do any more fighting now?" On 14 October, a Division memo ordered "all discussions of peace be suppressed."[11]

Finally, it must be remembered that the division advancing on the Kriemhilde Stellung had lost a third of its original strength, possibly its best men. The adverse impact of the Ourcq may be understood by a German soldier's words in 1916, "The tragedy of the Somme battle was that the best soldiers, the stoutest hearted men were lost; their numbers were replaceable, their spiritual worth never could be."[12]

To counter peace talk rumors and arouse the troops' fighting spirit, they were told that the harder they hit the enemy in the coming fight, the sooner he would yield.

The 42nd Division, when it entered the lines, was the left hand unit of V Corps. The I, V and III corps were scheduled to renew the offensive in the Meuse-Argonne Sector on 14 October.

The section of the Kriemhilde Stellung to be attacked by the Rainbow Division fronted Landres-et-St. Georges. The terrain was dominated by Cote de Chatillon, a conical, densely wooded hill bristling with German ordnance. Other area strong points included Musarde and Tuilerie Farms plus Hills 242 and 288.[13]

The Rainbow Division was ordered to attack at 0800 on 14 October. The 84th Brigade was to drive through the enemy lines and seize Cote de Chatillon. The 83rd Brigade was to capture the ridge east of Cote de Chatillon, seize the towns of St. Georges and Landres-et-St. Georges and the road running between those hamlets.

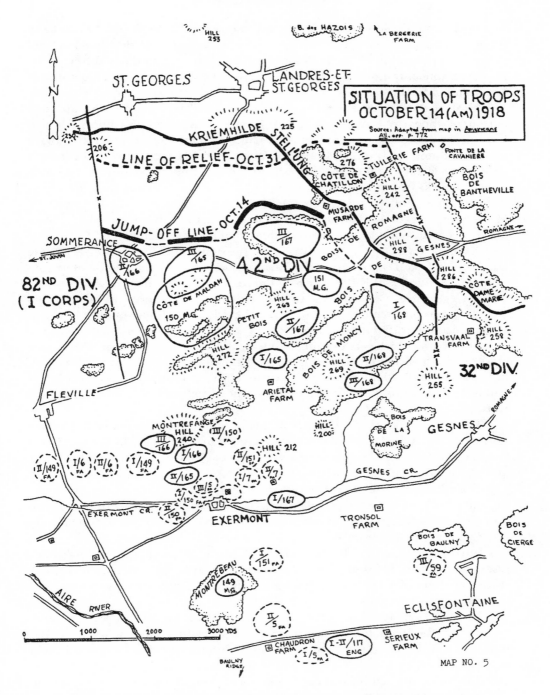

HILL 253

B. des HAZOIS

LA BERGERIE FARM

ST. GEORGES

LANDRES-ET-ST. GEORGES

SITUATION OF TROOPS OCTOBER 14 (AM) 1918

Source: Adapted from map in *Americans* All. off. P. 772

KRIEMHILDE STELLUNG

225

206

LINE OF RELIEF-OCT.31

276

TUILERIE FARM

FONTE DE LA CAVANIÈRE

CÔTE DE CHATILLON

HILL 242

BOIS DE BANTHEVILLE

JUMP-OFF LINE-OCT.14

MUSARDE FARM

ROMAGNE

SOMMERANCE

III/167

ROMAGNE

ST.JUVIN

III/165

42ND DIV

151 M.G.

HILL 288

GESNES

HILL 286

II/166

82ND DIV. (I CORPS)

CÔTE DE MALDAH

150 M.G.

HILL 263

II/167

I/168

CÔTE DAME MARIE

HILL 272

PETIT BOIS

I/165

BOIS DE MONCY

HILL 269

II/168

TRANSVAAL FARM

HILL 258

FLEVILLE

ARIETAL FARM

III/168

HILL 255

32ND DIV.

MONTREFANGE HILL 240

III/150

BOIS DE LA MORINE

GESNES

ROMAGNE

II/149 FA

I/6 FA

II/6 FA

I/149 FA

III/166

I/166

III/151

HILL 212

HILL 200

GESNES CR.

II/165

II/5 FA

I/7

I/150 FA

II/7

TRONSOL FARM

BOIS DE BAULNY

BOIS DE CIERGE

EXERMONT CR.

II/150 FA

EXERMONT

I/167

II/59 FA

AIRE RIVER

MONTREBEAU

149 M.G.

I/151 FA

ECLISFONTAINE

0 1000 2000 3000 YDS

II/5 FA

CHAUDRON FARM

I/5 FA

I-II/117 ENG

SERIEUX FARM

BAULNY RIDGE

MAP NO. 5

42nd Division in the battle of Landres-et-St. Georges (from Official Sources).

Corps and division orders called for a two hour bombardment by 42nd and 1st division artillery on enemy strong points, including Cote de Chatillon, Hill 288 and sections of the Bois de Romagne. Gas shells were to be used freely. The promised concentrations of artillery fire were not delivered, however, because of an ammunition shortage.

Most of the 25,000 High Explosive shells fired in the softening up bombardment appear to have been wasted. Proper registration of artillery fire had been prevented by enemy control of the air. The barrage preceding the attack was also limited with respect to the number of rounds fired. Smoke shells were used in the last few minutes of the barrage. No gas shells were fired in the initial or later attacks by the 42nd Division on the Kriemhilde Stellung.

The 168th Infantry got into the German trenches on Hill 288 by 1225. MacArthur recorded, "The battalion which took the hill was very badly shattered.... The position ... was superbly defended and heroically won."[14]

A number of hours later the division on the right of the Iowans took Romagne and flanked Cote Dame Marie. The 167th got within less than a kilometer from Cote de Chatillon and Hill 242 before the regiment was pinned down by enemy machine gun fire. General MacArthur estimated that there was at least 200 machine guns on Cote de Chatillon. He believed the position couldn't be taken without careful artillery preparation.[15]

The 165th, which was essentially out in the open, reached the dense wire cresting Landres-et-St. Georges ridge. The regiment was stopped by machine gun fire from Cote de Chatillon, as well as frontal fire from enemy positions below Landres-et-St. Georges and long range gas and shrapnel fire from the Bois des Hazois.

The 166th Infantry, attacking from below Sommerance with the 82nd Division on its left, halted at Hill 230 while that position was flanked by the latter division. The Ohios then moved toward their second objective, Hill 206, but they were quickly halted by machine gun fire.

At dusk on 14 October, the 84th Brigade was still well below Cote de Chatillon and its supporting strong points at Musarde Farm, Hill 242 and Tuilerie Farm. The 83rd Brigade, especially the 165th Infantry was out in the open, beneath the wire fronting the line from St. Georges to Landres-et-St. Georges.

During the night of 14-15 October, the Germans subjected the 83rd Brigade's reserves and artillery formations in Exermont to continuous bombardment. Gas shells were intermixed with high explosives. The interdictory fire degraded preparations for the next day's advance.

The 42nd Division made little progress in the rain and storms of 15 October. Elements of the 168th, following a series of unsuccessful attacks, managed to dig in within a half kilometer of Musarde and Tuilerie farms. The enemy still held most of Hill 242.

The 167th finished the day out in the open facing the machine guns of Cote de Chatillon. The Alabamas were reluctant to advance since patrols reported the wire fronting the German position was undamaged by the preparatory bombardment.[16]

Mechanical problems and casualties due to German interdictory fire turned back the promised tanks. Nevertheless, the 83rd Brigade continued its attacks toward St. Georges and Landres-et-St. Georges, advancing against "withering and well aimed machine gun fire [and] very active High Expolsives and gas shell fire."

The New Yorkers on the right of the attack were caught in enemy cross fire from Cote de Chatillon and enemy strong points in Sommerance. By late afternoon, the assault battalions of both regiments were reported to be, "badly shot up and pretty well disorganized."[17]

Around 1600, the 165th Infantry reported that the 1st, 2nd and 3rd Battalions were reduced to 186, 480 and 496 riflemen respectively. The Regiment's stoutest warrior, Major Donovan was incapacitated, wounded in the knee by a machine gun bullet. Dead of the 83rd Brigade, most of them from the 165th Infantry, were left on the enemy wire fronting St. Georges and Landres-et-St. Georges. Unfortunately, a number of them were still hanging there when V Corps broke through the position on 1 November.

Cochrane chides the 42nd Division for its reluctance to use gas during the attacks of 14 and 15 October. He maintains that, "the immediate situation demanded gas on the wired trenches before St. Georges and Landres-et-St. Georges, on the machine gun nests in the Cote de Chatillon, and on the hostile artillery in the Bois des Hazois and Bois L'Epasse. Division was reluctant to use gas during the attack, and most the 42nd would do was to plan a great smoke screen along the east west boundaries of the 83rd Brigade between its second and fourth objectives, to block flanking fire from superior enemy positions on the right and left. Even that wasn't carried out, owing to a change in Army plans."[18]

During the night of 15-16 October, orders were written for renewed attacks on the morrow. The 83rd Brigade, with tank support, was to break through the German lines and capture St. Georges and Landres-et-St. Georges. The 84th Brigade was to capture Cote de Chatillon

General Summerall was not pleased with the performance of the 42nd Division and not confident of success on the morning of 16 October. He visited the command posts of both brigades, the 165th and 166th Regiments and the 149th Field Artillery. He demanded answers as to why units had failed to seize their objectives. Summerall also wanted assurances that the next day's assaults would would be successful.

He was not satisfied with Lenihan's response and fired him as commander of the 83rd Brigade. Summerall's visit to the 165th Infantry did not go well either. Colonel Mitchell and some of his staff were also sacked.

The key to the German resistance facing the 42nd Division was clearly Cote de Chatillon. The 83rd Brigade could not advance as long it remained in German hands. Unknown to the Americans, however, the Germans had already conceded its loss.

At a meeting with General Menoher and Colonel Hughes (Division Chief of Staff), MacArthur proposed a do-or-die assault by the 84th Brigade on the troublesome German position. He suggested that the 151st Field Artillery in its entirety support the attack. His plan was proposed to Summerall and General Drum, Army Chief of Staff. The latter wanted a general attack. MacArthur persuaded the ranking officers that his plan would work. During a heated exchange, Summerall reportedly said, "Give me Chatillon or a list of 5,000 casualties!.," to which MacArthur was said to quickly respond, "All right general; we'll take it or my name will head the list."[19]

The attack order was suspended when it was learned that the Germans were going to launch a heavy counterattack on on V Corps' front. When the Boche assault did not materialize, 84th Brigade was ordered to attack as planned. The 83rd Brigade did not make an organized assault on 16 October.

The 151st Field Artillery bombarded the slopes of Cote de Chatillon for approximately 30 minutes and at 1000 battalions of the Alabama and Iowa regiments assaulted Tuilerie Farm, the crests of Hill 242 and Cote de Chatillon. Sixty machine guns on Hill 263 supported the advance of the 84th Brigade.

The Germans on Cote de Chatillon had been outflanked the previous day. During the morning of 16 October, the 32nd Division reached Pont de La Cavaniere, further threatening the Boche defenders with encirclement.

Finally, around 1600, after a series of determined assaults, the 84th Brigade seized Cote de Chatillon. The Germans on the heights retreated to Bois des Hazois.

Division casualties on 16 October were 391 men (killed—36, wounded—254 and gassed—101).[20] Total losses were far fewer than those sustained on 14 and 15 October. Luckily for MacArthur, his do-or-die promise to take Cote de Chatillon or leave himself and 5,000 dead on the prominence was not required.

The fall of Cote de Chatillon compromised the Kriemhilde Stellung. Those portions of the line still under enemy control, were considered outposts for the enemy's next defensive position, which was being established north of Landres-et-St. Georges.

At dusk on 16 October, the 42nd Division strengthened its positions and awaited orders. On 21 October, the 83rd Brigade extended to the right and took over the 84th Brigade's section of the front. The latter unit went into reserve status.

The Rainbow Division awaited orders to resume its attack on the Hindenburg Line. General Liggett, however, believed it was necessary for First Army to refit and reorganize before it resumed the attack. Accordingly, the 42nd Division was not allowed to exploit its success in piercing the Kriemhilde Stellung.

On 17 October, First Army Headquarters ordered V and III corps' divisions to systematically bombard enemy positions on their respective fronts. Since ammunition was limited, artillery fire was to be spotted. Gas shells were to be used freely. With respect to the latter, between 22 and 29 October, 9,589 gas shells were lobbed on enemy strong points in Landres-et-St. Georges.[21]

On 21 October, V Corps Headquarters issued preliminary orders for the next general assault. The 42nd Division, with the 83rd and 84th brigades from left to right, would assault St. Georges, Landres-et-St. Georges and Hill 253. These objectives were to be seized on the first day. Four days later, General Liggett shifted the weight of the attack toward the center of V Corps. First day objectives on the 83rd Brigade's front were advanced seven kilometers north of Landres-et-St. Georges to include Bois de Barricort. The attack was to be preceded by a two hour bombardment using High Expolsives and gas shells.

Summerall decided to have the 2nd Division make the assault, although the

83rd Brigade made a special request to lead the attack. It is probable that he wanted a regular army division to lead the expected breakthrough.

During the two hour preparation for the attack on 1 November, V Corps guns fired 187,317 shells, of which 15,009 were gas shells. (The attack of 14 October was preceded by bombardment of 25,000 High Explosives shells, none of which contained gas.)[22] Not unexpectedly, the attack was a walkover. The first day's advance swept ahead almost eight kilometers to the heights of Barricourt.

As a result of the fighting in the Argonne between 5 October to 1 November 1918, the Rainbow suffered 3,864 casualties: killed—701 men (including 225 men mortally wounded) and wounded—3,163 men.

Total casualties for the division were then 14,196 men. Assuming an initial strength of 27,000 men, battlefield casualties exceeded 52.6 percent of the division's original fighting strength.

Almost 3,000 soldiers were sick or otherwise incapacitated. In addition, the division's animals were in pitiable shape. The Rainbow was close to being used up.

165th Infantry at Landres-et-St. Georges

When the regiment headed for the Argonne Forest, its strength was 53 officers and slightly fewer than 3,000 men. The number of killed and wounded to that time totaled about 2,600 men. Considering losses of all kinds, nearly 3,000 of the Regiment's original strength of 3,600 men were lost to the unit for varying periods of time. If none of the wounded or sick returned to the outfit, and there were no replacements, then only 600 men of the 69th would be left. Most of the unit's wounded, considered "Fit for Service," however, were returned to the parent organization. According to Father Duffy, approximately half of the regiment's 2,983 men were from its original companies.[23]

It was about 8 months since the regiment entered the Luneville lines. Now, there was a new name next to almost every billet in the command structure of the regiment. Nevertheless, positions of authority were filled by men from the ranks. Although half of the 69th was comprised of relatively new men, regimental pride and traditions were maintained by the unit's veteran officers and noncoms.

The 165th marched to its positions before the Kriemhilde Stellung on 11 October. Ettinger's description of the scene is almost a parody of Father Corby's famous "Absolution at Gettysburg."

> Our regiment loved to sing on the march. To say our songs were risque would be putting it mildly. They were as bawdy as the collective imaginations of 3,000 horny men could conceive.
> On our last day of our journey to Exermont, the sun came out, and we were able to march into our staging positions during the late afternoon. To bolster our morale, I suppose, the officers let us sing. It was quite a sight to see the whole Regiment under march singing away at the top of their lungs. As a dispatch rider, I used to be able to watch them, but this time I was in the ranks with the mortar platoon. I happened to look up, and there was Father Duffy standing on a bluff at the side of the road, giving his benediction to the troops

as we were "banging away on Lulu" under full field pack and full throat. He didn't care what we were singing as long as we were alive and singing.

Some weeks later in the hospital at Allerey, I picked up an issue of the Literary Gazette, and there was as beautiful photograph of Father Duffy with arms outstretched in benediction as the regiment filed below. The caption read, "Father Francis P. Duffy, regimental chaplain of the 165th New York Infantry, blesses his troops as they march into battle singing, 'Onward Christian Soldiers.'"

Oh God, I laughed—a Protestant hymn no less![24]

The 3rd Battalion (Reilley) took over the front line just north of the Cote de Maldah, Companies M (Rowley) and I (Walsh) were in forward positions while Companies K (Guigon) and L (Given) were in woods behind them. The 2nd Battalion (Anderson) was north of Exermont near Hill 240 while the 1st Battalion (Kelly) was near Arietal Farm between Bois de Moncy and Petit Bois. The 2nd Battalion, 166th Infantry, was in Sommerance on the left flank of Reilley's men and the 3rd Battalion, 167th Regiment, was on the New Yorkers' right flank.

The Shamrock Battalion was subjected to continuous artillery fire while it was in the trenches waiting for the attack order. A number of men were killed and wounded as a result of the German shelling.

The section of the Kriemhilde Stellung facing the New Yorkers consisted of three lines of barbed wire and three lines of trenches. The first section of wire was formidable, it was breast high and at least 20 feet deep. The wire was fastened to iron supports firmly fixed in the ground. It was difficult for artillery to destroy the wire maze. Machine gun nests were cleverly positioned in the second line. Maxims concentrated near Musarde Farm and more importantly, Cote de Chatillon controlled the open field in front of the 3rd Battalion.[25]

The objectives of the 84th Brigade were Musarde Farm, Tuilerie Farm and then Cote de Chatillon. The ultimate objective of the 83rd Brigade was to sever the road between St. Georges and Landres-et-St. Georges. The 165th and 166th Regiments were going into the teeth of the German defenses across relatively open ground. The 84th Brigade was to start their assault three hours before that of the 83rd Brigade so that required regimental alignment could be maintained.

14 October. American artillery began bombarding key German positions at 0330. Fire was concentrated on strong points such as Cote de Chatillon and the immediate front line. There was a shortage of ammunition so the preparatory bombardment was far less intense as that which preceded the St. Mihiel Offensive. The 3rd Battalion went over the top at 0830, companies I and M in the advance with companies K and L in immediate support.

Corporal Hogan participated in the assault and gave this account:

> Companies I and M led off. They were in the fight from the first jump out of the trenches, some Germans in their anxiety to make an impression coming part way to meet them. We could plainly see the companies ahead. Their taut lines were meeting a very bad situation from the start and meeting it well. The Shamrock was off to take and pass its objectives.
> Even though the wood was very thick, the doughboys had their eyes opened, and many a beautiful individual fight developed unawares for the German doing execution from what he thought was safe hiding. Every bad tangle was a

machine gun nest, and every tree was a turret. I saw men in front jump head on into what appeared to be pathless thickets, and disappear, head and shoulders below ground. Later, they would emerge, their bayonets clotted with red.

A stinging fire, from all angles, was pouring over the rough field of action on us. The whole front was a series of individual actions and short range duels. The pace slackened a little, and companies L and K caught up. The Germans dropped a powerful barrage behind us, to cut us off, and their snipers in the high trees devoted to companies L and K, as offering fair targets in a safe field. Our casualties lessened somewhat when we reached the front line of fighting....

The fighting reached its highest possible point about eleven o'clock that morning, and hung at this point all day. Each man was putting into the fight all of his strength, all of his skill as a marksman, all of his acuteness of vision, and all that he had learned against men in cover.

The paths that led to the enemy machine gun nests were almost unthinkably bad, yet they were rushed, front on, again and again and again. Despite the intensity of our barrage, hundreds of these hidden forts, which vomited their endless streams of lead, were left ready to stop us. These were taken one at a time, in headlong charge, by encircling, by being stumbled upon accidentally, fallen into, and captured after silent arguments with blood dripping bayonets.

Our men fell everywhere along the line. They would break out before a thicket, and far ahead the rat-a-tat would sing and a man would lie clawing frenziedly at stones and tangled roots. They would straighten up and run forward toward a suspicious thicket, when crack! crack! from some tree ahead, and the doughboys would move forward, leaving some of their number in death convulsions on the ground and others sorely wounded. But sooner or later they got the man in the tree for full payment, and sooner or later they got the hidden machine gun men. They kept on until they got their price for the comrades they lost; and they kept on....

Between twelve and one o'clock we reached our objective, clothes torn, tongues hanging out, bathed in sweat, shin-sore and foot -sore. It was a small town and semi-clearing in the forest. Here the line paused for a breath, but it went on later and lived up to the Shamrock's record. However, it was from this general line that the 1st Battalion later took up the work.[26]

The 3rd Battalion continued to move ahead but at an increasingly slower rate as its casualties mounted. Corporal Hogan was seriously wounded in the left hand during the early afternoon. The German barrage prevented his retirement to the dressing station until after dark.

Hogan's index finger was shot away and the rest of his hand badly mangled. He recovered from his wound after three weeks in the hospital and then was assigned to limited duty. Shortly thereafter, Hogan was sent home. He was discharged from the army in January 1919 but participated in the homecoming parade.

Lt. Colonel Donovan was at the front and had overall command of the attacking units. Colonel Mitchell and Captain Merle-Smith (the regiment's operations officer) were in the command post at Exermont. By 1430, the 3rd Battalion had reached slopes under the German wire. Rowley and Walsh, commanders of companies I and M, were seriously wounded and out of action. The same was true for the back-up officers. Companies K and L had also suffered serious losses. In Donovan's opinion, the Third Battalion was used up and unable to push through the German wire. Donovan requested a 90 minute artillery barrage to facilitate relief of the 3rd by the 1st Battalion (Kelly). The operation was completed with considerable loss to both units.

In the late afternoon, the 1st Battalion advanced against the German positions using infiltration procedures. Kelly's men reached the Boche wire, but could not get through. The only passageway leading to the road was covered by machine guns. The attackers fell back a short distance from the edge of the wire. A number of their comrades were left hanging on the enemy wire. Major Kelly was ordered to hold his advanced position with companies A and C. They were to be jump-off sites for the next day's assault. Donovan established his command post on the reverse slope of a hill near Kelly's men.

The situation on the night of 14-15 October was as follows. The 168th Infantry had broken into the Kriemhilde Stellung and was threatening Hill 242. The Alabamas had advanced toward Musarde and Tuillerie Farms, both the strong points were still in German hands. The 165th, in spite of murderous fire from Cote de Chatillon, had driven the Boche from their advanced positions into the main line of the Kriemhilde Stellung while the Ohios had advanced beyond Sommerance.

The New Yorkers and part of the 167th Infantry were in a precarious situation. They were in exposed positions in front of Cote de Chatillon.

15 October. Orders were issued to continue the attack. This time the advance of the 83rd Brigade was to be supported by tanks. At 0715, divisional artillery opened up on the German lines. The expected tanks did not show up. Nevertheless, Kelly's men attacked. He quickly realized that his task could not be successful. Enemy fire from his front and Cote de Chatillon was murderous. Every man that reached the German wire was shot down.

Shortly after the advance began, Donovan was hit in the leg, the bullet passing through the bone. He refused to be evacuated and directed the battle from a command post established in a shell hole.

Around 1000, the tanks finally arrived, coming up the road from Sommerance. Things were looking better for the 1st Battalion. The clanking monsters, however, came under accurate artillery fire and a number of tanks were damaged. To the utter disappointment of Kelly's men, the hippos turned about and withdrew.[27]

The Germans counterattacked around 1100 but were driven off. About that time, Donovan realized that Kelly's men had enough. He ordered Anderson, who was near him, to bring the Second Battalion forward.

Kelly refused to retire without a written order from Donovan. The latter wrote the message and left the field in Anderson's hands. The actual relief began at 1200 and was aided by an unexpected barrage by division artillery. The purpose of the bombardment was to support an attack by the 2nd Battalion. That advance, however, had been canceled because of Merle-Smith's protest that Anderson's unit was the regiment's last fresh battalion.

Father Duffy encountered Donovan as he was being carried to a dressing station. He looked up from the stretcher and said with a smile, "Father, you're a disappointed man. You expected to have the pleasure of burying me over here."

"I certainly did, Bill, and you are a lucky dog to get off with nothing more than you've got."[28]

Donovan was in great pain after spending more than five hours in a shell hole with his shattered leg. His spirits were still high and he was confident that with tanks and proper artillery support, the regiment could get through the Kriemhilde Stellung.

It was a stalemate; the regiment was unable to take its final objective. According to Father Duffy, "The most glorious day in the history of our Regiment in the Civil War was Fredericksburg, where the old 69th in the Irish Brigade failed to carry the impregnable position on Marye's Heights, though their dead with the green sprigs in their caps lay in rows before it. Landres-et-St. George is our Fredericksburg and the Kriemhilde Stellung our Marye's Heights."[29]

The Iowans captured Hill 242 and most of Tuilerie Farm but retired from the latter after dark. Patrols from the 167th Infantry probed the wire in front of Cote de Chatillon and found it undamaged by the artillery fire. Except for a small part of its line still in the Bois de Romagne, the Alabamians were out in the open facing the Cote de Chatillon to the east and the line of the Kriemhilde Stellung to their front. On the left, the Ohios were north of Sommerance but also up against the German wire.

Night of 15-16 October. Menoher's staff realized that Cote de Chatillon was the linchpin of the German defenses in the Rainbow's sector. Colonel Hughes, chief of staff of the 42nd Division, described it this way:

> A careful study of the situation showed that the Cote de Chatillon was the key to the whole situation, not only because of its physical characteristics and the position which it occupied, but also because it was very strongly held by the Germans, who apparently after our first attacks had increased its garrison.
>
> The heavy flanking fire from it held up the Alabama regiment and was the main reason why the 83rd Brigade could not successfully break through the German position to its immediate front. It caused the heavy losses, particularly in the New York regiment. Nevertheless, they held on to the position to which they had advanced and from which each of their unsuccessful attacks was made, leaving behind as evidence the bodies of their dead in the German Wire.
>
> When there could no longer be any doubt that only by the capture of the Cote de Chatillon, the apex of the German position, could the Rainbow achieve its objectives, MacArthur asked permission to concentrate on the Cote de Chatillon and that the 151st Minnesota Field Artillery be placed directly under his command for the attack."[30]

During the early evening, generals Drum (Chief of Staff, First Army), Summerall and Menoher plus Colonel MacArthur discussed the tactical situation and then made plans for an attack the next day.

Per Field Order 38, the 83rd Brigade, supported by tanks, was again ordered to capture the road running between St. George and Landres-et-St. Georges. The brigade was to seize both towns and then establish a defensive line well to their north.

The 84th Brigade was to capture Cote de Chatillon and the woods around La Tuillerie Farm. The order emphasized the 83rd Brigade's attack, which was to be supported by an advance of the 82nd Division on its left. The 84th Brigade and the 32nd Division to its right were to exploit resultant German weaknesses on their front.

The Rainbow Division was bogged down and General Summerall was not happy. He visited command posts of some of his units to determine prospects for success on 16 October. He visited Colonel Henry Reilly, 149th Field Artillery, at his command post near Exermont. While there, he read a memorandum sent by Reilly to his brigade commander (67th Field Artillery Brigade). It recommended that the infantry (165th) be withdrawn from their advanced positions before the next attack, so the German line could be effectively bombarded without risk to the troops. It was also suggested that more artillery be used and that it should be concentrated on Cote de Chatillon.

After studying the memorandum, Summerall said good night to Reilly and left the dugout.[31] His next stop was the 165th's PC.

Father Duffy describes the meeting,

> On the evening of the 15th he [Summerall] came to our brigade and made a visit to our PC in Exermont to demand why our final objective had not been taken. He was not well handled, Colonel Mitchell is a good soldier, and one of the finest men in the world, but he is entirely too modest to say a strong word is his own defense. Everybody is familiar with the kind of man who, in spite of the merits of his case, makes a poor figure on the witness stand. Donovan who is an able lawyer and likes the give and take of battle, verbal or otherwise, would have sized up the Corps Commander's mood and would have been planning a new attack with him after the first ten minutes. Captain Merle-Smith stated the facts of the case—the enfilading fire from the Cote de Chatillon, the unbroken wire in our front, the inadequacy of artillery against it on account of lack of air service to register their fire, the failure of the tanks and the extent of our losses. General Summerall was in no mood for argument. He wanted results, no matter how many men were killed, and he went away more dissatisfied than he had come.[32]

General Menoher, per Summerall's order, relieved General Lenihan and Colonel Mitchell. He also sacked Captain Merle-Smith and Lieutenant Betty, the regimental adjutant. Later that night, Colonel Reilly replaced Lenihan. Lieutenant Colonel Charles H. Dravo, the Rainbow Division's senior machine gun officer, relieved Mitchell.

General Menoher asked Colonel MacArthur, then commanding the 84th Brigade (Colonel Brown having been sacked by Pershing on 8 August), whether his troops could take Cote de Chatillon the next day. MacArthur had an aerial photograph showing a passage through the wire fronting the Boche strong point. Nevertheless, MacArthur was not confident that his brigade could seize the position.

When General Summerall visited the 84th Brigade's Command, MacArthur described the strength of the obstacle preventing the advance of his command "as a series of trenches with dugouts and new wire with steel posts. It was strongly manned by both machine guns and infantry. One estimate put the number of machine guns at 200...."

In spite of the challenges, Summerall, as noted earlier, demanded that MacArthur's brigade take Chattilon or die trying.

MacArthur remembered his exact reply, "General Summerall, this brigade assures you that it will capture Cote de Chattilon. If this brigade does not capture Chatilon you can publish a casualty list of the entire brigade with the brigade commander's name at the top."

According to MacArthur, "Tears sprang into General Summerall's eyes. He was evidently so moved he could say nothing. He looked at me for a few seconds and then left without a word."[33]

General Summerall also visited the command post of the 166th Infantry. Apparently, Colonel Hough gave him acceptable reasons for his regiment's failure to seize its objectives. No officers in the command structure of the Ohios were removed. Summerall's blood lust was sated by his visit to Mitchell's PC.

Around 2345, V Corps ordered the 42nd Division to prepare for a German counterattack. The attack was expected along the section of line facing Cote de Maldah and Bois de Romagne. Information on the counterattack came from a German prisoner, who, when questioned, stated that the Germans were planning a large scale assault on V Corps' positions.

Upon receipt of the above order, the 42nd Division's headquarters canceled Field Order 38. The division readied itself for the expected Boche assault.

Henry J. Reilly, graduated from West Point with Douglas MacArthur in 1904. Reilly saw action in the Philippines as a captain of artillery. Charles Summerall, whom Reilly cited for gallantry on a number of occasions, served in his battery. When he returned to the States, Reilly was assigned to West Point as a a history instructor. In his spare time, he contributed military columns to the Chicago Tribune.

When war broke in 1914, Reilly resigned his commission so he could observe the war in France. He served as a volunteer ambulance driver on the Western Front in 1915. That experience gave him a renewed appreciation of the devastating power of artillery. Reilly returned to the States in 1916 and obtained a captaincy in the 1st Illinois Field Artillery. A short while later, he commanded the outfit on the Mexican Border. The 1st was federalized in 1917, becoming the 149th Field Artillery. Reilly, then its colonel began training his gunners for the rigors of modern war.[34] Reilly survived the war and went on to become a military historian of some renown. In 1936, his *Americans All: The Rainbow at War: Official History of the 42nd Division in the World War* was published.

Charles H. Dravo was also a West Point graduate and officer in the regular army before the war. He made an extensive study of Japanese machine gun deployment during the Russo-Japanese War, 1904–1905. Based on that experience, he created a training program for use of the weapon by the American Army. Later, he traveled to Europe to study German machine gun organization and training methods. When the Rainbow went to France, he was its senior machine gun officer. Dravo survived the war, receiving the following awards for service in France: Distinguished Service Medal, Legion of Honor and Croix de Guerre.

16 October. The expected German counterattack did not occur, so MacArthur was once again ordered to assault Cote de Chatillon. Elements of the 168th Infantry attacked Tuilerie Farm at 0530. Twice during the morning, the Iowans seized the site but on each occasion were forced out by the Boche counterattacks. However, at 1030, the 1st Battalion pushed through the farm and reached the crest of Cote de Chatillon. They were subsequently forced off the hill and retreated to its base.

Meanwhile, the Alabamas repulsed a local German counterattack and then pushed through the gap in the German wire known to MacArthur. They advanced through Musarde Farm and to the base of Cote de Chatillon. About 1500, elements of the 167th and 168th regiments overran the Germans on Cote de Chatillon. The Boche strong point was firmly in American hands.

The 165th remained in its position in front of the Kriemhilde Stellung. It did not attack but reorganized its decimated units. The Ohios also reorganized and strengthened their defenses, particularly in the small strip of woods southwest of Sommerance on the right of its sector.

After the capture of the Cote de Chatillon, the Rainbow ceased its attacks on the German positions.

Stand Down

On 17 October, the 84th Brigade took over the division's sector of the front line. The 83rd Brigade went into reserve status. Since General Liggett had ordered a "stand down" for the First Army, there was minimal fighting on the front line.

The troops camped out on the bare hillsides in little pits they dug for themselves. The men were poorly clothed. They were dirty, lousy, thirsty and usually hungry. Many of them were sick.

Colonel D.S. Fairchild, medical officer of the 42nd Division, commented on the condition of the troops,

> During the early days of the division's active campaigning, when the weather was warm and the soldiers were still in good condition both mentally and physically, the number of shock cases was relatively small. It was observed during this period that even those cases in severe shock responded gratifyingly to treatment. Youthful enthusiasm rose to the surface. The men laughingly recounted tales and experiences along the battle line. Furthermore, though recently snatched from the jaws of death, they eagerly inquired how long it would be before they could return to the line.
>
> In striking contrast was the clinical picture presented by the wounded during the closing weeks of the war. Not only were the shock cases greater in number, running from 17 to 20 percent of the severely wounded, but they were far graver in character and reacted very slowly to the most energetic treatment. Worn out by long fighting, with little chance for rest, exposed to the cold with insufficient protection or warmth, constantly wet and insufficiently fed by cold food because of the risk of building fires along the line, the men were at the low water mark of fitness both mentally and physically. Their reserve [was] gone so that the type then exhibited was more profound than that theretofore encountered. Soldiers with only moderate wounds began to arrive at the hospitals in deep shock, from which they often failed to rally under any form of treatment.[35]

The 83rd Brigade relieved the 84th Brigade on 21 October. The New Yorkers heard that an all-out attack was planned for 1 November and hoped to get another crack at the Germans. When orders for the advance were finalized, however, it was decided to use the rested Marine brigade of the 2nd Division instead of the 83rd Brigade as originally planned.

The officers of the 83rd Brigade protested the decision. An angry Colonel

Reilly sent a memo through channels to General Summerall requesting that the order be changed.[36]

> Headquarters 83rd Infantry Brigade
> American Expeditionary Forces
> France
> October 23, 1918
> From: Commanding Officer, 83rd Infantry Brigade
> To: Commanding General, 5th Army Corps, thru channels
> Subject: Attack by the 83rd Inf. Brigade.
>
> I. I hereby request that this Brigade, instead of being relieved by the 2nd Division or any part thereof, be allowed to make the attack now contemplated. The Colonels commanding the 165th and 166th Infantries are of the same opinion as am I, that the attack will be carried through should this permission be granted.
>
> HENRY J. REILLY
> Colonel, U.S.A, 149th F.A.,
> Cmdg. 83Rd Inf. Brigade.

The plan was not changed and on the night of 31 October–1 November a Marine battalion replaced the 3rd Battalion (Thomas Reilley) in the front lines. During the relief, harsh words were exchanged between the two groups of men. Major Reilley's description of the encounter follows:

> The night before the Marines jumped off as they were coming up to replace us I was in the Cote de Chatillon maybe forty yards from the nearest edge of the woods towards the town of Landres et St. Georges. There were wires behind us. We were through the wires, the first thickness anyhow. I heard a noise to the left. As we were supposed to keep quiet so as not to give away the jump-off I went toward the noise. I saw a crowd coming along the lines. They were making invidious remarks about the 42nd Division. They were razzing the outfit.
>
> I went up to them and said, "What in hell is all this noise about?" One fellow spoke up. He mentioned his name: I think it was Olsen. He said he was a major in command of the unit coming in to replace me in the jump-off. I asked him what the hell he meant coming through our lines and saying anything to the outfit. The conversation went back and forth. I got a little hot-headed.
>
> The basis of his argument was that the Marines would show the Rainbow how to get through the wire which had stopped them.
>
> I finally told him that if he made another crack at the outfit there would be a private war right there. It made me angry to have him roasting our outfit when he had not seen what we had been up against while I knew, having been in the middle of it.[37]

Thomas Reilley, a lawyer in civilian life, was a graduate of Columbia and New York universities. An athletic man at six foot three, he was a well known football player in his college days. Reilley survived the war and was awarded the Distinguished Service Cross for heroism in the Argonne Forest. The above incident was not the first, nor last, acidic exchange between the Marines and members of the 165th Infantry.

After their relief, the New Yorkers went into reserve status near Exermont.

While the 83rd Brigade was in the line, General Summerall issued an order, dated 26 October 1918, commending the 84th Infantry Brigade for its seizure of the Cote de Chatillon.

> This Brigade, under the command of Brigadier General Douglas MacArthur, has manifested the highest soldierly qualities and has rendered service of the greatest value during the present operations. With a dash, courage, and a fighting spirit worthy of the best traditions of the American Army, this Brigade carried by assault the strongly fortified Hill 288 on the Kriemhilde Stellung and unceasingly pressed its advance until it had captured the Tuilerie Farm and the Cote de Chatillon, thus placing itself at least a kilometer beyond the enemy's strong line of resistance. During this advance the enemy fought with unusual determination with a first class division and in many cases resorted to hand-to-hand fighting when our troops approached his rear. The conduct of this Brigade has reflected honor upon the Division, the Army and the States from which the Regiments came.[38]

Members of the 83rd Brigade believed that they also deserved credit for seizure of Cote de Chatillon and the Kriemhilde Stellung breakthrough.

In Henry Reilly's opinion,

> The fight of the 83rd Infantry Brigade in this battle is one of the best examples of the fact that ground gained and number of prisoners captured is far from being the rule with which to measure the military importance of a combat. If the 83rd Infantry Brigade and in particular its right regiment, the 165th Infantry, which occupied by far the most dangerous position of any regiment of infantry on any part of the whole Argonne front at this time, had not advanced to the immediate front of the main German position and had not desperately hung on there, the subsequent operations might have been in favor of the Germans.
>
> As long as the Brigade hung on they were a threat to the Germans in their immediate front with the result that the enemy's infantry and artillery could not come to the aid of the defenders of the Cote de Chatillon. Also the position of the 165th Infantry was such that the defenders of this hill could not ignore them in order to concentrate, first, on the Alabama Regiment alone, and later when the 168th Infantry had captured Hill 288 on that regiment as well as the Alabama one when their combined attack first threatened and then successfully carried the Cote de Chatillon.[39]

The heroic exploits of the 165th Infantry did not go entirely unnoticed. Three men of the Rainbow Division were awarded the Congressional Medal of Honor for valor during the Argonne Offensive. Two of them were members of the New York Regiment and the third was from the 167th. Citations for the 69th men follow:

October 14, 1918
Michael Donaldson
Sergeant, 165th U.S. Infantry, 69th New York

> The advance of his regiment having been checked by intense machine gun fire of the enemy, who were entrenched on the crest of a hill before Landres-St. Georges, his company retired to a sunken road to reorganize their position, leaving several of their number wounded near the enemy lines. Of his own volition, in broad daylight and under direct observation of the enemy and with utter disregard for his own safety, he advanced to the crest of the hill, rescued

one of his wounded comrades, and returned under withering fire to his own lines, repeating his splendidly heroic act until he had brought in all the men, six in number.[40]

October 15, 1918
William J. Donovan
Colonel, 165th U.S. Infantry, 69th New York

Colonel Donovan personally led the assaulting wave in an attack upon a very strongly organized position, and when our troops were suffering heavy casualties he encouraged all near him by his example, moving among his men in exposed positions, reorganizing decimated platoons, and accompanying them forward in attacks. When he was wounded in the leg by a machine gun bullet, he refused to be evacuated and continued with his unit until it withdrew to a less exposed position. [41]

During the lull in the fighting, Father Duffy had a chance to get some rest behind the lines in Esperance Farm. Unfortunately, his sleep at night was usually disturbed by the Boche:

Shell fire does not come back this far except occasionally, but the nights are often made hideous by enemy bombing planes. Aeroplanes carrying machine guns are futile things, but a plane at night dropping bombs is absolutely the most demoralizing thing in war. It is a matter of psychology. The man in front discharging his rifle has the hunter's exhilaration. Even shells can be dodged if not too numerous, and after a man has dropped on his face or jumped into a doorway and has escaped, that is the satisfaction that a hare must have when it eludes the dogs and pants contentedly in its hole. But when one lies at night and hears the deep buzz of a plane overhead, and most especially when the buzz ceases and he knows that the plane is gliding and making ready to drop something, the one feeling that comes is that if that fellow overhead pulls the lever at the right spot, a very, very wrong spot, it means sudden and absolute destruction. There is no way of getting away from it. One simply lies and cowers.[42]

This bloody chapter in the history of the 165th Infantry will be concluded with two amusing incidents reported by Father Duffy.

I got this story with no names mentioned and was too discreet to ask for them. A patrol was out for the purpose of getting in touch with the enemy. As they were ascending the reverse slope of a hill a young officer who was with two or three men in advance came running back, stooping low and calling breathlessly to the Lieutenant in command, "The Germans! The Germans! The Germans are there!" Nobody thought him afraid but his tone of excitement was certainly bad for morale. There was a sudden halt and a bad moment, but the situation was saved when a New York voice in a gruff whisper was heard, "Well, what the hell does that guy think we are out here looking for?—Violets?"[43]

We were short of officers during the Argonne fight and, since advancing under shell fire necessitates a deliberate scattering of men, a great deal depends upon the efficiency of our non-coms especially the sergeants. The result of their activity was that an extraordinary number of them were wounded. I came on Sergeants Tom O'Malley and Jim O'Brien of Company D, both wounded severely and bound for the rear.

"Tom," I said, "what did you want to get yourself hit for? We're short of officers as it is, and it's only men like you that can put this thing through."

"Well, Father," says Tom smilingly apologetic, "you see it's like this: a sergeant stands an awful fine chance of gettin' hit as things are goin now. We got a lot of new min that he's got to take care of to see that they don't get kilt; and whin the line moves forward, there's some of thim nades a bit a coaxin."[44]

During the time frame 5 October to 1 November, the regiment sustained 1,209 casualties, 200 killed and 1009 wounded. Seventy of the wounded subsequently died. Total casualties were then 3,535 men. Assuming zero replacements, the 165th had lost over 98 percent of its original strength of 3,600 men.

Breakthrough, 1 November

General Liggett ordered a full scale attack for 1 November. His troops were rested, supplies were plentiful and transportation problems were under control. In addition, the weather had improved significantly.

Liggett lined up seven divisions for the assault. The battle plan called for a straight ahead thrust by V Corps to capture Barricourt Ridge, then a westward push to flank Bois de Bourgogne, followed by linkage with the Fourth French Army near Boult-aux-Bois.

A few days before the attack, Liggett had the eastern edge of the Bois de Bourgogne saturated with mustard gas. Nine of 12 hidden German batteries were eventually put out of action.

At 0330 on 1 November, a tremendous artillery barrage plastered key German positions on the front between the Bois and Dun Sur Meuse. At 0530, the largest American Army ever deployed up to that date went over the top.

This time things went right and the attack was successful nearly everywhere. The next day, the Americans continued to make significant gains. By dusk on 3 November, elements of the 2nd Division were at Bois de Belval. By 4 November, elements of the American Army had crossed the Meuse River and by 5 November the First Army was running off the maps at headquarters.

Unjustified Sacking of Colonel Mitchell

The relief of Colonel Mitchell by Major General Summerall on the night of 15-16 October was an impulsive and unjustified act. Mitchell's sacking was also an insult to the hitherto unblemished and outstanding fighting record of the 165th Infantry. The tactical situation on that night was as follows:

After two days of hard fighting, the 165th Infantry had failed to breach the Kriemhilde Stellung and seize its objectives, the villages of St. George and Landres-et-St. Georges, plus the road between the two sites. The road ran parallel to the section of Kriemhilde Stellung in that area and was about a mile distant from the German lines.

The regiment's 2nd Battalion was hunkered down, out in the open, at the edge of the wire fronting the Kriemhilde Stellung. The 1st and 3rd battalions were well below half strength after suffering heavy casualties in a series of valor-

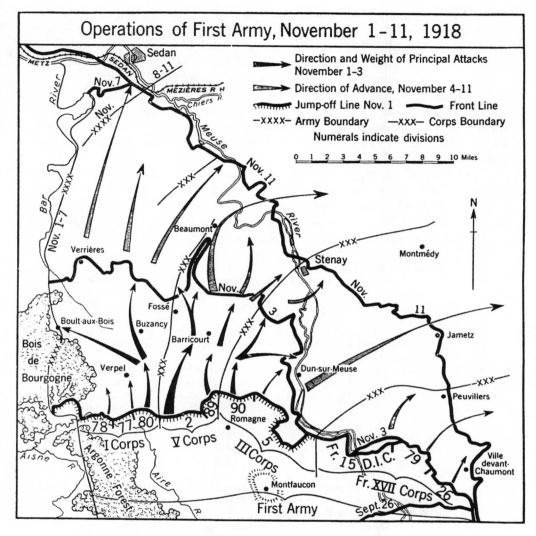

Meuse-Argonne plan of attack, 1 November 1918 (from Official Sources).

ous but futile attacks on the Boche lines. Corpses of their comrades hung on the German wire.

2nd Battalion patrols reported the barriers in front of the German positions were still in place. Division artillery, after two days of fighting, had failed to break up the enemy's extensive field of barbed wire.

Tank support had been quickly neutralized by German artillery.

Other factors that must be considered in evaluating the situation on the night of 15-16 October were:

The regiment's best combat officer, Lieutenant Colonel Donovan, was seriously wounded on 15 October, and out of action.

Colonel Mitchell was the fourth commander of the 165th since it arrived in

France. He was made colonel following the Battle of the Ourcq. At the time of his "canning," he had directed the regiment for slightly more than 50 days. By comparison, the other three regiments in the Rainbow Division were still led by their original colonel or lt. colonel; Screws (167th), Hough (166th) and Tinley (168th). General Summerall needed a scapegoat for the failed attacks and Mitchell was his man.

Everyone realized an armistice was in the works. Battalion and regimental officers were reluctant to hurl their infantry against German strong points in the forlorn hope that sheer weight of numbers would overwhelm enemy machine gun nests.

The last point is supported by a letter from Lloyd R. Ross to Henry J. Reilly in the summer of 1935. Ross served as a major in the Iowa Regiment and was considered a first class combat officer. He summed up the lessons learned by the Rainbow Division. The following paragraphs in his letter are directly applicable to the situation on the Kriemhilde Stellung front.

> There also existed all through the chain of command an ever present tendency to rush troops forward and keep pushing them against enemy machine guns without adequate support from machine guns, howitzers, and artillery. General officers (ie Summerall) and field officers were the guilty ones in this respect. They generally, had never commanded troops in large bodies and against a first class well armed enemy. Many of them employed the same driving tactics they used in smaller commands in the Philippine Islands and in other similar campaigns.
>
> They would not take the word of the officer in the front lines as to the opposing forces and weapons but kept driving troops forward inadequately supported by artillery. Along the Ourcq there were outstanding examples of this sort of thing. The artillery of the 26th Division was there but was not used to its full capacity. Men were constantly driven against machine guns well placed with ample ammunition and with orders to hold the Yankees back. Finally it dawned upon the General Officers they were sacrificing their infantry. Then they massed enough artillery to blow the machine guns loose and the way was cleared.
>
> Had artillery been turned loose on those positions the first day our infantry would have just walked over Hill 212 and the Germans would never have been able to organize along their next line.
>
> The same mistake was made in the Argonne, except the infantry had become wise to the game. We officers in command had determined that when stubborn resistance was met we would not sacrifice men against material but take our time and gain our ends in other ways. We moved more slowly perhaps but more surely and had more men alive at the end of the action. We attained our objectives but without enough artillery in support.
>
> Then a halt was called from October 18th until November 2nd. During that time there was brought in all of the available artillery. Large quantities of artillery ammunition was placed at the guns. All of it was turned loose on November 1st. Result, the Germans abandoned the positions leaving their artillery in position and retired to the Meuse. Of course the 2nd Division and the 89th Division had a walk through.[45]

There is no doubt that General Summerall was a ruthless, hard-bitten commander. He commanded the 1st Division during the Battle of Soissons. After three days of vicious fighting, the division had suffered more than 7,300 casualties.

When asked by a staff officer whether his division was capable of another attack, he was reputed to have said, "Sir, when the 1st Division has only two men left they will be echeloned in depth and attacking toward Berlin."[46]

One wonders whether Summerall would be leading those last two men.

It is likely that General Summerall wanted the 165th Infantry to continue its attacks against the German lines with the artillery and tanks at hand. It is equally probable that Colonel Mitchell and his staff were less than optimistic about their chances for success. Summerall wanted Mitchell to sacrifice his command so that V Corps and Summerall would continue to perform well in the eyes of General Pershing.

After the capture of Cote de Chatillon, there were no further attacks on the Kriemhilde Stellung until 1 November 1918. During that period of time the amount of artillery in the area was nearly doubled. Target areas were continuously shelled and doused with gas.

When the 2nd Division attacked the Kriemhilde Stellung on 1 November, it was a walkover. With the Cote de Chatillon in American hands and adequate artillery, Colonel Mitchell's regiment could have captured its objective on 16 October.

Finally, it is interesting to note that three of the four sacked officers were almost immediately reassigned. Brigadier General Lenihan reported to General Hunter Liggett, who shortly afterwards put him in command of a brigade in the 77th Division. Captain Merle-Smith returned to the regiment before the 1 November offensive and was given command of the 1st Battalion. Lieutenant Betty was also quickly returned to duty. Colonel Mitchell remained with the Regiment for a while and was then reassigned prior to the Armistice on 11 November 1918.

The regiment suffered 1,089 casualties during the period 5 to 19 October, including 185 killed and 904 men wounded. Almost all of those losses occurred during the attacks of 14 and 15 October. Assuming a strength of about 3,000 riflemen, Colonel Mitchell lost more than 36 percent of his command attacking Landres-et-St. Georges. Corresponding percentages for the 166th, 167th and 168th infantries during the same time frame were 16, 23 and 26 respectively. Obviously, the 165th, under Mitchell's leadership, had done its fair share of the fighting in front of the Kriemhilde Stellung.

Elton E. Mackin, in his memoirs *Suddenly We Didn't Want to Die*, provides a pertinent remembrance of Summerall via his address to members of the Marine brigade prior to their attack on 1 November:

> An army general came on a beautiful black horse and lectured us; telling combat men about the lay of the land ahead; telling men about a job to do along a route he'd mapped to reach the Meuse.
>
> He talked bare headed, his two starred helmet hanging from a saddle tie, his gloves tucked neatly in his Sam Browne belt. His riding crop, like his horse, was big and black and strong. He aimed it like a pointer, stressing things he wanted done, or slapped his boot leg to make a point. We gave him our full attention. He did not mince words. He made us understand,
>
> "You are the troops who taught the world how to take machine guns...."
>
> Men sneered sideways under the brims of old tin hats and muttered low beneath their breath. They understood.

"Before you there are twenty kilometers of machine guns. Go get them....
You'll bypass Landres-et-St. Georges. Keep outta there and never mind the goddamn souvenirs. Keep away from it because we're going to smother it with
gas....

"Now on those ridges, all your officers may be down, but you keep going,"
said the general. "I want to sit back in my headquarters and hear you carried
all your objectives on time....

"And I repeat, on those first ridges, go forward while you can still crawl. Top
that third ridge and settle down to keep all of those guns from being moved.
Do it with rifle fire if you have nothing else—you will be close to them."

And then he delivered his final punch, his closing line.

"And now I say, and you remember this. On those ridges, take no prisoners,
nor stop to bandage your best friend...."

For a while there was total silence. He studied us. We studied him. Finally, he
raised his arm in something of a salute. His riding crop made an arc against
the sky, a half waved gesture of good luck, farewell. The black horse turned to
trot away along a forest trail.

"Bastard!" a scarred buck sergeant said, talking half to himself, "Bastard, and
he's gonna sit and watch our progress on a map, says he. An' where will we
poor sonsabitches be? What in hell'd he call that place? Kriemhilde Stellung?
Him an' his three ridges. The bastard."[47]

CHAPTER 18

Race for Sedan

Sedan was a major target of the Franco-American Meuse-Argonne Offensive, since it straddled the key Metz-Sedan-Mezieres Railroad. The city was also important to the French because it was the site of a humiliating defeat by the Germans during the Franco Prussian War. For those reasons, it was targeted by the Fourth French Army.

General Pershing wanted the American First Army to have the honor of capturing Sedan. On 3 November, he met with the commanding officer of the Fourth Army, who surprisingly consented to American seizure of the city, if First Army got there first.

Pershing ordered his troops to seize the plum on the Meuse River. He instructed the I and V Corps to work together toward that end. He stated that boundaries were not to be considered binding. By this comment, Pershing meant the interface between French and American forces and not the flanks between the I and V Corps.

On 6 November, General Summerall ordered the 1st Division to capture Sedan. The division was his favorite and he wanted it to have the honor of seizing the prize. Accordingly, the 16th Infantry, in the midst of a very dark night moved across sectors assigned to the 77th and 42nd divisions. The result was chaos. American troops ended up shooting at each other. Douglas MacArthur, then commanding officer of the Rainbow Division's 84th Brigade, was captured and held as a German spy. The First Army was in considerable disarray and fortunate that the Germans didn't take advantage of its plight.

The French Fourth was then moving rapidly toward Sedan. Its command was confused by the irrational movement of the U.S. Divisions on its right flank. General Liggett was embarrassed. The commanding officer of I Corps, General Dickman, was furious that the 1st Division had moved into the 77th's area and disrupted his communications.

Liggett demanded an explanation for 1st Division's bizarre movements. Summerall cited Pershing's comment, "Boundaries will not be considered binding." Liggett and Dickman found Summerall's explanation unsatisfactory. Dickman wanted Summerall and the 1st Division's commander court martialed.[1]

Pershing and Liggett decided to let the incident drop. The 1st Division and

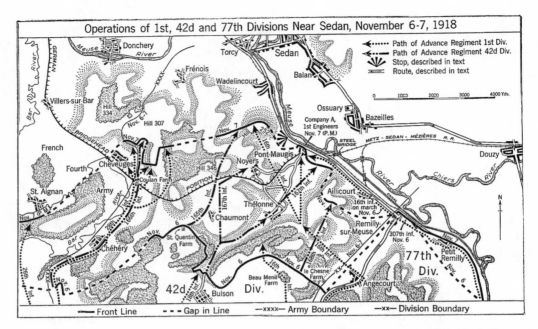

Operations of the 1st, 42nd and 77th divisions near Sedan, 6 and 7 November 1918 (from Official Sources).

Summerall were Pershing's favorites. If a National Guard division, such as the 42nd Division, had committed a similar blunder, heads would have rolled. Such an incident would have confirmed Pershing's low opinion of the "goddamn militiamen."[2] It is ironic that Summerall was spared. Pershing had canned a corps commander and three division commanders while Summerall sacked the 83rd Brigade commander and the colonel of the 165th Infantry for less obvious failings a few weeks earlier in the heat of the Meuse-Argonne Campaign.

Within two weeks of the above affair, General Pershing praised the 1st Division and its commander in American Expeditionary Force general orders. During the entire war, no other American division received such a citation.[3]

42nd Division Advances to Sedan

In early November, General Menoher was given command of the newly formed VI Corps. MacArthur assumed command of the Rainbow Division and Colonel Screws took his place as commander of the 84th Brigade.

Even though the Rainbow Division was in a jaded condition, it began its advance on 5 November with great enthusiasm. German rear guard units were brushed aside as the division began its movement in the general direction of Sedan. At 1700 on 6 November, the 165th and 167th Infantries passed the village of Thelonne and reached the Meuse River heights overlooking Sedan. On 6 November, elements of the 42nd Division were threatening Sedan. The New Yorkers seized two important German positions at the point of the bayonet on the morning of 7 November. That afternoon, a patrol of the 165th Infantry pushed into the town of Wadelincourt on the south bank of the Meuse across from Sedan.[4]

The high command decided to let the French Army capture Sedan, so the Rainbow Division eased its pursuit of the retreating Germans. The division had advanced 21½ kilometers in 29 hours.[5]

The Rainbow was relieved by the 77th Division on 10 November. The next day, the armistice was signed. In the race to Sedan, the division suffered 390 casualties; killed—83, and wounded—307 men (23 men subsequently died of their wounds).[6] Total wartime casualties for the 42nd Division were 14,586 men, approximately 54 percent of an average strength of 27,000 men. The Rainbow Division lost 37 men as prisoners during the Argonne Offensive. None were captured during the race to Sedan.

165th Infantry Reaches the Meuse

The 42nd relieved the 78th Division in the vicinity of Les Petites Armoises on 5 November. Except for new underwear and overcoats, the New Yorkers and the rest of the Rainbow were in the same ragged clothing worn in the Argonne Forest.

The 42nd Division moved out around noon. The regiments were aligned as usual, 168th, 167th, 165th, and 166th Infantries from right to left.

The regiment moved northward against weak German resistance. On 7 November, however, the 2nd Battalion (Bootz), which was in the lead, encountered determined German resistance at Hill 346, about a mile north of Chaumont.

Captain Bootz worked his battalion close to the German strong point. He then ordered platoons of Company G and H to take the hill via a bayonet charge. Father Duffy recorded, "With a great cheer our fellows swarmed up the crest and the daunted Germans, after a futile stand, grounded their arms, threw up their hands and surrendered."[7]

The 2nd Battalion suffered a significant number of killed and wounded in the assault. They were unfortunate losses since the armistice was only four days away.

After his Battalion captured Hill 346, Bootz saw khaki clad troops approaching his prize from flank and rear. He realized that the approaching American troops were not from his division. They were men of the 16th Infantry, 1st Division troops, who because of Summerall's misinterpretation of Pershing's orders for the capture of Sedan, blundered into the Rainbow's sector. Elements of the 16th Infantry came up the hill and claimed it as theirs. Bootz was not impressed, "This is my hill, and my line of advance. If you say its yours, show your booty. I have twenty five prisoners and twelve machine guns: What have you got to show for it ?"[8]

Bootz retained control of the hill. He informed Major Reilley that he was almost out of ammunition. Reilley's men moved through the 2nd Battalion. They then assaulted Hill 252, which was also carried at bayonet point. German machine gunners were cut down as they fired their weapons.

The Meuse river was in plain sight from the crest of Hill 252. Reilley sent a patrol to Wadelincourt, a village on the south shore of the river. The patrol was to seize the village, hold it and identify potential crossing sites.

Wadelincourt was strongly held; Major Reilley decided to wait until morning before he attacked the village. During the night, the Germans shelled his positions on Hill 252 from gun emplacements across the Meuse.[9]

The Allied high command decided the French were to capture Sedan. Accordingly, elements of the French 40th Division relieved the New Yorkers in their dugouts on Hills 346 and 252.

The French commander, as a matter of courtesy, invited a company from the 165th and 166th Regiments to enter Sedan with his troops. Company D was selected for the honor but through a screw up in orders, never participated in the ceremony.

On 8 November, the regiment marched back to Artaise, the next day to Les Petites Armoises, on the 10th to Vaux and by the 11th it was in Sirvy-les-Buzancy.

The regiment spent two days in Sivry-les-Buzancy and then moved on to Landres-et-St. Georges. The men of the regiment heard rumors of an armistice but discounted them. The village, which the New Yorkers had tried so hard to capture, was in ruins. The troops pitched their tents on hills surrounding the town. That night, official word of an armistice was received. Men raided munition stores for rockets of every kind. Later that night, the sky was filled with thousands of flares and signal lights. The hillsides around Landres-et-St. George were ablaze with bonfires. *Finie la guerre.* The war was over.

Father Duffy's feelings were mixed:

> My duties, like my feelings, still lay in the past with men from all companies. I went around the battlefield to pay, as far as I could, my last duties to the dead, to record and in a rough way to beautify their lonely graves, for I knew that soon we leave this place that their presence hallows, and never look upon it again.
>
> On the 15 November, in accordance with Division orders, a formal muster was held. Our strength was 55 officers and 1,637 men, with 8 officers and 43 men attached, 1,300 short of the number we had brought into the Argonne. Of the survivors, not many more than 600 were men who had left New York with the Regiment a little over a year ago. And most of these belonged to the Adjutant's office, Battalion and Company Headquarters, Kitchens, Band and Supply Company. In the line companies, there are about twenty-five riflemen to each company who are old timers and nearly all of these have wound stripes earned in earlier engagements. The great bulk of the old Regiment is in hospitals, convalescent and casual camps; some of them promoted, some transferred, hundreds of them invalided home, a great many, alas! buried on battlefields or in hospital cemeteries.[10]

CHAPTER 19

Armistice

On 8 November in a railway car in Compiegne Forest, Marshal Foch, and Sir Rosslyn Wemyss representing Allied armies and navies respectively, began meetings with representatives of the German government to negotiate a cease fire. Terms for the armistice were very harsh. Foch refused to grant a provisional truce. The war would go on until Germany agreed to Allied conditions. Foch eventually gave the German delegation 72 hours in which to accept or reject the armistice terms. The deadline was 1100 on 11 November.

Everyone knew of the pending cease fire, but the war went on. French forces on the flanks of the American armies all but stopped fighting until the armistice was settled one way or the other.

Foch was advised that the Germans accepted the Allied terms on 10 November. The document was signed by all parties around 0510 the next day. First and Second army headquarters were informed by 0630 that a cease fire would begin at 1100 that day. Nevertheless, the American Expeditionary Force continued operations, some units went over the top and took casualties right up until 1100. It was a shocking disregard for human life and prompted a Congressional investigation after the war.[1]

Pershing was annoyed with the French because their high ranking officials never said one word of thanks for all the American Expeditionary Force had done. He told General Haig that he would never forget "the bad treatment which they had received from the French and that it was difficult to exaggerate the feeling of dislike for the French which existed in the American Army."[2]

General Pershing rejected Foch's order for American units to assist in the rehabilitation of France by filling in trenches, rolling up barbed wire and reconstructing roads. The American general stated that "It would be unjust, and even criminal ... to use our soldiers as laborers."[3]

Paris Victory Parade

The Paris Victory Parade of 14 July 1919 was considered by many to be the greatest martial review of all time. The spectacle started on a pathetic note with a solemn procession of one thousand badly wounded veterans. The unfortunate group of ex-soldiers included blind, lame and mutilated men.

Then came the military pageantry. Foch and Joffre, carrying their marshals' batons and accompanied by a small escort, led the parade. They were followed by 1,500-man contingents representing each of the Allied nations. Units paraded in alphabetical order, Americans, Belgians, British, Czechs, Greeks, Italians, Japanese, Portuguese, Rumanians, Serbs and Poles. The French contingent, representing the host nation, was last.

Pershing, a magnificent figure on horseback, led the Americans. An officer rode behind the general carrying a large silk flag with a blue field studded with four gold stars. General Harboard, American Expeditionary Force Chief of Staff, cantered behind Pershing's flag. Ten yards farther back and riding abreast, came Pershing's three aides; Marshall, John G. Quekenmeyer and John T. Hughes. Next rode Henry T. Allen, the commander of the American troops still in Europe, and John L. Hines, who much later would succeed Pershing as army chief of staff. Then, riding eight abreast at ten yard intervals were four lines of American Expeditionary Force generals, thirty in all. The American Expeditionary Force band, "Pershing's Own," led the Composite Regiment. The latter unit consisted of a select group of officers and enlisted men, all over six feet in height, who were chosen from the best American outfits in Europe. The Composite Regiment carried ninety or more American and regimental flags. Apparently, the unit was a blaze of brilliant color.

The parade passed up the Avenue de la Grand Armee, through the Arc de Triomphe, down the Champs Elysees, by the Place de la Concorde, to the Boulevards and the Place de la Republique. The seven mile route was lined by an enthusiastic crowd of over two million that cheered the passing units.[4]

Following the parade, after the survivors of the greatest war the world had then known had received their much deserved adulation, it was time to honor the dead. A long line of French citizens walked in single file through the Arc de Triomphe and by the casket of the unknown soldier. Most of the mourners dropped single flowers on the coffin of the soldier, whose ghastly remains represented those unlucky ones who had not survived the holocaust. Throughout the summer afternoon, the somber line passed by the coffin. Later that night, the flower-draped sarcophagus stood alone in the silent darkness. To some, that was the most unforgettable site of the day.[5]

Occupation of Germany

The Third Army, with a strength of about 260,000 men, was activated on 7 November 1918 at Ligny-en-Pavois under Major General Dickman. The Rainbow along with the 1st, 2nd, 4th, 32nd, 89th and 90th Divisions was assigned to the Third Army. Its mission was to serve as the American of Occupation. Pershing eventually became dissatisfied with him and he was replaced by General Liggett.

Third Army ceased to exist after the Treaty of Versailles was signed on 2 July 1919. It was thereafter known as American Forces in Germany, until withdrawn in January 1923.

The Composite Regiment (courtesy of U.S. Army Military Institute).

42nd Division in Germany

The 42nd Division was stationed in the Kreis of Ahrweiler Sector from 15 December to 2 April 1919. The unit was then on the extreme left flank of the Army of Occupation.

The Rainbow began its journey of over 250 kilometers to Germany in mid–November. On Thanksgiving Day, the Division was in Luxembourg and on 2 December, crossed the Rhine into Germany. The Rainbow was the first American Expeditionary Force division to enter the Fatherland. The trek in Germany was made in miserable weather on bad roads. In spite of difficulties, the hike was performed in a fine manner, with individual units marching in close-knit, solid columns.[6]

While in Germany, the Rainbow's organization underwent a number of important changes. Major General Clement Flagler relieved MacArthur on 21 November 1917. The latter returned to the 84th Brigade while Screws resumed command of the 167th Infantry. Reilly was replaced by General Frank Caldwell. Colonel Reilly resumed command of the 149th Field Artillery. Lt. Colonel Dravo's well deserved promotion was put on hold and command of the 165th Infantry went to Colonel Charles Howland.[7]

Flagler, a regular, commanded 5th Division brigade and III Corps artillery during the St. Mihiel and Meuse-Argonne Offensives respectively. Howland, also a regular officer, previously led the 86th Division's 172nd Infantry Brigade. His outfit arrived in France near war's end and had seen minimal combat. Understandably, the New Yorkers did not hold Howland in high regard.[8]

Somewhat later, Flagler left the Rainbow to become Chief, Army Engineer School. Brigadier General George Gately, 67th Field Artillery Brigade, was his replacement. Surprisingly, MacArthur, who had commanded the Division for a short time under combat conditions, was passed over. It is probable that Pershing hadn't forgiven MacArthurs's earlier machinations which helped prevent the Rainbow's designation as a replacement division.[9]

General Menoher recommended MacArthur for the Congressional Medal of Honor. The latter had earned two Distinguished Service Crosses, seven Silver Stars and two wound stripes in France. Many Rainbow veterans believed MacArthur deserved the award and that once again Pershing's Chaumont Circle was paying him off for past politicking on behalf of the Rainbow.[10]

The Rainbow's distinctive shoulder patch, three equal arcs of red, yellow and blue, was approved on 29 October 1918. The badges, however, were not issued to the 42nd until after the Armistice. Patches provided by the Government during the occupation were too large to be smartly displayed on the soldiers' uniforms. In spite of the usual griping, the American Expeditionary Force refused to replace the oversized items with correctly manufactured patches. Enterprising veterans solved the problem. Cheaper and much sharper embroidered patches were obtained from a local German firm.[11]

On 16 March, the Rainbow was reviewed by Pershing and the commander in chief of the American Army of Occupation. Soon thereafter, elements of the 42nd began to leave for the United States. The last unit, the 117th Kansas Ammunition Train, arrived home on 1 May 1919. The 83rd Brigade was demobilized on 5 May at Camp Upton.

Each Rainbow veteran received a new uniform, pair of shoes and $60 from the government to ease his return to civilian life.

165th Infantry in Germany

The Fighting Sixty-Ninth began its march to Germany on 16 November 1918. The regiment crossed into Belgium at the Village of Fagny on 21 November. At that time, Colonel Reilly had been superseded by Brigadier General Caldwell. The regiment crossed the southern tip of Belgium and entered Luxemburg late the next day. The New Yorkers rested in Luxemburg until 1 December. On 3 December, the 165th Infantry crossed the Sauer River entering Germany at the Village of Bollendorf. Father Duffy recounted,

> The column came down along the river, the band in front playing, "The Yanks are Coming" and as we turned to cross the bridge, the lively Regimental tune of "Garry Owen." In front of us, above the German hill, there was a beautiful rainbow. As we marched triumphantly onto German soil, nothing more hostile greeted us than the click of a moving picture camera....
> The greatest surprise of our first week in Germany was the attitude of the

people towards us. We had expected to be in for an unpleasant experience.... We were received very peacefully, one might almost say cordially. Farmers in the fields would go out of the way to put us on the right road, children in the villages were as friendly and curious as youngsters at home; the women lent their utensils and often helped soldiers with their cooking, even offering stuff from their small stores when the hungry men arrived far ahead of their kitchens....

As for us, we are here in the role of victors, and our soldiers are willing to go half way and accept that for them also (unless somebody wants to start something) the war is a past issue....

Civilians hold grudges, but soldiers do not; at least the soldiers who do the actual fighting.... We fought the Germans two long tricks in the trenches and in five pitched battles and they never did anything to us that we did not try to do to them....

At any rate we were convinced from the beginning that our experiences as part of the Army of Occupation were not going to be as unpleasant as we expected.[12]

The regiment reached Remagen on the Rhine River by 15 December. The 165th spent the winter months of 1918-1919 comfortably billeted in the river city. During that period of time, Lieutenant Colonel Donovan and Major Hurley, still recovering from their wounds, returned to the regiment.

When Father Duffy celebrated midnight mass in Remagen's large parish church, he reminisced about past Christmases, "Christmas Mass on the Rhine! In 1916, our midnight mass was under the open sky along the Rio Grande; in 1917, in the old medieval church at Grand on the Vosges and now, thank Heaven, in this year of grace, 1918, we celebrated it peacefully and triumphantly in the country with which we had been at war."[13]

During the winter months the men were kept busy during the day in field training, infantry drill, range practice and athletics. Attention was paid to soldierly bearing and courtesy. After the armistice, the American Expeditionary Force made a determined effort to teach the many illiterate men in its ranks to read and write. The 165th had at least 200 men, mostly replacements from Southern states, who could not sign their names to the payroll. The educational work in the regiment was by far the best in the Rainbow Division.

While in Remagen, wounded officers returned to the regiment and eventually the organization of the unit approached something of its old composition. The 42nd was reviewed by General Pershing on 16 March 1919.

Father Duffy wrote,

It was a note-worthy military ceremony in an appropriate setting, by the banks of that river of historic associations. When he came to our Regiment the eyes of General Pershing were taken by the silver furls which covered the staff of our flag from the silk of the colors to the lowest tip. In fact, that staff is now in excess of the regulation length, as we have had an extra foot to get on the nine furls [battle rings] that record our battles in this war.

"What Regiment is this?" he asked.

"The 165th Infantry, Sir."

"What Regiment was it?"

"The 69th New York, Sir."

"The 69th New York. I understand now."[14]

The new furls on the regimental staff were for the following engagements:

- Luneville Sector, 21 Feb. to 23 March 1918
- Baccarat Sector, 1 April to 21 June 1918
- Esperance-Souain Sector, 4 July to 14 July 1918
- Champagne-Marne Defensive, 15 July to 18 July 1918
- Aisne-Marne Offensive, 25 July to 3 August 1918
- St. Mihiel Offensive, 12 Sept. to 16 Sept. 1918
- Essey and Pannes Sector, Woevre, 17 Sept. to 30 Sept. 1918
- Argonne-Meuse Offensive, 13 October to 31 October 1918
- Argonne-Meuse Offensive, Last Phase, 5 Nov. to 9 Nov. 1918.[15]

Shortly before the Rainbow's return to the U.S., Colonel Howland was relieved by Donovan. The still limping warrior was then promoted to Colonel.

General Pershing's inspection was in preparation for the division being sent home. On 2 April, the 165th boarded trains for Brest. After a short stay in the French port, the regiment embarked on two ships for the United States and on 21 April, the troops arrived, without incident, at Hoboken, New Jersey.

Members of the regiment celebrated their last night in France with a boisterous party. The Fighting Sixty-Ninth lived up to its name and the shindig ended up in a huge brawl. Arrival of the military police (MPs) intensified the fracas. Many of the veterans hated military police. Order was finally restored but not before a number of the soldier cops were hospitalized. The next day, a contingent of military police under the command of a captain attempted to arrest the riot ringleaders before they embarked for home. Colonel Donovan wasted no time in fruitless argument with the young officer. He deployed a platoon of New Yorkers with bayonetted rifles and ensured that all of his men got on board the ship for the States.[16]

CHAPTER 20

Homecoming, April 1919

On Monday afternoon, 21 April 1919, the S.S. *Harrisburg* entered New York Harbor. She was carrying the 1st and 2nd battalions plus the regimental staff of the 165th Infantry. When the ship was spotted in the lower harbor, a flotilla of small vessels got underway from the Battery to greet the homecoming veterans.

Two Navy scout boats led the procession. They were followed by the police launch patrol carrying Mayor Hylan, Governor Whelan and other dignitaries. Vessels in the welcoming column included the steamer *Grand Republic* carrying members of the 69th New York National Guard and various Irish American societies, Correction with gold star mothers aboard, Gowanus, Bay Bridge and Gaynor. The flotilla was enlarged by fire boats and scores of private vessels. Many of the ships had bands playing popular Irish melodies.

The *Harrisburg*, convoyed by the welcoming flotilla, proceeded up the North River to a debarkation site in Hoboken, New Jersey. A huge crowd greeted the arriving veterans at the dock.[1]

After *Harrisburg* was tied up, port officials went aboard the vessel to meet Donovan. The colonel made the following points during the debriefing:

- About 1,400 of the 3,507 men who originally sailed for France were returning to the States. Only 27 of the regiment's original complement of 108 officers were with Donovan's command. The rest were battlefield casualties, lost to disease or transferred to other commands.
- When the regiment left for France, more than 85 percent of its troopers were of Irish descent. Its losses were made up by replacements containing large numbers of Italian, Jewish and Native Americans. These men had the right attitude and helped maintain the regiment's fighting spirit.
- Donovan cited the contributions of Jewish Americans during the fighting in France. He stated that during the struggle in the Argonne Forest, adjutants of the 1st, 2nd and 3rd battalions were Jews.
- Another non–Irisher who made a significant contribution to the regiment's success in France was Major Henry Bootz. He was born in Germany and had four brothers in the kaiser's army. Bootz led the regiment's first raid on enemy's trenches in the Luneville Sector.[2]

Colonel Donovan was asked if reports were true that Father Duffy was in the trenches while fighting was going on. Donovan dodged the question neatly and replied,

> No one is allowed to go into the front line trenches except the officers and men on duty. It is a matter of life and death there, and too serious for any but those needed. I would rather you pictured Father Duffy as we saw him doing his great work for humanity and never shirking it no matter how late or how early the hour was. Here was this doctor of philosophy, doctor of divinity, a student of nature, taken away from his flock and transplanted amidst the scenes of devastation and bloodshed in Europe. This man of wonderful opportunity went there and was an inspiration to the officers and men of the 165th Regiment. His was the dirtiest and yet the most important work from the humanitarian standpoint, and so necessary to keep up the morale of the men. After we came in at night and laid down on the ground tired as dogs, Father Duffy, who was tired too, with his long hours under shell fire at the dressing station had to go out and bury the dead.[3]

The rest of the regiment returned to the United States on Friday, 25 April, aboard the confiscated German steamship *Prinz Fredarik Wilhelm*. The vessel was expected to make port on 22 April but was delayed by bad weather and the threat of floating mines. The exuberance of the welcome home greeting for the returning veterans was mollified somewhat by gale force winds across the bay and the presence of five other ships carrying American Expeditionary Force soldiers.

Major Van S. Merle-Smith was in command of the detachment which included elements of the Headquarters Company and the 3rd Battalion. The total number of soldiers was 48 officers and 987 men.

Company K of the Shamrocks was originally known as the Meagher Guards. (Company K of the 69th New York State Militia, the Irish Zouaves, commanded by then Major Meagher, fought with distinction at First Bull Run.) It consisted of 250 men when it left New York City for France. Only 66 men returned with the unit on Friday. The rest of the men were casualties, of which 60 were killed in action. Three men in Company K were awarded the Distinguished Service Cross. All of the returning soldiers had been wounded or gassed at least once.[4]

On Monday evening, Colonel Donovan sent a committee, including Lieutenant Colonel Anderson, Major John Mangan and Father Duffy to the Belmont Hotel for a conference with city officials on regimental matters. Donovan went with the troops to Camp Mills.

On Wednesday, Colonel Donovan and his staff were formally welcomed home by Mayor Hylan at City Hall, where Donovan was given keys to the city. After a brief meeting, the group went to the India House in Hanover Square for lunch as guests of the Benefit Fund of the 165th Infantry.

On Saturday night, almost all of the veterans were given overnight passes so they could attend a dinner dance at the armory. The affair was sponsored by the Mayor's Committee of Welcome to the Homecoming Troops. On the same evening, the regiment's officers attended a reception at the Waldorf Astoria Hotel.

The highlight of the homecoming celebration was a parade up Fifth Avenue on Monday, 28 April 1919. The regiment marched 80 blocks from the Washington Square Arch to a reviewing stand at 115th Street. On the day of the march, the skies were overcast. It was chilly and damp with a threat of rain. One of the veterans believed the weather provided "just a hint of Flanders."[5] Actually, it was typical St. Patrick's Day weather.

Colonel Donovan insisted that the parade be carried out with strict military decorum. His thoughts on the matter were reported in the *New York Times* prior to the event:

> In tribute to the members of the Regiment who perished in the service, a banner with more than 600 gold stars upon it, will be carried with the Regimental colors. When Colonel Donovan announced his original plans for the parade he said that no banners of any kind would be carried except the colors but after his conference in the armory with the organization of the "Gold Star Mothers," he decided that some symbol should be displayed in tribute to those who gave their lives that the Regiment might be victorious.[6]
>
> Even the wounded will be under strict military discipline. Donovan having issued orders to the men to maintain their dignity as members of a historic Regiment returning with the honors of war and receiving the respect and acclimation of their friends and admirers. He also issued a formal appeal to the public to accord to the Regiment a review that will not detract from the dignity of the officers and soldiers. One of his special pleas was that gifts should not be thrown upon the pavement so that the soldiers would yield to the irresistible temptation to scramble for them in the rest periods.[7]
>
> Colonel Donovan expressed his gratitude yesterday to the city for the welcome given to the Regiment and said that the soldiers of the Regiment had finished their job and would, "go back to work as ordinary citizens, not posing as heroes, or trying to live on any reputation made as soldiers."
>
> "What we have tried to do as a Regiment is to come home in the proper spirit as a military unit that has had some part in the fine effort of America," he continued. "We have come home trying neither to boast nor to knock."[8]

The parade consisted of five contingents. The first three units were the 1st, 2nd and 3rd battalions led by Majors Kelly, Meaney and Van S. Merle-Smith respectively. The 4th Battalion, led by Major Bootz, consisted of headquarters, supply and medical companies. The 5th Battalion was composed of over 700 wounded veterans. Each of these men had at least one wound strip on the right sleeve of his uniform. That unit was led by Major Thomas Reilley, who went overseas as a first lieutenant, was promoted on the field and then temporarily forced out of the fighting as a result of serious wounds.

Colonel Donovan broke a precedent of military pageantry by refusing to ride at the head of his regiment. By unanimous decision, the five battalion commanders and ranking staff officers also decided to march as they had in France. The men wore service uniforms, steel helmets and light field packs. The bayonets on their rifles were burnished to a silvery luster. The regiment paraded in close order formation. Platoons and companies marched in lines of 20 men. A few paces separated those units. There was about 15 paces between battalions. The troops looked sharp; they had been subjected to a rigorous inspection at Camp Mills before they entrained for the city.

Colonel Donovan, at the head of the parade, wore three wound stripes on his right sleeve. The embroidered eagles on his shoulders were so small they resembled the silver bars of a first lieutenant. Onlookers knew who the young officer was, however, by his position at the head of the regiment and the medals on his chest which included the Distinguished Service Cross and the Croix de Guerre.[9]

Father Duffy marched in the middle of a long line of staff officers that came directly behind Donovan and Lieutenant Colonel Anderson. Donovan and Anderson wanted Father Duffy to take a more prominent position in the parade. He insisted upon marching in a place commensurate with his rank as a major and regimental chaplain.

Orders for the parade were closely observed and the regiment moved out from Washington Square at 1350, ten minutes before the official start time. While on the Mexican border, a battalion of the regiment had set a divisional record for marching. In France, elements of the 165th Infantry set another record, hiking in excess of 32 miles over rough terrain in adverse weather. The regiment upheld those records on 28 April by covering 80 city blocks in less than two hours and in passing the reviewing stand in ten minutes, instead of 20 minutes as was estimated by parade planners.

The regiment was led by a field band of 60 pieces. The group had picked up an innovation overseas introduced by a black musician, and had 20 trumpeters in the first ranks. Each instrument was adorned with a small Irish banner, a golden harp on a green field. The band played music always associated with the 69th NY such as "The Wearing of the Green" and "Garry Owen."

Three flags carried at the head of the regiment told the story of the Fighting Sixty-Ninth. The first was the faded and tattered national banner carried by the troops in France. The second was an immense service flag with 644 gold stars and the third was the 69th's original battle flag. That banner, with its fewer stars, was also in tatters, having being torn by wind and Rebel bullets. The national flag was attached to a flagstaff adorned by 50 silver furls.

The paraders were enthusiastically received by their fellow New Yorkers and the event received considerable press coverage. Excerpts from the next day's *New York Times* provide concise descriptions of the happening:

> All along the route and particularly in front of St. Patrick's Cathedral, flowers were thrown upon the colors and upon the service flag in tribute to those who gave their lives as part of the price of victory. A group of girls in the reviewing stand, where Archbishop Hayes and other Catholic dignitaries sat, threw hundreds of roses upon the white folds of the service flag, and the soldiers coming behind avoided them carefully with their feet and then picked them up when opportunity came.
>
> Observance of strict rules of discipline among the veterans took nothing from the effect of the parade, nor did it detract from the enthusiasm of the crowds. Even among the wounded who rode in the automobiles, some preceding the combat troops and some following them, there was no relaxation, no lax of dignity and little sign that the men recognized in this acclamation and homage to them and their achievements anything more than just a serious job for them to be taken as a march to the front lines.
>
> Archbishop Hayes and other dignitaries of the New York Archdiocese reviewed the regiment from the Knights of Columbus stand in front of St. Patrick's Cathedral and were recognized by Colonel Donovan and the Regiment as an official reviewing party. All the officers passed at salute and the men at "eyes right." The Archbishop returned the salute by waving his berretta. It was here that groups of girls paid tribute to the dead by throwing flowers upon

The Regimental Band is shown passing St. Patrick's Cathedral on Fifth Avenue (courtesy of U.S. Army Military History Institute).

the gold star service flag. Some of them also presented bouquets of roses to Colonel Donovan and Father Duffy, who returned them to the girls so they could throw the flowers to the soldiers. Salutes to the colors also were given at the Arch of Liberty and at the Court of the Victorious Dead and at the Public Library.

Mrs. Aline Kilmer, widow of Joyce Kilmer, the poet and member of the staff of the New York Times who was killed at the Ourcq while he was serving as sergeant in the intelligence section of the 165th, sat in the stand in front of the cathedral with her seven year old son Kenton. One of the last poems written by Sergeant Kilmer in his service in France was entitled, "When the 69th Comes Home." It was set to music later and the old 69th played the aire yesterday.

In a section of the stand at 105th Street and Fifth Avenue were several Civil War veterans who had fought in the 69th New York Volunteers and other regiments of the Irish Brigade under the command of General Meagher. One of them was Patrick Tumulty, uncle of Joseph Tumulty, the President's secretary. He served in Company D of the 69th during the last eighteen months of the war, and remembers clearly the homecoming parade of the Regiment in lower Broadway on July 4, 1865. With him were John R. Nugent, who was lieutenant of his company, and many other veterans of the Irish Brigade.

In the official reviewing stand at 115th Street were Governor Al Smith, Mayor Hylan, Rudman Wanamaker—Chairman of the Mayor's Committee of Welcome to the Homecoming Troops, Major General Alexander of the 77th Division and

The regiment's color guard. The flag on the left is obviously badly torn. The silver furls on its flagstaff are barely visible. The cord held by the soldier in the next rank was used to keep the service flag unfurled. (Courtesy of U.S. Army Military Institute.)

Major General O'Ryan of the 27th Division. A considerable number of other dignitaries were present including Governor Cox of Ohio, Governor Burnquist of Minnesota and Governor Allen of Kansas all of whom were in NYC to welcome their constituents who were in the Rainbow Division.

Another officer in the reviewing party was Brigadier General William A. Mann, retired, who left his post as Director of the Bureau of Military Affairs to take command of the Rainbow Division when it was organized at Camp Mills. Colonel Charles D. Hine, who took the 165th overseas and was later transferred to General Pershing's staff, marched with Major Reilley's battalion.[10]

As we know, the 69th NY was created by Irish revolutionaries. From its inception, it was manned almost exclusively by men who wished Ireland free from British domination. In that respect, the troops that marched up Fifth Avenue were no different than their predecessors. Early in 1919, Sinn Fein leaders in Dublin had raised the Tricolor and declared Ireland a Republic. Nevertheless, the 165th paraded as American soldiers exhibiting no allegiance to any flag but the Stars and Stripes. The following paragraph from the *New York Times* article covering the parade supports the observation that the regiment had become "Americanized."

The service flag is escorted by the color guard (courtesy of U.S. Army Military Institute).

None of the colors or emblems adopted by the Sinn Fein convention in Dublin were carried by any man in the parade but the tricolor chosen there as an emblem was used in decorating the official reviewing stand in front of the Metropolitan Museum of Art. There were three flagstaffs on the small stand on the east side of the avenue where the reviewing party sat. One flew the state flag, the second flew the flag of the city and the flag of the regiment was on the third. The front part of the stand was decorated with American colors, and in a position slightly less prominent was the orange, white and green of the Dublin convention.[11]

As the regiment passed by the reviewing stand and into history, its members had every reason to hold their heads high. They had more than equalled the sterling record of their illustrious progenitors, the 69th New York State Militia and Fighting 69th of the Irish Brigade.

The homecoming celebration was concluded by a dinner for the entire regiment in the Hotel Commodore. The event was sponsored by the Trustees of the Benefit Fund of the 69th, who were all members of the Friendly Sons of St. Patrick. Short speeches were made by Colonel Donovan, Father Duffy, Mayor Hylan and

General Mann. Another speaker who received an enthusiastic ovation was Brigadier General Lenihan.

The veterans were given overnight passes with orders to report to the armory at 0900 for transport to Camp Mills. Two days later the regiment was once again mustered out of federal service.

CHAPTER 21

Combat Effectiveness

In this section, the military accomplishments of the American Expeditionary Force, 42nd Division and 165th Infantry are assessed. The American Expeditionary Force's contribution toward the Allied victory on the Western Front is considered first. The impact of the American breakthrough in the Meuse-Argonne Offensive is evaluated by contrasting the opinions of a number of well known military historians. Next, Braim's methodology for appraising the divisions in Pershing's Army is presented. Ratings tabulated in his *The Test of Battle* are discussed with emphasis on the combat record of the Rainbow. Finally, the combat records of the 165th and its fellow regiments are compared using a number of performance criteria.

How Good Was the American Expeditionary Force?

Shortly after the war ended, the Allies began to "poor mouth" the American Expeditionary Force's military capabilities and downplay its contributions toward winning the struggle. Prominent Allied leaders minimized the American effort on the Western Front so they could weaken President Wilson's influence at the Versailles peace talks.

Total American battle losses on the Western Front were 361,189 men, heavy casualties considering they occurred during a period of about seven months. That number, however, was dwarfed by those of the British and French, who sustained 2,722,152 and 4,865,000 casualties respectively on the same front after more than fifty-one months of combat.[1] Understandably, senior British and French officers considered the late arriving Americans to be military upstarts.

The American Meuse-Argonne Campaign was eventually successful, but British Expeditionary Force and French offensives during the same time frame made more significant gains against the Germans. President Wilson believed General Pershing's modest military successes reduced his diplomatic clout at the peace talks.[2]

The magnitude of the American Expeditionary Force's contribution toward victory on the Western Front is debated to this day. Specifically, what impact did the Meuse-Argonne Offensive have on Ludendorff's decision to seek an armistice?

Many historians believe it was the realization that the U.S. would soon field an overwhelming force in France, that forced Germany to throw in the towel. On the other hand, supporters of Pershing and his staff are convinced that the American breakthrough on the Meuse-Argonne Front forced Ludendorff to seek a cease fire. Detractors of the American Expeditionary Force counter with the argument that the French and British stopped Ludendorff's spring offensives and then made greater gains than the Americans during the last months of the war. Strong support for the American Expeditionary Force, however, was provided after the war by Ludendorff, who stated, "The American infantry in the Argonne won the war...."[3]

General Ludendorff's comments were certainly appreciated by the rank and file of the 165th Infantry.

Representative opinions concerning the significance of the Meuse-Argonne Offensive and the American Expeditionary Force's contribution to victory are presented in following paragraphs. Negative, neutral and positive positions are provided by Hart, Braim and Mossier.

Captain B.H. Liddell Hart is considered by many to be the foremost authority on World War I. His short history, *The Real War, 1914–1918,* is a precise source of accurate information about the conflict. In the thirties, the retired British officer reviewed General Pershing's book, *My Experiences in the World War.* He challenged the general's contention that the American battlefield contribution was decisive. In Hart's opinion, the American total reinforcement was vital to victory, but the American military breakthrough in the Meuse River–Argonne Forest Campaign was not the most decisive action of 1918.[4]

Paul F. Braim, a professor of history at Emory-Riddle University, has written four books and numerous articles on military affairs. In his *The Test of Battle,* he presents the following observations on the American Expeditionary Force: "It is concluded that the Meuse-Argonne Campaign was a decisive action, but it was not the only nor the most decisive offensive of the war. For the Americans it was a hard won victory, won only in the last stages and at a great cost in lives. It was a victory produced mostly by improperly trained leaders and soldiers, and it was won by determination, esprit and the exhaustion of the enemy. The victory was a tribute to the vitality and strength of the United States when sorely tried. The losses should have served as a lesson of the price of military unpreparedness. That lesson was not learned...."[5]

John Mossier is a full professor of English at Loyala University in New Orleans. His background as a military historian dates from his role in developing an interdisciplinary curriculum for the study of World Wars I and II, a program funded by the National Endowment for the Humanities.

Mossier concluded that the British and French generals routinely lied about battlefield results and corresponding casualties. Allied losses were minimized and German losses were exaggerated. He opens his book, *The Myth of the Great War,* with a statement by Lloyd George, British Prime Minister during World War I, which supports his contention: "The reports passed on to the ministers were, as we all realized much later, grossly misleading. Victories were much overstated. Virtual defeats were represented as victories, however limited their scope. Our casualties were understated. Enemy losses became pyramidal. That was the way the military authorities presented the situation to the Ministers—that was their active propaganda in the Press. All disconcerting and disparaging facts were suppressed in the reports from the front by the War Cabinet—every bright feather of success was waved and flourished in our faces."[6]

Mossier, as a result of his studies, believes the American Expeditionary Force won the war on the Western Front, "But America's role in the war was absolutely decisive. The string of German battlefield successes stopped abruptly on the entry into the line of the newly formed American divisions, the course of the war changed drastically, and members of the Oberste Heeresleitung, the General Staff of the German Army (the OHL), recommended that Germany seek terms. When Wilson hinted to the Allies that he would seek his own peace unless his famous Fourteen Points were adopted, they caved in. The Great War was won on the ground by American soldiers deployed as an American force, and operating largely against the wishes and suggestions of the senior French and British commanders, who thought American troops should be distributed into Allied units as replacements for Allied losses to minimize their importance."[7]

The debate goes on.

How Good Was the Rainbow Division?

When President Wilson federalized the National Guard in the summer of 1917, most senior army officers had serious misgivings about the militia's military prowess. The big question on their collective minds was, "Would the National Guard fight?"

Regular Army officers had a low opinion of their opposite numbers in the militia. In many cases, guard officers held higher rank than their jealous counterparts of the same age in the regular army. Pershing believed the National Guard was commanded by marginally qualified, political generals.

Most military historians consider the Rainbow to be one of the better combat divisions to serve in France. The 2nd, with its hard fighting Marine brigade, was undoubtedly the best such organization in the American Expeditionary Force. The 1st was probably the second best division in Pershing's army. The 42nd Division should be considered a solid third with respect to fighting capability.

Braim's assessment of 29 divisions that saw action in France supports the above selection of best units. The 27th and 30th divisions, which fought with the British Expeditionary Force throughout the war, were not included in his study. Outfits were compared with respect to five performance criteria: days in the front line, distance advanced against fire, awards for valor, battlefield casualties, and prisoners captured.

Days in the Front Line. Days in the front line is the sum of days in quiet and active sectors. As expected, those units among the first to arrive in France (1st, 26th, 42nd and 2nd Divisions) had the most days in the trenches. The 1st Division leads in this evaluation category with 127 days in quiet sectors and 93 days in active sectors for a total of 220 days. The next four divisions were the 26th,

42nd, Second and 77th divisions, with total days of 193, 164, 137, and 113 respectively.

Some organizations such as the 3rd, 30th and 36th divisions had all of their trench time in active sectors; 86, 56 and 23 days respectively.[8]

Distance Advanced Against Fire. Ground gained against the Germans depended on many factors, including quality of opposing troops, mission requirements, nature of ground being contested, etc.

The 77th Division led in this evaluation category with a value of 44.5 miles. The next four divisions were the 2nd, 42nd, 1st and 89th divisions with values of 37.5, 34.0, 32.0 and 30.0 miles, respectively.

When the above mileage figures are normalized versus days in active sectors, the ranking in this performance category becomes 89th, 42nd, 77th, 2nd and 1st divisions with comparative values of 1.07, 0.87, 0.67, 0.57 and 0.34 miles per day respectively.[9]

Awards for Valor. Awards considered are the Congressional Medal of Honor and the Distinguished Service Cross, the nation's highest and second highest decorations. Oak Leaf Clusters (second award for a given decoration) are also tabulated for each division.

Winning a medal in combat is dependent upon a number of factors in addition to heroism. Contingencies include luck, timing, survival of witnesses and command structure of the individual's military organization. Nevertheless, the number of medals won by a given unit is a measure of that group's military effectiveness.

The 2nd Division leads in this evaluation category with seven Medals of Honor, 693 Distinguished Service Crosses and 13 Oak Leaf Clusters, a total of 686 awards. The next four divisions prominent in this category are the 1st with 420, 3rd with 332, 30th with 319 and 26th with 276. The 42nd Division ranked seventh with 248 awards.

Braim lists two Medals of Honor for the 42nd Division. The correct number should be five; 165th—three and 167th—two, making the total number of awards 248 and not 245.[10]

Battlefield Casualties. Casualties considered include battle deaths, mortally wounded, wounded, and those evacuated for sickness.

Relatively high battlefield casualties could be the result of military incompetence, bad luck and poor training or other factors. Braim, Fox and other military historians, however, believe there is a positive relationship between battlefield casualties and military proficiency. The better units are those most often deployed where enemy lead is thickest.

It is a stretch to assume that the number of casualties sustained by a division due to sickness is a measure of military proficiency. It could be argued that casualties resulting from sickness are primarily due to poor sanitary practices, medical incompetency and poor morale.

The better divisions in the American Expeditionary Force, including the Rainbow, suffered relatively less debilitating illnesses such as trench foot and other maladies caused by prolonged exposure to the elements. Casualty lists that include evacuees for sickness work against the Rainbow's rating with this discriminator.

Nevertheless, the 42nd Division scored high in this category. The 2nd Division led with 25,232 casualties. The next four units were the 1st, 3rd, 28th and 42nd divisions with 23,496, 18,468, 17,003 and 16,107 casualties respectively.[11]

Prisoners Captured. Braim maintains, correctly I believe, that the number of prisoners captured by a unit is a positive measure of that organization's military effectiveness. With respect to prisoners, the 42nd Division had a reputation in enemy quarters for not taking many German captives.

While the 42nd Division was slugging it out with the Kaiser's troops in the Marne salient, German newspapers reported incidents in which Rainbows killed German soldiers who were trying to surrender. The charges, which included the slaughter of helpless wounded, focused on fighting during the Champagne Defensive on July 15.

The hard hitting New Yorkers and Alabamas had a reputation in the American Expeditionary Force for taking few prisoners in the heat of combat. This was probably true when bayonet wielding Rainbows reached Boche machine gunners who fired their weapons until they were about to be overrun and then attempted to surrender.

A formal inquiry was convened reference the above allegations. During the course of the investigation, numerous officers were questioned. Fifteen company grade officers gave written depositions. All their testimonies denied the charges. Inquiry results were forwarded to Chaumont and reviewed. The matter was subsequently pigeon holed.[12]

The 2nd Division leads this category with a total of 12,026 prisoners. The next four divisions are the 1st, 89th, 33rd and 30th with 6,469, 5,061, 3,987 and 3,848 prisoners respectively. The 42nd Division is ranked 17th in this category with 1,317 prisoners.[13] Maybe the Germans were correct in their assessment of the Rainbow Division.

Consolidated Factors. Totaling the indicators for each division yields the following ranking; 2nd, 1st, 3rd, 26th and 42nd divisions with factor totals of 37, 31, 22, 20 and 19. When the factors are normalized versus days in combat, the ranking becomes 2nd, 42nd, 26th, 28th, 1st and 77th divisions.[14]

Why was the Rainbow Division such a good fighting organization? I believe it was due to the synergistic combination of the following factors.

The division was not thrown together. Secretary of War Baker and Douglas MacArthur, carefully selected the guard units comprising the division. Its four infantry regiments had outstanding service records on the Mexican border.

The division's general officers were exceptional men. Major General Menoher was a classmate of General Pershing and considered a capable officer. His chief of staff, MacArthur, survived the war and eventually rose to the rank of five star general.

In early 1916, many of the British Expeditionary Force's divisions were newly organized and hastily trained units. Almost all of these outfits, part of "Kitchener's Army," performed poorly on the Somme. Some units, however, possessing relatively high levels of social cohesion, demonstrated surprisingly good combat effectiveness in spite of limited military expertise. Social commonality, such as identification with a distinct locale or specific industry, generated competitive spirit and pride in one's formation, characteristics that enhance martial proficiency.[15]

All of the Rainbow's units sprang from distinct areas of the nation. Thus each possessed significant measures of geographic cohesion. This was especially true for the New York and Alabama regiments. As we know, the former derived its strength from the crowded, combative Irish-American wards of New York City. Its progenitor was the distinctly Irish Catholic Fighting Sixty-Ninth. The 167th's parent, the Fourth Alabama, was organized in the Deep South by people who vividly remembered the sting of defeat in the Civil War and subsequent humiliation of military occupation. Soldiers of the 167th identified themselves with the Confederate South and the "lost cause." The 166th and 168th regiments, from essentially rural areas, also possessed an "us against the world" attitude, but to a lesser degree than that of the New York and Alabama units.

Diversity in backgrounds created a healthy rivalry between individual regiments. The New Yorkers, for example, considered themselves better than the hayseeds in the other regiments. On the other hand, the Alabamians did not want Yankees to out perform them. This was especially true for their Civil War nemesis, the 69th New York. The sometimes-not-so-friendly diversity contributed to the overall excellence of each regiment.

The Rainbow held the Baccarat Sector for 82 days while the Allies were responding to Ludendorff's offensives. During that period of time, the division depended on itself. The infantry learned to respect the work of the artillery and vice versa. Engineers, signal battalions, medical teams and supply units learned to cooperate for the general good of the division.

How Good Was the 165th New York?

The fighting characteristics of the Rainbow Division's infantry regiments were compared using a procedure based on Braim's methodology to evaluate the military prowess of American Expeditionary Force divisions.

Three of the five discriminators used by Braim were not employed in the regimental evaluation. It is assumed that individual units would receive essentially the same grade for the following performance criteria: days in the front line, distance advanced against fire, and prisoners captured.

Another discriminator was added to the remaining two, significant achievements. In this evaluation category, important tactical successes attributed to the regiments were considered and compared.

In summary, performance discriminators used in this evaluation were significant achievements, awards for valor, and battlefield casualties.

Significant Achievements

The following successes were considered:

Aisne-Marne Offensive. Capture of Croix Rouge Farm, a critical German strong point, by two battalions of the 167th Infantry supported by a battalion of the 168th and 165th Infantries on the right and left flanks respectively. Reilly recorded, "Despite the heaviest kind of enemy fire, particularly from machine guns placed in the farm and along the farther edges of the clearing in such a way as to enfilade the attacking troops, despite heavy and continuous losses, the Iowans drove the Germans out of and made their own position along the Croix Rouge Farm–le Chennel Road, while the Alabamians took the farm and held it. The bayonet was freely used.

"Too much credit cannot be given the troops who carried out this successful assault."[16]

Aisne-Marne Offensive. Crossing of the Ourcq River, and capture of Meurcy Farm. On the Ourcq River, the 165th Infantry put up what has been called one of the great fights of the war when it forced a crossing without artillery support and, fighting alone on the enemy's side of the river with its flanks unsupported, engaged a Prussian Guard Division and forced it to retire. Subsequently, the 165th Infantry captured Meurcy Farm, a German strong point near the river, at the point of the bayonet.

Aisne-Marne Offensive. The 166th Infantry captured Seringes-et-Nesles and Hill 184, German strong points on the extreme left of the Rainbow's front, after three days of see-saw fighting. The Ohio regiment's successful assault on the town culminated in a vicious hand to hand struggle. Hill 184 was seized in conjunction with the French 62nd Infantry.

Aisne-Marne Offensive. The 168th Infantry, with support from the Alabamas, captured Sergy, a stoutly defended town on the right of the 42nd's sector. The 84th Brigade suffered heavy losses in the operation. The next day, the Iowans were driven from the site. Later, the 3rd Battalion 47th Infantry supported by the Iowans captured Sergy for good.

St. Mihiel Offensive. Rapid advance to Halimont and Hassavant Farm by Donovan's Battalion. The 165th Infantry spearheaded the Rainbow's assault during Pershing's first successful offensive of the war.

Meuse-Argonne Offensive. Capture of Hills 288 and 242, important strong points in the Kriemhilde Stellung. The positions were captured by the 168th Infantry via a determined assault in which the attacking battalion suffered severe losses.

Meuse-Argonne Offensive. Capture of Cote de Chatillon, a linchpin in the Kriemhilde Stellung. On 16 October, this hilly bastion, which was seized by the 167th Infantry after the Iowans took Hill 288, prevented the advance of the Rainbow on 14 and 15 October. It was overrun by a heroic bayonet attack. Per Reilly, "In other words, the key position of the enemy, the Cote de Chatillon, fell into American hands as the result of a combined attack of the Alabama and Iowa regiment, to whom the division of the honors must be equally made...."[17]

It must be remembered that while the 84th Brigade was assaulting Cote de Chatillon and Hill 288 on 14, 15 and 16 October, the 83rd Brigade was out in the open at the edge of the German wire fronting the Landres-et-St. Georges Sector of the Kriemhilde Stellung. The sacrifice of the 165th and 166th Infantries aided the 84th Brigade in its ultimately successful attack on the Cote de Chatillon.

Race to Sedan. The 165th Infantry led the Rainbow Division's push to Sedan. On 7 November, the Regiment's 2nd and 3rd Battalions captured German strong points, hills 252 and 346, by gallant bayonet attacks. The next day, the regiment held the high ground dominating the river crossing to Sedan at Wadlincourt. until relieved by French forces.

Unit Citations. The French government awarded decorations for especially meritorious conduct in action during the war to 156 elements of the American Expeditionary Force, varying in size from a section to a brigade. The following Rainbow units received awards; Croix de Guerre with Palm: 167th Infantry, Company F and Croix de Guerre with Silver Star: 168th Infantry, Company B plus 168th Infantry, Stokes Mortar Section, Headquarters Company.[18]

Rank. The author, considering the above information, arrived at the following qualitative rankings; first—167th and 168th Regiments, Second—165th and 166th Regiments.

Awards for Valor

The regiments were compared with respect to the number of Medals of Honor and Distinguished Service Crosses won by their members. Data with respect to lesser awards are provided for information purposes only.

The Medal of Honor was introduced during the Civil War in 1861. It is the nation's highest award for valor and is given to enlisted men and officers for bravery in action involving conflict with the enemy. Recipients must distinguish themselves in an outstanding manner. The medal is awarded after a stringent investigation is performed to ensure a candidate is worthy of the citation.

The Congressional Medal of Honor was awarded to three members of the 165th Infantry, Sergeant Richard O'Neil (Meurcy Farm), Private Michael A. Donaldson (Landres-et-St. Georges) and Lieutenant Colonel William J. Donovan (Landres-et-St. Georges) plus two members of the 167th Infantry, Private Thomas C. Niebaur (Cote de Chatillon) and Corporal Sidney E. Manning (Ourcq River).

The Distinguished Service Cross is the nation's second highest award for valor. Introduced in January 1918, it is awarded to service personnel who distinguish themselves by extraordinary heroism against an armed enemy under circumstances which do not warrant the Medal of Honor. A recipient of a second award is identified by an oak leaf cluster on the medal's ribbon. The 165th, 166th, 168th and 167th Infantries received 84, 47, 40 and 36 Distinguished Service Crosses respectively. Donovan of the New York Regiment was authorized to wear the medal with an oak leaf cluster.

The Distinguished Service Medal was also instituted in 1918. The medal is awarded to any person in the army for exceptionally meritorious service in the field or post of duty. The 165th received two, 166th was awarded one and 168th one.

The Legion of Honor was instituted by Napoleon in 1802 for distinguished military and civil service. It is France's highest award and during World War I, it was only conferred for gallantry in action or 20 years distinguished military or civil service. The 165th received seven, 168th five and 166th two awards.

The Medaille Militaire was established by France in 1852. It is awarded to officers and enlisted men for single acts of valor or especially meritorious service.

FIG. 5-35 AWARDS FOR VALOR

REGIMENTS / AWARDS	165 [1,5]	166 [2]	167 [3,5]	168 [4]
CONGRESSIONAL MEDAL OF HONOR	3	0	2	0
DISTINGUISHED SERVICE CROSS WITH OAK LEAF	84 1	47	36	40
DISTINGUISHED SERVICE MEDAL	2	1	0	1
FRENCH LEGION OF HONOR	7	2	0	5
FRENCH MEDAILLE MILITAIRE	4	1	1	2
FRENCH CROIX DE GUERRE WITH PALM	104 1	46	14 1	74
ORDER OF LEOPOLD [BELGIUM]	2	0	1	0
ORDER OF THE CROWN [BELGIUM]	0	1	1	2
CROIX DU GUERRE [BELGIUM]	0	2	0	1
CROCE DE GUERRA [ITALY]	2	0	0	1

SOURCES
1. Francis P. Duffy, *Father Duffy's Story* (Garden City, NY: Garden City Publishing Company, 1919), 243–44.
2. R.M. Cheseldine, *Ohio in the Rainbow* (Columbus, Ohio: The F.J. Heer Printing Company, 1924), 347–49.
3. William H. Amerine, *Alabama's Own in France* (New York: Eaton and Gettinger, 1919), 333–36.
4. John H. Taber, *The Story of the 168th Infantry* (Iowa City, Iowa: State Historical Society of Iowa, 1925), 288–91.
5. American Battle Monuments Commission, *American Armies and Battlefields in Europe, A History Guide and Reference Book* (Washington, D.C.: Government Printing Office, 1948), 72–73, 243–244.

It is the equivalent of Britain's Distinguished Conduct Medal. The 165th received four, the 168th was awarded two, and the 167th and 166th Infantries were awarded one each.

The Croix de Guerre was instituted by France on 8 April 1915. During World War I, it was open to officers and enlisted men of the French and Allied armies who were cited for bravery in military dispatches from an officer commanding an army, corps, division, brigade or regiment. Each award was identified as to the level of the dispatch. Emblems on the ribbon indicate the citation's importance; Army Dispatch-small bronze laurel branch, Corps Dispatch-silver gilt star, Divisional Dispatch-silver star and Brigade or lower-bronze star. The awards listed in the table "Awards for Valor" were totaled without regard to class of dispatch.

The 165th, 168th, 166th and 167th Infantries received 104, 74, 46 and 14 Croix de Guerres respectively. One member of the Alabama Regiment received the award twice. It should be noted that many officers in the American Expeditionary Force believed the French were too liberal in awarding the Croix de Guerre. Major General Liggett made the following comment in his memoir, "It would be an exaggeration to say that decorations were as difficult to avoid after great victories as poppies on tag days, yet the French prodigality with the Croix de Guerre

Comparative Battlefield Casualties

	165	166	167	168
Wounded	2451	1584	2239	2289
Died of Wounds	170	129	138	175
Killed in Action	558	256	485	404
Total Casualties	3179	1969	2862	2867

Source: "42nd Division, Summary of Operations in the World War," American Battle Monuments Commission, United States Government Printing Office, 1944.

was outdone only by Germany's reckless flinging about of her Iron Cross in a besieged country, where metal was scarce. The French were most generous with our Army...."[19]

The Order of Leopold was Belgium's highest award for valor during World War I. It was awarded for extraordinary military or civil service. Awards were made in various grades. The 165th received two and the 167th regiment received one award. Other Belgian awards for valor were the Order of the Crown and the Croix de Guerre. The 166th, 168th and 167th Infantries were awarded three, three and one of the rewards respectively.

The Italian equivalent of the French and Belgian Croix de Guerres was the Croce di Guerra. The 165th received two and the 168th infantry received one of the Italian awards.

The 165th Infantry, with three Medals of Honor and 84 Distinguished Service crosses, is clearly superior in this evaluation category and is ranked first. The 167th Infantry is ranked second. The other two regiments are ranked third.

Battlefield Casualties

The number of soldiers that were killed in action, wounded or died of their wounds are tabulated in the table "Comparative Battlefield Casualties." Data are presented for specific periods of time during the Champagne-Marne Defensive, Aisne-Marne Offensive, St. Mihiel Offensive and Meuse-Argonne Offensive. Losses sustained while training in the Luneville and Baccarat sectors were not compared.

The 165th Infantry suffered a total of 3,179 casualties during the comparative time frames and is ranked first. The Alabama and Iowa regiments suffered a total of 2,867 and 2,862 casualties respectively and are ranked second in this category. Surprisingly, the 166th Infantry sustained a significantly lower number of killed and wounded, 1,969 men. The 166th Ohio ranked third in this category.

Comparative Performance

The accompanying evaluation matrix was used to make a qualitative comparison of the regiment's fighting prowess. The three "performance discriminators" were weighted with respect to relative importance in the evaluation procedure. Significant achievements, awards for valor, and battlefield casualties

PERFORMANCE DISCRIMINATOR	DIS. VALUE		REGIMENT			
			165	166	167	168
SIGNIFICANT ACHIEVEMENTS	3	RANK	2	4	1	2
		SCORE	9	3	12	9
AWARDS FOR VALOR	2	RANK	1	2	2	2
		SCORE	8	6	6	6
BATTLEFIELD CASUALTIES	1	RANK	1	4	2	2
		SCORE	4	1	3	3
TOTAL SCORES			21	10	21	18

5-37 EVALUATION MATRIX

were given numerical values of 3, 2, and 1 respectively. A multiplier was obtained for each regiment within an evaluation category. This multiplier was based on a regiment's ranking within an evaluation category. A ranking of first rated a multiplier of 4, a ranking of second a multiplier of 3, a ranking of third a multiplier of 2 and a ranking of last a multiplier of one. The product of corresponding multiplier and discriminator values provided the relative scores for each regiment per performance category. The three scores awarded to each regiment were then summed to provide the total scores.

Based on this qualitative analysis, the regiments are ranked as follows; 165th (21 points), 167th (21 points), 168th (19 points) and 166th Ohio (15 points). The New York and Alabama regiments are rated equal with respect to fighting capabilities. The 168th Infantry is ranked a close second and the 166th third.[20]

Epilogue

In 1938, a service was held in the 69th Armory in memory of those killed in France. Ettinger's recollections include the following about Father Duffy:

> Early on the morning of October 15, 1918, Sherwood and I were reminiscing about home. I wanted to smoke and had plenty of tobacco and paper for making cigarettes, but, damn it, I didn't have a match. Consequently, I went over to the next foxhole to get some matches.
>
> In the next foxhole was our color sergeant, Bill Sheahan and another doughboy I didn't know. I got some dry matches from them and squeezed back into our foxhole. No sooner had I rolled and lit a cigarette than there was a terrible explosion! Both Sherwood and I were stunned and buried in mud. We managed to dig ourselves out of our hole, heard loud shouts, and discovered that the shell had landed in the adjacent foxhole where the two men had been. There was no Bill Sheahan, and the other fellow had both legs blown off. He was being carried down the slope to the aid station, but you could tell it was useless.
>
> Everyone was mystified as to what had happened to Sheahan. I told Tom Fitzsimmons he had been in that hole, because I had spoken to him only a few minutes before the shell exploded. At dawn we looked around and soon came across what appeared to be a piece of roast beef strapped by a web belt, and the initials "W S" were burned into the belt. Those were the mortal remains of Bill Sheahan.
>
> Twenty years later, in 1938, we held a service in the 69th Regiment Armory in memory of our comrades who had been killed during the war. A beautiful plaque was unveiled on which were engraved the names of the men who had died in France. A man sitting next to me introduced himself as the brother of William Sheahan; then he introduced me to a woman next to him, who was Bill's sister. They had traveled all the way from Ireland for the occasion. I was nonplussed when he told me that during the war, Bill's body had been returned to his hometown in Ireland for burial. I wondered what in God's name had been returned. Then his brother confided, "You know, Father Duffy told us that he was killed by shell concussion, and there wasn't a mark on his body."
>
> Although shocked, I managed to reply, "Father was right, sir, that's what happened."[1]

In January 1940, Warner Bros. Studios invited regiment veterans to the Waldorf Astoria for a review of their new movie, *The Fighting Sixty-Ninth*. Ettinger's reminiscences of the affair were recorded in his book.

He recalled that Bill Donovan and Alex Anderson (then colonel of the regiment) were on the dais with actors Jimmy Cagney, Pat O'Brien and George Brent. O'Brien and Brent played Father Duffy and Wild Bill Donovan in the film. The guest of honor was Governor Herbert Lehman.

The highlight of the evening, in Ettinger's opinion (he thought the movie was corny) was the following radio address by General MacArthur from Manila.

> No greater fighting regiment has ever existed than the One Hundred and Sixty-fifth Infantry of the Rainbow Division, formed from the old Sixty-ninth of New York. I cannot tell you how real and how sincere a pleasure I feel tonight in once more addressing the members of that famous unit. You need no eulogy from me or from any other man. You have written your own history and written it in red on your enemies' breast, but when I think of your patience under adversity, your courage under fire, and your modesty in victory, I am filled with an emotion of admiration I cannot express. You have carved your own statue upon the hearts of your people, you have built your own monument in the memory of your compatriots.
>
> One of the most outstanding characteristics of the Regiment was its deep sense of religious responsibility inculcated by one of my most beloved friends—Father Duffy. He gave you a code that embraces the highest moral laws that will stand the test of any ethics or philosophies ever promulgated for the uplift or man. Its requirements are for the things that are right and its restraints are for the things that are wrong. The soldier, above all men, is required to perform the highest act of religious teaching—sacrifice. However horrible the results of war may be, the soldier who is called upon to offer and perchance to give his life for his country is the noblest development of mankind. No physical courage and no brute instincts can take the place of the divine annunciation and spiritual uplift which will alone sustain him. Father Duffy, on those bloody fields of France we all remember so well, taught the men of your Regiment how to die that a nation might live—how to die unquestioning and uncomplaining, with faith in their hearts and the hope on their lips that we might go to victory.
>
> Somewhere in your banquet hall tonight his noble spirit looks down to bless and guide you young soldiers on the narrow path marked with West Point's famous motto—duty, honor, country.
>
> We all hope that war will come to us no more. But if its red stream again engulfs us, I want you to know that if my flag flies again, I shall hope to have you once more with me, once more to form the brilliant hues of what is lovingly, reverently called by men at arms, the Rainbow.
>
> May God be with you until we meet again.[2]

Notes

Unit Insignia

1. Information Sheet, 69th Infantry, Department of the Army, The Institute of Heraldry, pp. 1–2 and Army Lineage Book, Volume II: Infantry, pp. 477–479.

2. Stein, *U.S. Army Heraldic Crests*, p. 1.

3. Johnson and Buel, eds. *Battles and Leaders of the Civil War, Volume 2*, pp. 167–168. The idea for corps badges originated with Major General Butterfield, General Hooker's Chief of Staff. Devices for the First, Second, Third and Fifth Corps were a circle, trefoil, diamond and Maltese cross respectively. Within each organization, badges for the First, Second and Third Divisions were red, blue and white respectively.

4. Powers, *The Sixty Ninth Regiment of New York, Its History, Heraldry, Traditions and Customs* (pamphlet), p. 2.

5. Ibid., p. 4.

Introduction

1. Powers, *The Sixty Ninth Regiment of New York, Its History, Heraldry, Traditions and Customs,* and *The Army Lineage Book, Volume II: Infantry,* pp. 477–479. The 69th New York is accorded the battle honors of the original New York State Militia, the 69th New York Volunteers and the 69th New York National Guard Artillery. The latter two regiments were provided with cadre personnel from the parent militia unit. The New York National Guard Artillery (182nd New York Infantry) was the 1st Regiment of Corcoran's Legion. The 69th New York per-petuates the traditions of the other Irish Brigade regiments, defunct since the end of the Civil War.

2. Powers, p. 1.

3. Fox, *Regimental Losses in the American Civil War, 1861–1865*, p. 118. Published in 1889, Fox's work is a reliable source of statistical data based on official records.

4. Ibid., p. 67. The First Division, Second Corps, lost more men killed and wounded than any other division in the Union Army. Aggregate casualties were 2,287, 11,724 and 4,833 men killed, wounded (including mortally wounded) and missing.

5. Braim, *The Test of Battle*, pp. 150–155.

6. Lonn, *Foreigners in the Union Army and Navy*, pp. 71, 74 and 75.

7. Ibid., p. 653.

8. Powers, pp. 1–2.

9. Lonn, p. 646.

10. Welsh, *Irish Green and Union Blue, The Civil War Letters of Peter Welsh* (eds., Kohl and Richard), p. 102.

11. Daniel Chisholm joined the 116th Pennsylvania in February 1864. He fought in Grant's final campaigns which ended with General Lee's surrender at Appomattox. Chisholm survived the war and penned a personal chronicle of his experiences in the federal army. Also included in the notebook is the diary of fellow soldier and neighbor Samual Clear. W. Springer and J. August Shimrak edited Chisholm's work and published *The Civil War Notebook of Daniel Chisholm* in 1989. The work provides valuable insights into the wartime experiences of a soldier in the Irish Brigade.

12. Bacevich, *Diplomat in Khaki*, pp. 73, 77.

13. Duffy, *Father Duffy's Story.*

14. Albert Ettinger was born in Haworth, New Jersey, on 3 April 1900. Ettinger's father was half German and half Irish, while his mother's parents were born in Ireland. Although he had a German last name, he was three-quarters Irish. Ettinger's father, who became New York City Superintendent of Schools, was for a period of time the city's Amateur Welterweight Boxing Champion. Young Albert took after the senior Ettinger and was an intelligent, scrappy young man. Albert Ettinger died of cancer at his home in Sarasota, Florida, in November 1984.

15. Hogan, Martin J., *The Shamrock Battalion of the Rainbow.*

Chapter 1

1. O'Flaherty, *The History of the Sixty Ninth Regiment of the New York State Militia, 1852–1861,* p. 4.

2. Ibid., pp. 42–43.

3. Ibid., p. 133.

4. Ibid., p. 190.

5. Lane, "Colonel Michael Corcoran, Fighting Irishman," *The History of the Irish Brigade* (ed. Seagrave), pp. 13–17.

6. O'Flaherty, p. 188.

7. Ibid., pp. 206–207.

8. Ibid., p. 220.

9. Ibid., p. 225.

Chapter 2

1. Ketchum (ed.), *The American Heritage Picture History of the Civil War,* p. 12.

2. Gallagher, *Civil War, American,* Encarta, pp. 1–29.

3. Phisterer, *Statistical Record of the Armies of the United States,* Battle No. 36, p. 85.

4. Styple (ed.), *Writing and Fighting the Civil War,* p. 27. *The New York Sunday Mercury* routinely published correspondence from Civil War soldiers. These letters, written from the field, provide eyewitness accounts of the struggle. William B. Styple selected 500 letters from over 3,000 candidates for editing and subsequent inclusion in a book, *Writing and Fighting the Civil War.* General Todleben, referenced in the soldier's letter, was a Czarist engineer serving during the Crimean War, 1854 to 1856. He implemented innovative fortification procedures during the siege of Sebastopol, which initially stymied the Anglo-French forces.

5. Lonn, *Foreigners in the Union Army and Navy,* p. 119.

6. Hankinson, *First Bull Run 1861,* pp. 59–61 and Davis, *Battle at Bull Run,* pp. 178–188.

7. O'Flaherty, *The History of the Sixty Ninth Regiment of the New York State Militia, 1852–1861,* pp. 286–289.

8. Report of Col. Andrew Porter, Sixteenth U.S. Infantry. *Official Records of the War of Rebellion* [Hereafter referred to as OR], Series I, Vol. II/Ser. 2, pp. 383–387.

9. Garcia, "The Fighting Sixty Ninth New State Militia At Bull Run," *The History of the Irish Brigade* (ed. Seagrave), p. 54.

10. Fox, *Regimental Losses in the American Civil War, 1861–1865,* p. 426. The First Minnesota suffered the highest losses of any Federal Regiment at Bull Run, with 42 killed, 108 wounded, and 30 missing, for a total of 180. The Sixty Ninth's numbers were 38, 59 and 95 for an aggregate of 192. The 79th New York's numbers were 32, 51, 115 for an aggregate of 198.

11. O'Flaherty, pp. 299–302.

12. O'Flaherty, *The History of the Sixty Ninth Regiment in the Irish Brigade, 1861–1865,* pp. 26–33.

13. Lysy, *Blue for the Union, Green for Ireland,* pp. 36–37.

14. Ibid., p. 9.

15. Ibid., p. 45.

16. Lane, "Colonel Michael Corcoran, Fighting Irishman," *The History of the Irish Brigade* (ed. Seagrave), p. 26.

17. Ibid., pp. 32–33.

18. Conyngham, *The Irish Brigade and Its Campaigns,* pp. 540–541. David P. Conyngham was born in County Tipperary, Ireland. As a young man he was involved in the aborted and relatively bloodless rebellion by the "Young Irelanders" in 1848. He first came to the United States in 1861 as a war correspondent for an Irish newspaper. He joined General Meagher's staff in December 1862 and served with the brigade until the general's resignation after Chancellorsville. Later, Conyngham travelled with Sherman's Army. He was wounded

while carrying dispatches during the Battle of Resaca, Georgia. After the war, he joined the editorial staff of the *New York Herald*. Conyngham published *The Irish Brigade and Its Campaigns* in 1867. According to David J. Eicher in *The Civil War in Books, An Analytical Bibliography*, p. 359. "This is a valuable albeit early and occasionally confused treatment of a famous unit in the Army of the Potomac."

Conyngham died in April 1883 and was buried in Calvary Cemetery, the final resting place of many comrades in arms. Above synopsis of Conyngham's life was extracted from L.F. Kohl's Introduction, *The Irish Brigade and Its Campaigns*, pp. x–xxx.

Chapter 3

1. Hankinson, *First Bull Run 1861*, p. 86.
2. Symonds, *A Battlefield Atlas of the Civil War*, p. 55.
3. Phister, *Statistical Record of the Armies of the United States*, Battle Nos. 353, 354, 355, 356 and 357; p. 104.
4. Walker, *History of the Second Army Corps*, pp. 62–63.
5. Ibid., p. 62.
6. O'Brien, "Sprig of Green: The Irish Brigade." *The History of the Irish Brigade* (ed. Seagrave), p. 73.
7. Jones, *Lee's Tigers*, p. 110.
8. Conyngham, *The Irish Brigade*, pp. 219–220.
9. Priest, *Antietam, The Soldier's Battle*, pp. 163, 170, 180–183 and 207.
10. Johnson and McLaughlin, *Battles of the Civil War*, p. 67.
11. Conyngham, p. 308.
12. Fox, *Regimental Losses in the American Civil War, 1861–1865*, pp. 36–37, and 204.
13. Spink, "Colonel Richard Byrnes: Irish Brigade Leader," *The Irish Brigade* (ed. Seagrave), pp. 119–131.
14. Smith, *Fredericksburg 1862*, pp. 62–63.
15. Kelly, "The Green Flags of the Irish Brigade," *The History of the Irish Brigade* (ed. Seagrave), p. 203.
16. O'Flaherty, *The History of the Sixty Ninth Regiment in the Irish Brigade 1861–1865*, p. 205.

17. Fox, p. 204.
18. Ibid., p. 204.
19. McCarter, *My Life in the Irish Brigade* (ed. O'Brien), pp. 141–144.
20. O'Brien, p. 66.
21. Lonn, *Foreigners in the Union Army and Navy*, p. 512.
22. O'Flaherty, pp. 199–200. The expanded comment, made by General Lee a number of years after the war's end, was: "The Irish soldier fights not so much for lucre as through the reckless love of adventure…. The gallant stand which his [Meagher's] bold brigade made on the heights of Fredericksburg is well known. Never were men so brave. They ennobled their race by their splendid gallantry."

Chapter 4

1. Sears, *Chancellorsville*, p. 14.
2. Foote, *The Civil War, A Narrative, Fredericksburg to Meridian*, p. 640.
3. Ibid., p. 793.
4. Ibid., p. 877.
5. O'Flaherty, *The History of the Sixty-Ninth Regiment in the Irish Brigade, 1861–1865*, p. 238.
6. O'Brien, "Sprig of Green: The Irish Brigade," *The History of the Irish Brigade* (ed. Seagrave), p. 78.
7. O'Flaherty, p. 189.
8. McCarter, *My Life in the Irish Brigade* (ed. O'Brien), p. 16.
9. Athearn, *Thomas Francis Meagher, an Irish Revolutionary in America*, p. 1.
10. Corby, *Memoirs of Chaplin Life*, pp. ix to xvii.
11. O'Brien, "The Irish Brigade in the Wheatfield," *The History of the Irish Brigade* (ed. Seagrave), p. 105.
12. Ibid., p. 110.
13. Murphy, *Kelly's Heroes, The Irish Brigade at Gettysburg*, p. 38.
14. O'Brien, pp. 106–107.
15. McPherson, *For Cause and Comrades*, p. 166.
16. Welsh, *Irish Green and Union Blue, The Civil War Letters of Peter Welsh* (eds. Kohl and Richard), p. 109.
17. Berstein, *The New York City Draft Riots*, p. 18.
18. Ibid., p. 23.
19. Ibid., p. 54.

20. Walker, *History of the Second Army Corps*, p. 312. "In consequence of the riotous resistance to the conscription act in New York City, Colonel S.S. Carroll commanding First Brigade, Third Division, Second Corps, was in July ordered to the East with the Fourth and Eighth Ohio and Fourteenth Indiana. From the Second Division (Second Corps), those excellent regiments the First Minnesota and the Seventh Michigan were also dispatched for duty." None of the Irish brigade's regiments were sent to New York City during the riots.

21. Foote, *The Civil War, A Narrative, Fredericksburg to Meridian,* p. 637.

22. Cook, *Armies of the Streets,* p. 91.

23. Ibid., p. 177.

24. Ibid., pp. 192–209. Using official records, it can be definitely stated that 105 people lost their lives in the Draft Riots. When unsubstantiated casualties are included, the death toll rises to 119 persons. During the course of the insurrection, 35 soldiers and 32 policemen were seriously wounded while 128 civilians, both rioters and victims, were seriously injured. All but a very few of the large number of Irish Catholics on the Metropolitan Police Force remained faithful to their duty.

The New York Times estimated that the number of active rioters reigned from two to three thousand. The crowds filling the streets were mostly spectators.

25. The following quotations from Berstein's *The New York City Draft Riots* provide a succinct description of the Union League Club and its reaction to the riots: "No one better articulated the Union League Club view than Frederick Law Olmstead. The designer of Central Park first promoted the idea of a wartime 'club of true American aristocracy.' Such an institution, originating in New York but spreading to Washington and other Northern cities, would bring the prestige and social influence of a national business and cultural elite to the work of cultivating loyal opinion among the middle and upper classes. The Club membership list began with men of ancient New York lineage such as John Jay, James Beekman and Robert Stuyvesant. But it deliberately included as well, scientist Oliver Wolcott Gibbs, literati Henry T. Tuckerman and George Bancroft, respected professionals such as physicians William Van Buren and Cornelius Agnew and lawyer George Templeton Strong, loyal capitalists Robert Minturn and James Brown and clergyman Henry W. Bellows" (p. 55).

"That the Union Leaguers came to champion military rule, recommend bloody punishment of the Irish rioters and their well-to-do sympathizers, and use the Club to raise a black regiment and march it through the city" (p. 131).

26. Berstein, p. 49.

27. Ibid., p. 157.

28. Holzer, *Witness to War, The Civil War 1861–1865,* p. 162.

29. Ibid., pp. 162–163.

30. Welsh, p. 102.

31. Ibid., p. 110.

32. Ibid., p. 115.

Chapter 5

1. Symonds, *A Battlefield Atlas of the Civil War,* p. 81.

2. Ibid., p. 85.

3. McPherson, *Battle Cry of Freedom, The Civil War Era,* p. 778.

4. Wright, *The Irish Brigade,* pp. 54–55.

5. Swinton, *Army of the Potomac,* pp. 425–426.

6. Mulholland, *The Story of the 116th Regiment, Pennsylvania Volunteers in the War of the Rebellion* (ed. Kohl), p. 186.

7. Rhea, *The Battle of the Wilderness, May 5–6, 1864,* p. 392.

8. Chisholm, *The Civil War Notebook of Daniel Chisholm* (eds. Menge and Shimrak), p. 13.

9. Rhea, p. 398.

10. Ibid., p. 425.

11. Chisholm, p. 13.

12. Ibid., p. 15.

13. Welsh, *Irish Green and Union Blue, The Civil War Letters of Peter Welsh* (eds. Kohl and Richard), p. 156.

14. Ibid., pp. xvii, 157–158.

15. Rhea, pp. 292–293; Matter, *If It Takes All Summer, The Battle of Spotsylvania,* pp. 255–256.

16. Chisholm, pp. 15–16.

17. Matter, pp. 259–260.

18. Rhea, p. 293.

19. Matter, pp. 308–310.

20. Ibid., p. 311.

21. O'Brien, "Sprig of Green: The Irish Brigade," *The History of the Irish Brigade* (ed. Seagrave), p. 86.

22. Chisholm, pp. 17–18. Clear's entry for 18 May describes his wounding:

"The ball passed through the cartridges, struck the knife and then struck the belt plate with such force that it nearly sent it through me. When I first looked at the place it was as black as the hide of the darkest African. It felt like a square scantling had been punched through me. I do not think I ever felt so sick. I threw up everything that was in my stomach and I came near it and all my insides with it. I laid for about two hours and then dragged myself back to the troops supporting us."

On 20 May, Clear had his side dressed by a hospital surgeon. He refused admittance to the hospital and after a cursing by the doctor returned to his unit. He stayed on duty and the soreness gradually disappeared.

23. Foote, *The Civil War a Narrative, Red River to Appomattox*, p. 237.

24. Walker, *History of the Second Army Corps*, p. 487.

25. Furguson, *Not War but Murder*, p. 149.

26. Ibid., p. 171.

27. Spink, "Colonel Richard Byrnes: Irish Brigade Leader," *The History of the Irish Brigade* (ed. Seagrave), p. 171.

28. Conyngham, *The Irish Brigade*, p. 549.

29. Chisholm, p. 20.

30. Swinton, p. 488.

31. Walker, p. 522.

32. Corby, *Memoirs of Chaplin Life* (ed. Kohl), p. 239.

33. Ibid., p. 238.

34. Trudeau, *The Last Citadel*, pp. 4–7.

35. Johnson and McLaughlin, *Battles of the Civil War*, p. 147.

36. O'Brien, "The Irish Brigade in the Wheatfield," *The History of the Irish Brigade* (ed. Seagrave), pp. 98, 99 and 109.

37. Murphy, *Kelly's Heroes, The Irish Brigade at Gettysburg*, p. 51.

38. O'Flaherty, *The History of the Sixty-Ninth Regiment in the Irish Brigade, 1861–1865*, p. 344.

39. Trudeau, pp. 78–80.

40. McPherson, *For Cause and Comrades, Why Men Fought in the Civil War*, p. 166.

41. An ailing Moroney was mustered out of Federal service with the rest of the Regiment on 30 June 1865. He died a few months later in a military hospital.

42. Chisholm, p. 26.

43. Trudeau, p. 125.

44. Conyngham, pp. 471–473 and OR, Ser. I, Vol. XLII, Pt. I, No. 45, p. 291.

45. Walker, p. 574.

46. Ibid., p. 599.

47. Trudeau, p. 189.

48. Conyngham, p. 479.

49. Phisterer, *Statistical Record*, Battle 2,011, p. 197.

50. O'Flaherty, pp. 360–363.

Chapter 6

1. Symonds, *A Battlefield Atlas of the Civil War*, p. 113.

2. Ibid., p. 115.

3. Chisholm, *The Civil War Notebook of Daniel Chisholm* (eds. Menge and Shimrak), pp. 68–69.

4. Humphreys, *The Virginia Campaign, 1864 and 1865*, pp. 320–321.

5. Conyngham, *The Irish Brigade*, p. 516.

6. Fox, *Regimental Losses in the American Civil War*, pp. 169, 202, 204 and 217 and OR, Ser. 1, Vol. XLVI, Pt. 1, No. 34, pp. 200–201.

7. Conyngham, p. 518 and OR, Ser. I, Vol. XLVI, Pt. 1, No. 35, pp. 728–729.

8. Ibid., p. 519. Brigadier General William Hays took command of the Second Corps following Hancock's wounding at Gettysburg. On 12 August 1863 General Governeur K. Warren replaced Hays as the Second Corps' commanding officer.

9. Walker, *History of the Second Army Corps*, pp. 671–672.

10. OR, Ser. I, Vol. XLVI, Pt. 1, No. 32, pp. 724–725 and No. 35, pp. 728–729.

11. Conyngham, p. 522.

12. Ibid., pp. 523–524.

13. Ibid., pp. 541–542.

14. "Our Returning Veterans," *New York Herald*, July 3, 1865, p. 1.

15. "Independence Day," *New York Herald*, July 6, 1865, pp. 1–2.

16. "The Glorious Fourth," *New York Herald*, July 6, 1865, p. 6.

17. Ibid., p. 6.
18. Ibid., p. 7.
19. Chisholm, p. 26.

Chapter 7

1. Fox, *Regimental Losses in the American Civil War*, p. 118.
2. Conyngham, *The Irish Brigade*, p. ix.
3. Fox, pp. 118, 169, 202, 204, 217 and 292.
4. Ibid., p. 3.
5. Ibid., p. 204.
6. Lonn, *Foreigners in the Union Army and Navy*, p. 646.
7. Jones, *The Irish Brigade*, p. 255.

Chapter 8

1. Ferguson, *The Pity of War*, p. 146.
2. Hart, *The Real War, 1914–1918*, p. 35.
3. Preston, *Lusitania*, pp. 303–361.
4. Terraine, *The Great War*, p. 223.
5. Mossier, *The Myth of the Great War*, p. 241.
6. Hart, pp. 202–204.
7. Strachan, *World War I, A History*, p. 64.
8. Terraine, p. 237.
9. Paschal, *The Defeat of Imperial Germany*, 1917–1918, pp. 46–51.
10. Mossier, p. 284.
11. Laffin, *A Western Front Companion, 1914–1918*, p. 98.
12. Strachan, p. 258.
13. Smythe, *Pershing, General of the Armies*, p. 96.
14. Braim, *The Test of Battle*, p. 46.
15. Smythe, p. 131.
16. Paschall, pp. 160–161.
17. Strachan, p. 280.
18. Smythe, p. 158.
19. Ibid., p. 170.
20. Hart, pp. 429–438.
21. Paschal, pp. 170–178.
22. Smythe, p. 234.
23. Harris, *Duty, Honor, Privilege*, pp. 275–295. The 107th Regiment was the federalized progeny of the Seventh Regiment, New York City's so-called silk stocking regiment. The 69th and Seventh regiments have always had respect and good feelings for each other.
24. Hart, pp. 439–448.
25. Ferguson, p. 295. Number of dead include deaths from disease. Figures for Great Britain include those for British Empire. Sources: *War Office, Statistics of the Military Effort*, pp. 237, 352–7; Terraine, *Smoke and the Fire*, p. 44 and J. Winter, *Great War*, p. 75.
26. Harvey (Encarta), *World War I*, p. 43.
27. Ferguson, pp. 403–409.

Chapter 9

1. Braim, *The Test of Battle*, p. 15.
2. Ibid., pp. 16–17.
3. Duffy, *Father Duffy's Story*, p. 13.
4. Ibid., p. 13.
5. Hogan, *The Shamrock Battalion of the Rainbow*, p. 7.
6. Ibid., p. 8.
7. Ettinger, A.M., and Ettinger, A.C. *A Doughboy with the Fighting Sixty Ninth*, p. 6.

Chapter 10

1. Braim, *The Test of Battle*, p. 19.
2. Ibid., p. 19.
3. Smythe, *Pershing, General of the Armies*, p. 91.
4. Braim, p. 21.
5. Smythe, p. 37.
6. Reilly, *Americans All, the Rainbow at War*, p. 27.
7. Smythe, pp. 61–62.
8. Ibid., p. 87.
9. Cheseldine, *Ohio in the Rainbow*, pp. 36–43.
10. Amerine, *Alabama's Own in France*, pp. 30–46.
11. Taber, *The Story of the 168th Infantry*, p. 2.
12. Ettinger, A.M., and Ettinger, A.C., *A Doughboy with the Fighting Sixty Ninth*, p. 7.
13. Ibid., p. 9.
14. Ibid., p. 9.
15. Duffy, p. 336.
16. Canfield, *A Collector's Guide to the 03 Springfield*, pp. 40–41.
17. Gawne, *Over There! The American Soldier in World War I*, p. 34.

18. Braim, p. 23.
19. Ibid., pp. 23–24.
20. Ibid., p. 28.
21. Smythe, p. 72.
22. Ibid., p. 72.
23. Braim, p. 30.
24. Ibid., p. 40.

Chapter 11

1. Smythe, *Pershing, General of the Armies*, p. 27.
2. Ibid., pp. 33–34.
3. Ibid., p. 59.
4. Ibid., p. 8.
5. Ibid., p. 87.
6. Wolf, *A Brief History of the Rainbow Division*, p. 8.
7. Ibid., p. 10.
8. Duffy, *Father Duffy's Story*, p. 338.
9. Ibid., p. 339.
10. Farwell, *Over There*, p. 83.
11. Cooke, *The Rainbow in the Great War, 1917–1918*, pp. 36–38.
12. Duffy, p. 344.
13. Ibid., p. 54.
14. Cochrane, *The 42nd Division Before Landres-et-St. Georges*, p. 5.
15. Hogan, *The Shamrock Battalion of the Rainbow*, p. 49.

Chapter 12

1. Reilly, *Americans All, The Rainbow at War*, pp. 121–122.
2. Cochrane, *The 42nd Division Before Landres-et-St. Georges*, pp. 8–9.
3. Ibid., p. 9.
4. Casualty figures for deployment in Lorraine Sectors, 17 March to 22 March and 29 March to 21 June, from Cochrane. Casualty figures developed from data presented in Reilly's *American All*. Other data presented in Figure 5-13 from American Battle Monuments Commission's *42nd Division, Summary of Operations in the World War*, pp. 15, 16, 32, 33, 50, 91 and 92.
5. Duffy, *Father Duffy's Story*, p. 348.
6. Ibid., p. 350.
7. Ibid., pp. 50 and 71.
8. Reilly, p. 165.
9. Ibid., pp. 162–163.
10. Ibid., pp. 163–164.
11. Ibid., p. 164.
12. Duffy, p. 208.
13. Cochrane, p. 75.
14. Bacevich, *Diplomat in Khaki*, p. 73.
15. Reilly, p. 212.
16. Duffy, p. 96.
17. Bacevich, p. 74.
18. Duffy, p. 99.
19. Ibid., pp. 114–115.
20. Ibid., p. 208.

Chapter 13

1. Smythe, *Pershing, General of the Armies*, pp. 107–108.
2. Ibid., p. 129.
3. Ibid., p. 132.
4. Ibid., p. 137.
5. Marshall, *World War I*, p. 374.
6. Smythe, p. 138.
7. Ibid., p. 138.
8. Ibid., p. 140.
9. Ibid., p. 140.

Chapter 14

1. Duffy, *Father Duffy's Story*, p. 130.
2. Smythe, *Pershing, General of the Armies*, p. 151.
3. Duffy, p. 125.
4. American Battle Monuments Commission (ABMC), *42nd Division, Summary of Operations in the World War*, pp. 15–16.
5. Reilly, *Americans All, The Rainbow at War*, p. 272.
6. Wolf, *A Brief Story of the Rainbow Division*, p. 24.
7. Duffy, pp. 125–126.
8. Reilly, p. 274.
9. Duffy, pp. 129–130.
10. Reilly, p. 277.
11. Duffy, pp. 139–140.
12. Ibid., p. 135.
13. Reilly, p. 273.

Chapter 15

1. Reilly, *Americans All, The Rainbow at War*, p. 307.
2. Ibid., p. 307.
3. Smythe, *Pershing, General of the Armies*, p. 157.

4. Ibid., p. 157.
5. Ibid., pp. 158–159.
6. Ibid., p. 159.
7. Reilly, pp. 493–494.
8. Ibid., pp. 319–320.
9. Wolf, *A Brief Story of the Rainbow Division*, pp. 31–32.
10. Ibid., pp. 32–33.
11. Ibid., p. 34.
12. ABMC, *42nd Division, Summary of Operations in the World War*, pp. 32–33.
13. Reilly, pp. 382–383.
14. Ibid., p. 385.
15. Hogan, *The Shamrock Battalion of the Rainbow*, pp. 157–158.
16. Reilly, p. 387.
17. Duffy, p. 175.
18. Hogan, pp. 170–171.
19. Duffy, pp. 205–206.
20. Reilly, p. 391.
21. Ibid., p. 392.
22. Ibid., p. 401.
23. Ibid., p. 392.
24. Ibid., p. 394.
25. Ibid., p. 394.
26. Ibid., p. 396.
27. ABMC, *American Armies and Battlefields in Europe*, pp. 72–73.
28. Reilly, pp. 468–469.
29. Ibid., p. 389.
30. Ibid., p. 389.
31. Duffy, pp. 216–217.
32. Ibid., p. 220.
33. Ibid., p. 222.
34. ABMC, *American Armies and Battlefields in Europe*, p. 72.
35. Duffy, p. 223.
36. Ibid., pp. 224–225.
37. Ibid., p. 226.

Chapter 16

1. Smythe, *Pershing, General of the Armies*, p. 176.
2. Ibid., pp. 177–178.
3. Ibid., p. 184.
4. Ibid., pp. 185–186.
5. Wolf, *A Brief Story of the Rainbow Division*, pp. 40–42.
6. Duffy, *The Father Duffy Story*, p. 236.
7. Reilly, *Americans All, The Rainbow at War*, pp. 563–564.
8. Duffy, p. 243.
9. Farwell, *Over There*, p. 222.

10. Ibid., p. 222.
11. Ibid., p. 222.
12. Duffy, pp. 254–255.

Chapter 17

1. Smythe, *Pershing, General of the Armies*, p. 190.
2. Ibid., pp. 190–191.
3. Ibid., p. 192.
4. Ibid., p. 196.
5. Ibid., p. 196.
6. Ibid., p. 204.
7. Sherwood, *Diary of the Rainbow Division*, p. 26. Near the war's end, divisional insignias were worn on the left shoulder of uniform overcoats. That of New York's 77th Division was an embroidered Statue of Liberty. According to Sherwood, men in the other divisions good naturedly razzed troopers sporting the emblem. They claimed the insignia represented a French mademoiselle looking for the Lost Battalion.
8. Smythe, p. 206.
9. Cochrane, *The 42nd Division Before Landres-et-St. Georges*, p. 42.
10. Smythe, pp. 208–209.
11. Cochrane, pp. 39–40.
12. Moran, *The Anatomy of Courage*, p. 108.
13. Wolf, *A Brief Story of the Rainbow Division*, p. 46.
14. Cochrane, p. 46.
15. Ibid., p. 46.
16. Ibid., p. 51.
17. Ibid., p. 52.
18. Ibid., pp. 52–53.
19. Ibid., p. 53.
20. Ibid., p. 55.
21. Ibid., p. 58.
22. Ibid., pp. 66–67.
23. Duffy, *The Father Duffy Story*, p. 257.
24. Ettinger, A.M., and Ettinger, A.C., *A Doughboy with the Fighting 69th*, p. 169.
25. Duffy, pp. 264–265.
26. Hogan, *The Shamrock Battalion of the Rainbow*, pp. 237–242.
27. Duffy, p. 274.
28. Reilly, *Americans All, The Rainbow at War*, p. 697.
29. Duffy, p. 276.
30. Reilly, pp. 657–658.
31. Ibid., pp. 661–663.

32. Duffy, pp. 276–277.
33. Reilly, pp. 659–660.
34. Cooke, *The Rainbow Division in the Great War, 1917–1918*, p. 33.
35. Hallas, *Doughboy War, The American Expeditionary Force in World War I*, pp. 156–157.
36. Reilly, p. 748.
37. Ibid., p. 755.
38. Ibid., p. 666.
39. Ibid., p. 738.
40. ABMC, *American Armies and Battlefields in Europe*, p. 243.
41. Ibid., p. 243.
42. Duffy, p. 288.
43. Duffy, p. 285.
44. Duffy, p. 286.
45. Reilly, pp. 518–519.
46. Smythe, p. 157.
47. Mackin, *Suddenly We Didn't Want to Die*, pp. 225–227.

Chapter 18

1. Smythe, *Pershing, General of the Armies*, p. 228.
2. Ibid., p. 230.
3. Ibid., p. 230.
4. Wolf, *A Brief Story of the Rainbow Division*, pp. 51–52.
5. Ibid., p. 52.
6. ABMC, *42nd Division, Summary of Operations in the World War*, p. 91.
7. Duffy, *The Father Duffy Story*, p. 301.
8. Ibid., p. 302.
9. Ibid., pp. 303–304.
10. Ibid., p. 305.

Chapter 19

1. Friedel, *Over There, The Story of America's First Great Overseas Crusade*, pp. 343–347. During the period of time just before the magic hour, 1100 11 November 1918, a number of AEF units conducted offensive operations. Some outfits went sent over the top by commands unaware of the impending cease fire. Other HQs knew the Armistice was at hand but callously ordered some of their units to attack, realizing casualties would be incurred. Harry G. Rennagel, 101st Infantry, 26th (Yankee Division), reported that elements of his command were sent forward to seize enemy positions. The purpose of the operation was to eliminate a concavity in the 26th's line. His detachment jumped off at 1035. At 1055, a *Minenwerfer* landed on his command. Five men were wounded; one mortally, two critically and two seriously. The unfortunate soldier died at 1105.
2. Smythe, *Pershing, General of the Armies*, pp. 246–247.
3. Ibid., p. 236.
4. Smythe, *Pershing, General of the Armies*, pp. 256–257.
5. Ibid., p. 257.
6. Wolf, *A Brief Story of the Rainbow Division*, p. 54.
7. Cooke, *The Rainbow Division in the Great War*, pp. 203–204.
8. Ibid., pp. 203–204.
9. Ibid., p. 235.
10. Ibid., p. 235.
11. Ibid., p. 218.
12. Duffy, *The Father Duffy Story*, pp. 309–312.
13. Ibid., p. 315.
14. Ibid., p. 324.
15. Ibid., p. 355.
16. Cooke, p. 238.

Chapter 20

1. "Old 69th Men Got Hearty Welcome on Arriving Home," *New York Times*, Tuesday, April 22, 1919, Page 1, Column 1.
2. Ibid., p. 2, columns 1 and 2.
3. Ibid., p. 2, column 2.
4. *New York Times*, Saturday, April 26, 1919, "Rainbow Soldiers Here on Leviathan," p. 2, columns 3–5.
5. "Acclaim the 69th in Final Review," *New York Times*, Tuesday, April 29, 1919, p. 1, column 1.
6. "Old 69th Regiment to Parade Monday," *New York Times*, Wednesday, April 23, 1919, p. 2, column 3.
7. Ibid., p. 3, column 4.
8. Ibid., p. 3, column 4.
9. *New York Times*, Tuesday, April 29, 1919, p. 2, column 1.
10. Ibid., p. 2, columns 1–4.
11. Ibid., p. 2, column 3.

Chapter 21

1. Mossier, *The Myth of the Great War*, p. 12. Totals include prisoners of war who were later repatriated. Included figures for wounded are for cases, not individuals.

2. Braim, *The Test of Battle*, p. 151.

3. Smythe, *Pershing, General of the Armies*, p. 237.

4. Hart, *The Real War, 1914–1918*, pp. 461–469.

5. Braim, p. 177.

6. Mossier, p. 1.

7. Ibid., p. 7.

8. Braim, p. 187.

9. Ibid., p. 188.

10. Ibid., p. 189.

11. Ibid., p. 190.

12. Cooke, *The Rainbow Division in the Great War, 1917–1918*, p. 112.

13. Braim, p. 191.

14. Ibid., p. 15.

15. Ibid., p. 153.

16. Reilly, p. 323.

17. Ibid., p. 665.

18. *Army Lineage Book, Volume II; Infantry*, pp. 487 and 489.

19. Liggett, *AEF, Ten Years Ago in France*, p. 268.

20. Cooke, pp. 134–135 and 61. Cooke would not agree with my rankings. He believed the 84th Brigade and 167th Infantry were the best such outfits in the Rainbow Division. After discussing the relief of Brigadier General Brown by Colonel MacArthur, following the former's poor showing on the Ourcq River, Cooke made the following statement, "Very quickly, the 84th Brigade with its regiments of Alabamians and Iowans became the best in the Rainbow as the Argonne Fighting would demonstrate" (pp. 135–136).

Early in his book, Cooke identifies the 167th Regiment as the best such unit in the 42nd. As a result of its service in the Luneville Sector, he writes, "The 167th Infantry Regiment was quickly developing into the most aggressive and combat proficient unit in the Rainbow" (p. 61).

Cooke might agree with the following rankings; *first* 167th Infantry; *second* 165th and 168th Infantries, and *third* 166th Infantry.

Epilogue

1. Ettinger, *A Doughboy with the Fighting 69th*, pp. 183–184.

2. General Douglas MacArthur, address by short wave radio, Manila to Veterans of 69th NY at Waldorf Astoria Hotel, 24 January 1940.

Bibliography of Works Cited

Books

Amerine, William H. *Alabama's Own in France*. New York: Eaton and Gettinger, 1919.

Athearn, Robert G. *Thomas Francis Meagher: An Irish Revolutionary in America*. New York: Arno Press, 1976.

Bacevich, A.J. *Diplomat in Khaki, Major General Frank Ross McCoy and American Policy*. Lawrence: University Press of Kansas, 1989.

Berstein, Iver. *The New York City Draft Riots: Their Significance for American Society and Politics in the Age of the Civil War*. New York: Oxford University Press, 1990.

Braim, Paul F. *The Test of Battle*, 2nd rev. ed. Shippenburg, PA: White Mane Books, 1998.

Canfield, Bruce N. *A Collector's Guide to the 03 Springfield*. Lincoln, RI: Andrew Mowbray, 1989.

Cheseldine, R.M. *Ohio in the Rainbow, Official Story of the 166th Infantry, 42nd Division in the World War*. Columbus, OH: F.J. Heer, 1924.

Chisholm, Daniel. *The Civil War Notebook of Daniel Chisholm: A Chronicle of Daily Life in the Union Army* (eds. Springer Menge and August Shimrak). New York: Orion Books, 1989.

Cochrane, Rexmond C. *The 42nd Division Before Landres-et-St. Georges*. Maryland: Army Chemical Center, U.S. Army Chemical Corps Historical Office, 1959.

Conyngham, Captain D.P. *The Irish Brigade and Its Campaigns*. New York: William McSorley and Co., Publishers, 1867.

Cook, Adrian. *The Armies of the Streets, The New York City Draft Riots of 1863*. Lexington: The University Press of Kentucky, 1974.

Cooke, James J. *The Rainbow Division in the Great War, 1917–1918*. Westport, CT: Praeger, 1994.

Corby, William. *Memoirs of Chaplain Life: Three Years with the Irish Brigade in the Army of the Potomac* (ed. Lawrence F. Kohl). Bronx: Fordham University Press, 1992.

Davis, William C. *Battle at Bull Run*. Mechanicsburg, PA: Stackpole Books, 1977.

Duffy, Francis P. (Chaplain, 165th Infantry), *Father Duffy's Story*. New York: Garden City Publishing Co., Inc., 1919.

Eicher, David J. *The Civil War in Books: An Analytical Biography*. Chicago: University of Illinois Press, 1961.

Ettinger, Albert M., and A. Churchill Ettinger (eds.). *A Doughboy with the Fighting Sixty Ninth: A Remembrance of World War I*. Shippensburg, PA: White Mane Books, 1992.

Farwell, Bryan. *Over There: The United States in the Great War, 1917–1918*. New York: W.W. Norton, 1999.

Ferguson, Niall. *The Pity of War*. New York: Basic Books, 1999.

Foote, Shelby. *The Civil War: A Narrative*. New York: Vintage Books, 1986.

Fox, William F. *Regimental Losses in the American Civil War, 1861–1865*. New York: Albany Publishing Co., 1889.

Freidel, Frank. *Over There: The Story of America's First Great Overseas Crusade.* Canada: Little, Brown, 1964.

Furguson, Ernest B. *Not War but Murder: Cold Harbor, 1864.* New York: Alfred A. Knopf, 2000.

Gawne, Jonathan. *Over There! The American Soldier in World War I.* Mechanicsburg, PA: Stackpole Books, 1986.

Greenwood, Paul. *The Second Battle of the Marne, 1918.* Shrewsbury, U.K.: Airlife, 1998.

Hallas, James H. *Doughboy War: The American Expeditionary Force in World War I.* Boulder, CO: Lynne Riener, 2000.

Hankinson, Alan. *First Bull Run 1861: The South's First Victory.* London: Osprey, 1990.

Harris, Stephen L. *Duty, Honor, Privilege: New York's Silk Stocking Regiment and the Breaking of the Hindenburg Line.* Washington, D.C.: Brassey's, 2001.

Hart, Captain B. H. Liddell. *The Real War, 1914–1918.* New York: Little, Brown, 1930.

Hogan, Martin J. *The Shamrock Battalion of the Rainbow.* New York: D. Appleton, 1919.

Holzer, Harold. *Witness to War: The Civil War, 1861–1865.* New York: Berkley, 1996.

Humphreys, General Andrew A. *The Virginia Campaign, 1864 and 1865.* New York: Charles Scribner's, 1883.

Johnson, Curt, and Mark McLaughlin. *Battles of the Civil War.* New York: Barnes and Noble, 1995.

Johnson, Robert U., and Clarence C. Buel. *Battles and Leaders of the Civil War, Volumes I–IV.* New York: The Century Magazine, 1888.

Jones, Paul. *The Irish Brigade.* Washington, D.C.: Robert B. Luce, 1969.

Jones, Terry L. *Lee's Tigers.* Baton Rouge: Louisiana State University Press, 1987.

Ketchum, Richard M. (ed.). *The American Heritage Picture History of the Civil War.* New York: American Heritage, 1960.

Laffin, John. *A Western Front Campanion, 1914–1918.* Phoenix Mill, U.K.: Allan Sutton, 1994.

Liggett, Major General Hunter. *AEF: Ten Years Ago in France.* New York: Dodd, Mead, 1927.

Lonn, Ella. *Foreigners in the Union Army and Navy.* Baton Rouge: Louisiana State University Press, 1951. Reprint, Westport, CT: Greenwood, 1969.

Lysy, Peter J. *Blue for the Union and Green for Ireland.* Notre Dame, Ind.: Archives of the University of Notre Dame, 2001.

Mackin, Elton E. *Suddenly We Didn't Want to Die.* Novato, CA: Presidio, 1993.

Marshall, S.L.A. *World War I.* Boston: Houghton Mifflin, 2001.

Matter, William D. *If It Takes All Summer: The Battle of Spotsylvania.* Chapel Hill: University of North Carolina Press, 1988.

McCarter, Private William. *My Life in the Irish Brigade: The Civil War Memoirs of Private William McCarter, 116th Pennsylvania Infantry* (ed. Kevin E. O'Brien). El Dorado Hills, CA: Savas, 1996.

McPherson, James M. *Battle Cry of Freedom: The Civil War Era.* New York and London: Oxford University Press, 1988.

_____. *For Cause and Comrades, Why Men Fought in the Civil War.* New York and London: Oxford University Press, 1997.

Moran, Lord. *The Anatomy of Courage.* Boston: Houghton Mifflin, 1967.

Mossier, John. *The Myth of the Great War.* New York: Harper Collins, 2001.

Mulholland, St. Clair A. *The Story of the 116th Regiment, Pennsylvania Volunteers in the War of the Rebellion* (Ed. Lawrence F. Kohl), Bronx, N.Y.: Fordham University Press, 1996.

Murphy, T.L. *Kelly's Heroes, The Irish Brigade at Gettysburg.* Gettysburg, PA: Farnsworth House Military Impressions, 1997.

O'Flaherty, Patrick D. *The History of the Sixty Ninth Regiment in the Irish Brigade, 1861–1865.* New York: Privately Printed, 1986.

_____. *The History of the Sixty Ninth Regiment of the New York State Militia, 1852–1861.* Dissertation for Ph.D., Department of History, Fordham University, N.Y., 1963.

Paschal, Rod. *The Defeat of Imperial Germany, 1917–1918.* New York: Da Capo Press, N.Y., 1994.

Phisterer, Frederick. *Statistical Record of the Armies of the United States.* New York: Charles Scribner's, 1883.

Preston, Diana. *Lusitania: An Epic Tragedy.* New York: Walker, 2002.

Priest, John M. *Antietam: The Soldier's Battle.* New York and London: Oxford University Press, 1989.

Ray, Frederic E. *Alfred R. Waud, Civil War Artist.* New York: The Viking Press, 1974.

Reilly, Henry J. *Americans All, The Rainbow at War. Official History of the 42nd Division in the World War,* 2nd ed. Columbus, OH: F.J. Heer, 1936.

Rhea, Gordon C. *The Battle of the Wilderness, May 5 and 6, 1864.* Baton Rouge: Louisiana State University Press, 1994.

Seagrave, Pia Seija (ed.). *The History of the Irish Brigade: A Collection of Historical Essays.* Spotsylvania, VA: Sergeant Kirkland's Museum and Historical Society, Inc., 1997.

Sears, Stephen W. *Chancellorsville.* Boston: Houghton Mifflin, 1996.

Sherwood, Elmer W. *Diary of a Rainbow Veteran.* Indiana: Moore-Langan, 1929.

Smith, Carl. *Fredericksburg 1862: Clear the Way.* Oxford, U.K.: Osprey, 1999.

Smythe, Donald. *Pershing, General of the Armies.* Bloomington: Indiana University Press, 1986.

Stein, Barry J. *U.S. Army Heraldic Crests.* Columbia: University of South Carolina Press, 1993.

Strachan, Hew. *The Oxford Illustrated History of the First World War.* Oxford, U.K.: Oxford University Press, 1998.

Styple, William B. (ed.). *Writing and Fighting the Civil War: Soldier Correspondence to the New York Sunday Mercury.* Kearny, N.J.: Belle Grove, 2000.

Swinton, William. *Campaigns of the Army of the Potomac: A Critical History of Operations Into Virginia, Maryland and Pennsylvania from the Commencement to the Close of the War, 1861–1865.* New York: Charles P. Richardson, 1866.

Symonds, Craig L. *A Battlefield Atlas of the Civil War.* Baltimore: The Nautical and Aviation Publishing Company of America, 1983.

Taber, John H. *The Story of the 168th Infantry.* Des Moines: The State Historical Society of Iowa, 1925.

Terraine, John. *The Great War.* Hertfordshire, U.K.: Woodsworth Editions, 1998.

Trudeau, Noah Andre. *The Last Citadel: Petersburg, Virginia, June 1864–April 1865.* New York: Little, Brown, 1991.

Van Every, Dale. *The AEF in Battle.* New York: D. Appleton, 1928.

Walker, Francis A. *History of the Second Army Corps.* New York: Charles Scribner's, 1886.

Welsh, Peter. *Irish Green and Union Blue: The Civil War Letters of Peter Welsh* (Eds. Lawrence F. Kohl and Margaret C. Richard). Bronx: Fordham University Press, 1986.

Wolf, Walter B. *A Brief Story of the Rainbow Division.* New York: Rand McNally, 1919.

Wright, Steven J. *The Irish Brigade.* Springfield, PA: Steven Wright, 1992.

Government Documents

Ainsworth, Brigadier General Fred C. and Joseph W. Kirkley. *The War of the Rebellion: Official Records of the Union and Confederate Armies.* Washington, D.C.: Government Printing Office, 1901.

American Battle Monuments Commission. *American Armies and Battlefields in Europe: A History Guide and Reference Book.* Washington, D.C.: Government Printing Office, 1948.

_____. *42nd Division, Summary of Operations in the World War.* Washington, D.C.: Government Printing Office, 1944.

Center of Military History. *United States Army in the World War, 1917–1918: Military Operations of the American Expeditionary Forces.* Washington, D.C.: U.S. Army, 1990.

The Army Lineage Book, Volume II: Infantry. Washington, D.C.: Government Printing Office, 1953.

Pamphlets

Powers, Lt. Colonel Kenneth H. *The Sixty Ninth Regiment of New York: Its History, Heraldry, Traditions and Customs.*

Newspapers

New York Herald, July 3, 1865.
New York Evening Post, July 3, 1865.
New York Evening Post, July 5, 1865.
New York Times, July 3, 1865.
New York Times, July 5, 1865.
New York Daily Tribune, July 6, 1865.
The Evening Post, July 3, 1919.
The Evening Post, July 5, 1919.
New York Herald, July 3, 1919.
New York Herald, July 5, 1919.
New York Daily Tribune, July 6, 1919.

Encyclopedia

Microsoft Encarta Encyclopedia 2000, Civil War American (Gallagher, Gary, contributor). Microsoft Corporation, 1993–1999.
Microsoft Encarta Encyclopedia 2000, World War I (Harvey, Donald J.). Microsoft Corporation, 1993–1999.

Reference Bibliography

Bilby, Joseph G. *Remember Fontenoy! The 69th NY and Irish Brigade in the Civil War.* Hightstown, NJ: Longstreet House, 1995.

Catton, Bruce. *Bruce Catton's Civil War.* New York: The Fairfax Press, 1984.

_____. *The Coming Fury.* New York: Doubleday & Company, 1961.

Cecil, High, and Peter H. Liddle. *Facing Armageddon: The First World War Experienced.* South Yorkshire, U.K.: Pen and Sword Books, 1996.

Commager, Henry Steele (ed.), *The Blue and the Gray.* New York: Fairfax Press, 1982.

Davis, William C. *Death in the Trenches.* Alexandria, VA: Time-Life Books, 1986.

Eisenhower, John S.D. *Yanks.* New York: Free Press, 2001.

Ellis, John. *Eye Deep in Hell: Trench Warfare in World War I.* Baltimore: The Johns Hopkins University Press, 1976.

Evans, Martin Marix. *Retreat, Hell! We Just Got Here!* Oxford, U.K.: Osprey, 1998.

Freeman, Douglas Southall. *Lee's Lieutenants.* New York: Charles Scribner's, 1944.

Furguson, Ernest. *Chancellorsville, 1863: The Souls of the Brave.* New York: Alfred A. Knopf, 1992.

Fussell, Paul. *The Great War and Modern Memory.* New York and London: Oxford University Press, 1975.

Gallagher, Gary W. *The First Day at Gettysburg: Essays on Confederate and Union Leadership.* Kent, OH: The Kent State University Press, 1992.

_____. *The Second Day at Gettysburg: Essays on Confederate and Union Leadership.* Kent, OH: The Kent State University Press, 1992.

Gilbert, Martin. *The First World War: A Composite History.* New York: Henry Holt, 1994.

Graves, Robert. *Good Bye to All That.* New York: Doubleday, 1929.

Gregory, Barry. *Argonne 1918: The AEF in France.* New York: Ballantine, 1972.

Hancock, Cornelia. *South After Gettysburg: Letters of Cornelia Hancock from the Army of the Potomac* (ed. Henrietta Stratton Jacquette). Philadelphia: University of Pennsylvania Press, 1937.

Hill, Jim Don. *The Minute Man in Peace and War: A History of the National Guard.* Harrisburg, PA: Stackpole, 1964.

Johnson, J.H. *1918: The Unexpected Victory.* London: Cassell Military Paperbacks, 1997.

Johnson, Rossiter. *Campfires and Battlefields: A Pictorial Narrative of the Civil War.* New York: The Civil War Press, 1967.

Keegan, John. *The First World War.* New York: Alfred A. Knopf, 1999.

Langville, Leslie. *Men of the Rainbow.* New York: The O'Sullivan Publishing House, 1993.

Love, Captain Edmund G. *The 27th Infantry Division in World War II.* Washington, D.C.: Infantry Journal Press, 194.

MacDonald, John. *Great Battles of the Civil War.* New York: Macmillan, 1988

McDonald, Jo Ann M. *A Walk in Time, Give Them the Bayonet.* New York and London: Oxford University Press, 1997.

McPherson, James C. *Antietam, Crossroads of Freedom.* New York and London: Oxford University Press, 2003.

Palfry, Winthrop F. *The Antietam and Fredericksburg.* New York: Charles Scribner's, 1882.

Palmer, Frederick. *Our Greatest Battle [The Meuse-Argonne].* New York: Dodd, Mead, 1919.

Patrick, Marsena A. *Inside Mr. Lincoln's Army: The Diary of General Marsena Rudolf Patrick, Provost Marshal General, Army of the Potomac* (ed. Davis S. Sparks). New York: Thomas Yoseloff, 1994.

Pfanz, Henry W. *Gettysburg: The Second Day.* Chapel Hill: University of North Carolina Press, 1987.

Rhea, Gordon C. *Cold Harbor, Grant and Lee, May 26–June 3 1864.* Baton Rouge: Louisiana State University Press, 2002.

_____. *To the North Anna River.* Baton Rouge: Louisiana State University Press, 2000.

Sears, Stephen W. *To the Gates of Richmond: The Peninsular Campaign.* New York: Ticknor and Fields, 1992.

Sorrel, G. Moxley. *Recollections of a Confederate Staff Officer.* New York: Neale, 1905.

Stevens, Norman. *Antietam 1862, Classic Battles.* Oxford, U.K.: Osprey, 1994.

Toland, John. *No Man's Land, 1918—The Last Year of the Great War.* New York: Doubleday, 1980.

Tompkins, Raymond S. *The Story of the Rainbow Division.* New York: Boni and Liveright, 1919.

Trudeau, Noah Andre. *Bloody Roads South: The Wilderness to Cold Harbor, May–June 1864,* New York: Ballantine Books, 1989.

Truslow, Marion A. *Peasants Into Patriots: The New York Irish Brigade Recruits and Their Families, in the Civil War Era, 1850–1890.* Ph.D. Dissertation, New York University, 1994.

Tuchman, Barbara. *The Guns of August 1914.* London: Constable, 1962.

Watson, Peter. *War on the Mind, The Military Uses and Abuses of Psychology.* New York: Basic Books, 1978.

Winter, J.M. *The Experience of World War I.* New York: Oxford University Press, 1989.

Index